敦煌文化·译丛（汉英对照）

Dunhuang Culture in Translation: A Series

主编 姜秋霞

副主编 [美]安瑞 柳菁

遗响千年

敦煌的影响

Dunhuang: Its Everlasting Impact

刘进宝 著 曾丽馨 译

甘肃教育出版社

图书在版编目（CIP）数据

遗响千年：敦煌的影响 = Dunhuang:Its Everlasting Impact：汉英对照 / 刘进宝著；曾丽馨译. -- 兰州：甘肃教育出版社，2021.11

(敦煌文化·译丛 / 姜秋霞主编)

ISBN 978-7-5423-5145-6

Ⅰ. ①遗… Ⅱ. ①刘… ②曾… Ⅲ. ①敦煌学一文化史一汉、英 Ⅳ. ①K870.6

中国版本图书馆 CIP 数据核字(2021)第 133356 号

遗响千年——敦煌的影响

Dunhuang: Its Everlasting Impact

刘进宝　著　　曾丽馨　译

责任编辑　李慧娟
封面设计　石　璞
内文设计　方　圆
图片支持　敦煌研究院

出　版　甘肃教育出版社
社　址　兰州市读者大道 568 号　730030
网　址　www.gseph.cn　　E-mail　gseph@duzhe.cn
电　话　0931-8436105（编辑部）　0931-8773056(发行部)
传　真　0931-8773056
淘宝官方旗舰店　http://shop111038270.taobao.com

发　行　甘肃教育出版社　　印　刷　山东新华印务有限公司
开　本　787 毫米 × 1092 毫米　1/16　　印　张　21.25　　字　数　312 千
版　次　2021 年 11 月第 1 版
印　次　2021 年 11 月第 1 次印刷
书　号　ISBN 978-7-5423-5145-6　　定　价　88.00 元

“丝绸之路·敦煌文化翻译”工程

编 委 会

“丝绸之路·敦煌文化翻译”工程是甘肃文化翻译中心在甘肃省委宣传部的领导下所实施的文化翻译工程，旨在助力共建“一带一路”，弘扬丝路文化和敦煌文化，推进敦煌文化国际交流与传播，推动中国文化“走出去”。

“敦煌文化·译丛”为“丝绸之路·敦煌文化翻译”工程系列成果之一。

阳关龙勒山烽燧　王　金　摄

Beacon Tower at the Longle Mountain of Yangguan Pass (Photo by Wang Jin)

“敦煌文化·译丛”简介

近年来，在“中华文化走出去”“讲好中国故事”与共建“一带一路”的大背景下，充分展示了中华民族文化自信的敦煌文化，以其丰富的内涵和独特的魅力吸引着全世界的目光。越来越多的海内外人士渴望掀起敦煌文化神秘的面纱，走近敦煌，从而走进敦煌。“敦煌文化·译丛”的编纂，以“敦煌文化走出去”为目标，以“讲好敦煌故事”为原则，对外传播敦煌文化，交流敦煌学思想，传承敦煌精神。

一、丛书内容

“敦煌文化·译丛”在传播内容上重视知识的可接受度，甄选了既有学术价值，又便于普及的敦煌学著作和敦煌文化读物进行翻译。所选书籍均为敦煌学著名专家所著，集学术性与科普性于一体，且呈现出一定的系统性，主题逐步涵盖敦煌文化完整版图，着力打造出相对全面的敦煌文化外宣丛书体系。本系列译丛采用中外语言对照的编纂方式，传播敦煌文化，交流敦煌学研究思想等。

“敦煌文化·译丛”以开放的模式分期分批编辑出版。第一辑包含《丝路明珠：敦煌》《艺苑瑰宝：莫高窟壁画与彩塑》《箫管霓裳：敦煌乐舞》及《遗响千年：敦煌的影响》四部作品的汉英对照读本。

《丝路明珠：敦煌》（郑炳林、李军著）以敦煌的历史、地位和周边名胜古迹为主题，分别讲述了从新石器时代、两汉、魏晋南北朝到西夏、元、明、清各个不同朝代历史背景下敦煌的发展和变迁；论述了丝绸之路开通后，敦煌作为中西交通线路上的重要枢纽、中西贸易的中转站和中央王朝经营西域的军事重镇的历史地位;介绍了包括莫高窟、榆林窟等佛教石窟,玉门关、阳关等城池关隘,及鸣沙山、月牙泉等自然景观在内的敦煌周边历史文化名胜和古迹。全书脉络清晰,语言生动,集资料性、故事性和知识性于一体,既突出了敦煌的地域文化特点,又展现了敦煌厚重的历史内涵,使这颗沉睡在茫茫大漠之中的璀璨明珠在世人面前焕发出夺目的光华。

《艺苑瑰宝:莫高窟壁画与彩塑》(赵声良著)概括介绍了敦煌彩塑和壁画的基本风貌,包括塑像、佛像画、飞天、故事画、经变画、山水画、装饰画等单元,并阐述了包含其中的文化价值、历史价值、艺术价值,展示出千年中国美术的脉络。这本书还对古代印度、中亚艺术与中国艺术的交流与融合作了分析,全书浸透着作者全方位学术研究的成果,以及自豪自信的文化情怀。文笔流畅,深入浅出,图文并茂,雅俗共赏,把博大精深的敦煌艺术成功地传达给了读者。

《箫管霓裳:敦煌乐舞》(王克芬、柴剑虹著)以敦煌莫高窟为主题,分别介绍了敦煌乐舞的人文背景及源流、经变画中的天宫乐舞、世俗画里的歌舞、特色鲜明的民族舞蹈、生动活泼的童子舞姿、敦煌乐舞的文化特征等内容。作者用凝练、简洁、流畅的笔触,以敦煌莫高窟壁画、彩塑为着眼点,文解图义,栩栩如生地展示了敦煌莫高窟壁画中丰富多彩的佛国乐舞形象。全书凝练紧凑,主题鲜明,语言流畅,专业性与普及性兼顾,为中外读者了解与欣赏敦煌乐舞打开了一扇大门。

《遗响千年:敦煌的影响》(刘进宝著)以敦煌文献的整理刊布与敦煌艺术探索和文艺创作为主题,分别介绍了敦煌学的产生背景、敦煌文献在各国的研究概况、中外文化艺术名人与敦煌的故事、敦煌艺术光辉照耀下的文学艺术创作成果、敦煌文物的保护及研究等内容。作者用通俗易懂、生动活泼的语言,将专业性与普及性融为一体,让读者与敦煌渐行渐近,相知相亲,向世人展现了敦煌文化在中国和世界所产生的深远影响。全书图文并茂、材料翔实、叙述生动,吸引中外读者走进敦煌辉煌灿烂的文化圣殿与艺术宝库。

这四部作品涵盖了敦煌文化中的重要板块,系统阐释了敦煌文化的历史发展、艺术价值与人文精神。一方面,从本体视角出发介绍敦煌的历史地理知识;另一方面,从认识视角出发展示敦煌文化艺术中最为人感知的两张名片——壁画雕塑与音乐舞蹈；最终，从价值视角出发凸显敦煌文化及敦煌学在全世界产生的影响。本系列译丛将促进敦煌艺术之美的国际化交流，补充与敦煌乐舞相关的深度双语语料，拓展敦煌历史地理相关的系统语言资料，为“敦煌在中国、敦煌学在世界”这一国际化命题提供了必要参考。

二、译介特点

“敦煌文化·译丛”以“传播敦煌文化，交流敦煌学思想”为主旨，采用“中英对照”的形式讲述敦煌故事、阐释敦煌精神。在译介方式上，运用多元的翻译策略和方法，进行文本对比与转换。在原文阐释上，一方面通过系统查阅历史文献、背景资料、中外敦煌学研究成果等，深刻理解原文语义；另一方面通过译者与原作者的对话与沟通，精准把握敦煌文化的精髓要义。在外文表达上，注重信息的有效表达，通过“中西合璧”的模式展开翻译，由中外译者通力合作，以“读者接受”为主导，运用适切的话语方式，综合的翻译方法，进行语言转换。译文尽可能贴近英语读者的表达习惯、思维模式、语言风格和理解能力，使所译作品不仅在文字上实现了“走出去”，同时使其文化内涵真正能够“走进去”，力图实现文化的深度传播。

“敦煌文化·译丛”的总体翻译原则：在充分理解和尊重原文的基础上，对于汉英语言文化中存在对应概念和表达的内容，尽量忠实于原文的内容和风格，力求准确再现原文的语言和文化信息。在遵循翻译基本原理的前提下，根据汉英两种语言和文化之间的差异，综合运用“归化”“异化”“融合化”等翻译策略，对原文部分内容进行适度的增减编改，灵活采用节译、概译、编译和解释性翻译等方法进行语言文本的转换。

“敦煌文化·译丛”的基本翻译方法：

1. 对于原文中文化概念和术语的翻译，一般采用我国官方出版物和官方网站中已有的外文表达。

2. 对于中国的历史朝代，在外文文本中补充了公元纪年法中的年份信息。但对于个别年代信息有争议的历史朝代，则不再标注年份。

3. 对于历史官衔名称，以“传播历史文化，兼顾读者理解”为目的，采用

“音译+名词”“音译+释义”等方法，一方面保留原有的文化特质，另一方面使读者易于接受；对于官衔、官职修饰词语过多的情况，则采用意译或概译的方法进行语义对应；对于官职官衔名在不同历史时期，虽名称未变，但语义内涵发生变化的，根据其语境中相应的含义进行转换。

4. 对于原文中出现的书籍名称，首先遵循“名从历史”“名从主人”的原则，沿用已有的译名。如果已有译名为汉语拼音，则在保留原有名称的基础上，增补英文译名；无英译文的书籍名称，则采用常规翻译方法进行文本对应。

5. 对于原文中的引文（如诗词、古籍文献），根据引文的作用进行有选择性的转换。若引文为核心论点，或用于描写相应的文化内容，且上下文未对引文内容进行解释或重述，则全文翻译；若引文仅用于衬托或强化相应的文化内容，且相关内容已在上下文说明或提及，则进行概译或省译。

6. 对于一些描写壁画形象的直白语言，为提升其艺术美感，采用“优化”的策略和“解释性翻译”的方法，进行语篇结构的扩充对应。

7. 对于宗教文化概念，首先采用已有的英文表达；对于有固定梵语表达的佛教概念，则采用“回译法”进行转换；没有约定俗成表达的宗教概念、中国本土宗教概念及其他宗教与中国文化相融合后产生的概念，则根据情况采用音译、直译或意译进行文本对应。

8. 对于需要补充文化背景信息的内容，一般采用“译者注”的方式进行补充说明，以便更有效地提高阅读理解力。包括但不限于下列情况：一是对于一些在历史演变过程中语义发生变化的文化名称，采用“译者注”的方式加以说明，如“刺史”这一官职名称，分别译为Inspector / Governor / Prefect，并通过“译者注”说明同一名称在不同历史时期因其职责发生变化采用不同译文的背景信息。二是对于一些特殊地名，为避免产生阅读障碍，在翻译的同时加“译者注”进行说明，如不以行政区划命名的大地区概念（中原、西域等），翻译的同时，通过“译者注”明确其内涵和范围；含有古代行政区划“州”“郡”“府”“县”“道”等的地名，在翻译行政区划词的同时适当增加“译者注”解释其含义；由于历史原因更改地名的，亦通过“译者注”加以阐明。三是当同音异义词音译后在译文中无法分辨时，也采用“译者注”的方式加以区分。

9. 本译丛遵循一致性原则，运用统一的翻译策略和方法，但同时也存在一些体现译者个体风格的差异化表达。

三、几点说明

1. 中文文本之外附加的内容，如附录等，经与中文作者沟通，不再收录。

2. 中文文本中个别问题需要进行勘误时，英译文转换正确的语义内容，同时增加必要的说明。

3. 本译丛在翻译过程中参考了大量国内外相关著作、辞典、图册、音像资料、网络资料及数据库等，具体参考目录将在每本书后单另列出。

最后需要说明的是，敦煌文化翻译是一项十分具有挑战性的工作，难点很多，难度很大。因此，作为“丝绸之路·敦煌文化翻译”工程的第一辑译丛，在翻译中难免存在许多不足之处，甚至可能有误译和错译之处。我们真诚期待广大读者、专家学者批评指正！

致　谢

“敦煌文化·译丛”在策划、翻译、出版过程中得到甘肃省委宣传部、中国外文局、兰州大学敦煌学研究所等单位的大力支持；在翻译过程中得到了著作者的翻译授权和学术指导；同时得到了甘肃省人民政府新闻办、兰州城市学院等单位的支持，在此一并感谢。

“敦煌文化·译丛”编委会

An Introduction to *Dunhuang Culture in Translation: A Series*

In recent years, Dunhuang culture—an emblem of the pride of Chinese civilization—has increasingly attracted the world's attention with its profound significance and unique charms. This has taken place against the backdrop of "Chinese culture going global," "telling China's story to the world," and the joint pursuit of the Belt and Road Initiative. Ever-increasing numbers of people both internationally and domestically want Dunhuang's veil of mystery to be lifted. Through reading this series, people can become more familiar with Dunhuang, paving the way to really "get into" Dunhuang. Thus, along the principles of "Dunhuang culture going forth into the world," as well as "telling Dunhuang's story," the *Dunhuang Culture in Translation* series has been compiled with the goal of communicating the concepts of Dunhuang culture, carrying on the spirit of Dunhuang, and promoting Dunhuang to an international audience.

Series Content

The *Dunhuang Culture in Translation: A Series* emphasizes appropriateness for its readers, selecting works in the field of Dunhuang studies which embody academic value and also can be made accessible to a general audience. All the books in this series were written by well-known experts in the field of Dunhuang studies, blending academic knowledge with popular science and presenting information in a systematic way, and using a compilation method in both Chinese and English. The topics cover the essential part of Dunhuang culture, resulting in a relatively comprehensive framework for disseminating this subject to the world. The translated volumes in this series use a Chinese-English format to promote Dunhuang culture and academic exchanges of Dunhuang studies.

Dunhuang Culture in Translation is a multi-volumed, inclusive series published in sets. The first set in the series includes four bilingual volumes: *Dunhuang: Pearl of the Silk Road*; *Art Treasures: Murals and Painted Sculptures in Mogao Caves*; *Raiment of Rainbows and Feathers: Music and Dance from the Dunhuang Murals*; and *Dunhuang: Its Everlasting Impact.*

Dunhuang: Pearl of the Silk Road (by Zheng Binglin and Li Jun) takes as its subject matter the history of Dunhuang as well as its surrounding attractions. It traces Dunhuang's development and changes against the historical background of different periods, from the Neolithic Age, the Han Dynasty, Wei, Jin, Northern and Southern dynasties to the Western Xia, Yuan, Ming, and Qing dynasties. This volume explores the opening of the Silk Road and Dunhuang's historical status as an important crossroads for Sino–Western exchanges, the part it played as an important hub for Sino–Western trade, and its role as a military center for the Central Plains' operations in the Western Regions. It introduces the Buddhist rock–cut cave temples of the Mogao Caves and the Yulin Caves, historical and cultural sites such as the Yangguan and Yumen passes, and surrounding natural scenic spots including the Mingsha Mountain and the Crescent Moon Spring. The whole book is presented with clear ideas and vivid language, integrating factual data, literary narrative, and scholarly expertise. It not only highlights the regional cultural characteristics of Dunhuang, but also reveals its profound historical connotations as well, making this bright pearl, sleeping in the vast desert, glow with its brilliance for the world to see.

Art Treasures: Murals and Painted Sculptures in Mogao Caves (by Zhao Shengliang) outlines the basic features of Dunhuang sculptures and murals, including polychromed statues, Buddhist iconography, apsaras, narrative paintings, sutra illustrations, landscape paintings, decorative motifs, and other elements, expounding their cultural, historical, and artistic value in addition to tracing the course of Chinese art for thousands of years. This volume, steeped in Dr. Zhao's comprehensive academic research and brimming with pride in Chinese culture, also analyzes the exchange and synthesis of visual arts from ancient India, Central Asia, and China. The writing is fluent and easy to understand, with copious illustrations accompanying the text. Sharing an appreciation of both the sophisticated and the popular, it successfully conveys Dunhuang's broad and profound art to its readers.

Raiment of Rainbows and Feathers: Music and Dance from the Dunhuang Murals (by Wang Kefen and Chai Jianhong) takes the Mogao Caves as its subject, introducing the cultural background and origins of Dunhuang music and dance, images of palace entertainment depicted in sutra illustrations, singing and dancing as found in secular paintings, distinctive ethnic dances, the lively lotus child dance, and more. The authors use concise and natural language to discuss the murals and the painted sculptures of the Mogao Caves, explaining the meaning of the images and vividly revealing the rich Buddhist and Chinese music and dance images found in Dunhuang wall paintings. Compact and concise, the book's themes are clear and the language is articulate, with an emphasis on balancing professional scholarship with accessibility to the public, opening the door for readers at home and abroad to understand and appreciate the performing arts of Dunhuang.

Dunhuang: Its Everlasting Impact (by Liu Jinbao) takes the compilation and classification of Dunhuang manuscripts, the exploration of Dunhuang art, and Dunhuang literary creation as its themes. It introduces the background of Dunhuang studies as a field, the research overview of Dunhuang manuscripts in various countries, the famous names behind Dunhuang studies both in China and around the world, and the literary and creative achievements in Dunhuang art, as well as the research, and conservation of Dunhuang relics. The author uses easy-to-understand, lively and dynamic language to integrate scholarship with mass-market appeal, allowing readers to "get closer" to Dunhuang, showing the profound influence of Dunhuang culture in China and internationally. The book's pictures and texts, informative materials, and vivid narrative style encourage both Chinese and English-speaking audiences to truly enter the brilliant cultural temples and treasure houses of Dunhuang.

The four works in this set form a system of their own, covering important areas of the Dunhuang cultural sphere, and systematically explaining the historical development, artistic value, and humanistic spirit of Dunhuang culture. On the one hand, the main objective of the books sets out to introduce the history and geography of Dunhuang, while on the other hand, it explores two of the most well-known aspects of Dunhuang arts: the visual arts and the performing arts. Finally, judging from its value, the set highlights the influence of Dunhuang culture and Dunhuang studies around the world. This collection of translations aims to promote international understanding of the aesthetics of Dunhuang art, supplement in-depth bilingual works related to Dunhuang music and dance, expand systematic language materials related to Dunhuang history and geography, and provide a must-have language reference for researchers of Dunhuang studies both in China and overseas.

Special Features of the Translation

Dunhuang Culture in Translation is organized around the themes of promoting Dunhuang culture and transmitting Dunhuang thought, telling the stories of Dunhuang, and expounding the spirit of Dunhuang in a Chinese-English format. In terms of translation methods, this series uses multiple strategies and methods to compare and translate texts. In terms of the interpretation of the original text, on the one hand, we can deeply understand the semantics of the original text through systematic review of historical documents, background materials, and research results in Dunhuang studies in China as well as internationally; on the other hand, we can accurately grasp the essence of Dunhuang culture through dialogue and communication between the translators and the original authors. In terms of foreign language expression, special attention has been paid to the effective expression of information. The translation has been done according to a Sino-Western model. The Chinese and English language translators have closely cooperated with one other, with reader accessibility as their primary consideration, using appropriate discourse modes and comprehensive translation methods to exchange languages. The translation is as close as possible to the idiomatic expression, modes of thought, language style, and reading comprehension of English-language readers, so that the translated text of the works not only achieves a "going out" in a literary sense, but simultaneously also allows the cultural connotations to truly "go in" and achieve a deep transmission into the readers' conceptualization.

The overarching translation principles of the *Dunhuang Culture in Translation: A Series* are as follows: on the basis of understanding and respecting the original text, for those expressions which have a corresponding concept and expression in English language and culture, the translation strives to accurately reproduce the original language and cultural information, faithful to the content and style of the original Chinese text. Moreover, on the premise of following standard principles of translation, according to differences between Chinese and English languages and cultures we have comprehensively employed translation strategies such as domestication, foreignization, and fusion to appropriately add, delete, edit, and modify the original content. We have adopted a flexible mixture of approaches such as abridged translation, generalized translation, compilation, and interpretative translation for language and text conversion.

The basic translation methods for the *Dunhuang Culture in Translation: A Series* are as follows:

1. For the translation of cultural concepts and terminology in the original text, foreign language expressions found in official publications and official websites of China have generally been used.

2. For historical dynasties, information for the dates using AD and BC has been added to the foreign language text. However, for historical dynasties with dates in dispute, the year is not noted.

3. For the translations of historical titles of official rank, our purpose is to enhance exchanges of history and culture, taking into account the readers' understanding. Thus, we have employed methods such as "*pinyin* transliteration + nouns," and "*pinyin* transliteration + gloss," on the one hand, retaining the original cultural characteristics of the titles, and, on the other hand, allowing readers to easily accept the title names. For official titles with multiple versions or modifiers, free translation or generalized translation methods have been used for semantic correspondence; for official titles from different historical periods, when the name has remained unchanged, but the semantic connotation has changed, the meaning has been conveyed according to the appropriate context.

4. For the titles of Chinese books, the principles of "using historical names" and "using names created by the original parties" have been followed. If an existing title is in *pinyin*, the English translation has been added on the basis of keeping the original name; if there is no English translation of the name of the classic text, conventional translation methods have been applied.

5. For citations or quotations in the original text (such as poems, classics), selective conversion has been carried out according to the function of the citation. If a quotation or citation functions as a core idea or is used to describe corresponding cultural content, and the context does not explain or restate the citation content, the full text is translated; if the quotation is only used to highlight or strengthen the corresponding cultural content, and the relevant content has been explained or mentioned in the context, general translation or deletion has been applied.

6. For certain basic, straightforward language describing mural imagery, in order to enhance their artistic beauty, "optimization" strategies and interpretative translation methods have been applied to expand the text.

7. For religious and cultural concepts, we have first adopted existing English terms and expressions where they exist; for Buddhist concepts with fixed, conventional Sanskrit names, we have used the back translation method to convert the terms from Chinese back into their original Sanskrit again. Religious concepts that are not expressed by conventional usage or fixed terms, native Chinese religious concepts, and concepts arising from the fusion of other religions and Chinese culture have been rendered by transliteration, literal translation or free translation based on the situation or context.

8. For the content that needs to be supplemented with cultural background information, we have generally used footnotes as supplementary explanations, in order to more effectively improve the readers' comprehension. This includes but is not limited to the following situations: First, for some cultural names whose semantics have changed in the course of historical evolution, we have used footnotes to explain them. For example, the official title of "*cishi*" is translated variously as Inspector, Governor, or Prefect, and a footnote is used to explain that the title for this post was modified over time due to changes in the position's responsibilities in

different historical periods. Second, for special place names, footnotes have been added to avoid confusion. For example, the concept of large geographical regions such as the Central Plains, the Western Regions, and so forth, was provided with footnotes to clarify their meaning and scope. Footnotes have been provided for place names with ancient administrative divisions such as "*zhou*" "*jun*" "*fu*" "*xian*" "*dao*" etc., where necessary or appropriate. Changes in place names due to historical reasons have also been clarified through the addition of footnotes. Third, when homophones cannot be distinguished in the translation after transliteration, footnotes or annotations have also been used to distinguish them.

9. This translation series follows the principle of consistency and uses unified translation strategies and methods, but some terms and expressions may vary and reflect the individual style of the translators.

Special Points for the Readers' Consideration

1. Appendices, indices, and glossaries in the original Chinese versions are not included in the volumes of this set, which is permitted by the original authors.

2. Where individual issues in the Chinese text have required correction, the information in the English translation has been presented in the corrected, revised form, and explanations have been added where necessary.

3. This translation series relies on a large number of Chinese and English language reference works, dictionaries, atlases, audiovisual materials, internet resources, and databases during the translation process. A specific bibliography is listed separately at the back of each volume.

One final thing to be said is that Dunhuang culture translation is a very demanding task, with many difficulties and great challenges. Therefore, as the first series in the Silk Road Dunhuang Culture Translation Project, there are inevitably many shortcomings in the translation, and there may even be mistranslations and errors. We sincerely encourage criticism and correction from readers, experts, and scholars in the field.

Acknowledgements

The *Dunhuang Culture in Translation* : *A Series* received strong support from the Publicity Department of the Gansu Provincial Party Committee, China Foreign Languages Publishing Administration, Institute of Dunhuang Studies of Lanzhou University, and other governmental offices in the planning, translation, and publication process of this series. Throughout the translation process, permission, authorization, and guidance were granted by the authors of each volume. The Information Office of the People's Government of Gansu Province, Lanzhou City University as well as other governmental offices and leaders all gave their encouragement and support to this project. We extend our heartfelt thanks and gratitude to them all.

Editorial Committee of *Dunhuang Culture in Translation: A Series*

目录

Contents

目录

Contents

《丝路花雨》演出海报

Poster for “The Rain of Flowers Along the Silk Road”

序言一

1975年,中国与英国签订了教育交流协议,恢复了中断将近10年的留学生互换项目。我作为首批留学生之一,同14位同学到英国学习。与此同时,英国学生也到中国留学。很多年以后,我遇到其中一位当年曾经在北京大学留学的英国学者,那时她已经是大英图书馆的东亚部负责人。她告诉我正在做的一件事情就是和中国文物局合作,把大英图书馆收藏的来自敦煌的历史资料复制给中方,以此加深两国专家围绕敦煌学的研究活动。可见因为历史上的多种原因,大量敦煌资料流散在海外,这对中国是一种损失,但是也催化了国外对敦煌的关注。

然而,敦煌学不局限于仅仅流散在海外的史料研究,真正的研究中心永远在敦煌,永远在中国。比如石窟代表的敦煌文化就是搬不走的,敦煌背后的历史和哲学思想是搬不走的。近些年,中国学者对敦煌的研究成绩斐然,加之敦煌文化的博大精深,非常有必要通过翻译,把中国学者的研究成果,把敦煌文化的精华,大张旗鼓地传播出去。特别是"一带一路"倡议不仅强化了中国与沿线国家的经济活动,也拉近了文化上的联系。民心相通首先要以文明互鉴为依托,以文化传播为纽带,达到美美与共。敦煌文化重要,对外传播更为重要。然而,集历史、艺术、宗教为一体的敦煌学覆盖历史时段长,涉及艺术门类全,代表的宗教影响深,反映的社会发展广,要翻译成外文实在太难了。

令人欣喜的是,以甘肃文化翻译中心姜秋霞教授领衔的团队卧薪尝胆、呕心沥血达六年,终于把首批共四部中英文对照版的"敦煌文化·译丛"呈现给国内外的读者。这四部图书分别是《丝路明珠:敦煌》《艺苑瑰宝:莫高窟壁画与彩塑》《箫管霓裳:敦煌乐舞》和《遗响千年:敦煌的影响》。这套图书的出版标志着我国首次有计划、成规模地、系统地把敦煌文化最新的研究成果用英文对外介绍。四本书用当代的语言把一个中国故事的过去与现在讲述给国际受众。这个翻译出版项目成就有多大,其艰难历程就有多长。翻译难,中译外更难,敦煌文化的翻译难上加难。这六年来,姜教授的团队经历了多少艰辛,比如为寻找一个准确的词汇花费多少心血,为精准传达一个观点熬去多少时光,读者只需翻阅一下这四本书,就会一目了然。

既然难度这么大,为什么还要翻译?姜教授说:“翻译,不仅仅是语言的转换,更是对文化的阐释。翻译敦煌文化,不是简单的话码转换,也不是单纯的信息传递,更重要的是解释和阐释敦煌文化和历史遗存蕴含的哲学思想、人文精神、价值理念、道德规范;弘扬和传承蕴含其中的中华民族的文化精神、文化胸怀和文化自信。”通过她的话我感到,敦煌文化翻译反映了译者的一种家国情怀、对外传播的理想抱负和迎难而上的治学精神。没有坚定的信念、远大的抱负和刻苦的工作干劲,译者早已在翻译任务的困难面前望而却步。所以,在向译者团队表示祝贺的同时,我更想向他们表示崇高的敬意。

一套丛书有那么大的意义吗? 文明互鉴需要文化信息的交流,做好对外交流就是要拿出外国人读得懂、看得明白的作品来。展示文化自信,需要拿出难啃的硬骨头成果来。这套丛书就是文化自信的产物,敦煌文化对外传播的最新之作。

然而,“敦煌文化·译丛”的意义不仅仅在作品上。丛书的翻译还是翻译团队不断成熟的一个过程。“敦煌文化·译丛”是“丝绸之路·敦煌文化翻译工程”的第一期项目。启动后译者发现翻译的难度极大,文化概念的翻译难度尤其大。于是翻译团队又启动了“敦煌文化中英对照术语库”的编制工作,并在《敦煌文化关键词》完成后,再开始推进“敦煌文化·译丛”的工作。“敦煌文化·译丛”第一辑四部图书以及衍生作品的问世见证了一支年轻的翻译队伍从无到有、从小到大、从弱到强的发展壮大。而作为设在兰州城市学院的一个团队,译者们作为教师也在培育着更加年轻的译者。他们的精神和经验必然让他们带出一支对外传播的人才队伍。

“敦煌文化·译丛”的意义还在于填补了“一带一路”建设的一个空白。敦煌,曾经是古代丝绸之路的重镇,如今是“一带一路”建设的重要支点。丛书给敦煌乃至甘肃省的对外文化交流提供了精品之作，增添了灿烂的文化光彩。讲好中国故事，传播中国声音不是一句口号，需要一部部的作品来支撑和实现。“敦煌文化·译丛”不仅展示了一段辉煌的历史，更彰显了中国文化自信和文化繁荣在新时代的成果。四部作品宣扬的不仅仅是中国历史上的文化积累，它们所介绍的四个方面更是代表中国在文明互鉴过程中的四颗璀璨明星，反射中国文化发展的过去，照亮中国文化传承的当今，预示中国文化生生不息的未来。

也正因为如此，我们期待“丝绸之路·敦煌文化翻译工程”的下一个项目。

中国外文局原副局长
中国翻译协会常务副会长　黄友义

2020 年 10 月

Foreword I

In 1975, China and the United Kingdom signed an educational exchange agreement, resuming the exchange program for foreign students which had been suspended for nearly 10 years. I went to the UK to study with 14 classmates as part of the first group of these students. At the same time, British students also came to study in China. Some years later, I ran into one of the British scholars who had studied at Peking University when I was studying in the UK. At the time we met, she was already head of the Department of Oriental at the British Library. She told me that she was working on a joint project with the State Bureau of Cultural Relics, replicating historical documents and materials from Dunhuang held in the British Library, in order to facilitate Dunhuang research by experts from our two nations. Due to various historical reasons, a large amount of Dunhuang materials were scattered in various places overseas. This may have been a loss for China, but it also catalyzed foreigners' attention on Dunhuang.

However, Dunhuang studies is not limited merely to the study of historical materials scattered around the world. The real center of research has always been in Dunhuang and in China. For example, Dunhuang culture, as represented by its cave temples, is irremovable. Likewise, the history and philosophical thought behind Dunhuang is also deeply rooted here. In recent years, Chinese scholars have made outstanding achievements in the study of Dunhuang, and, coupled with the profundity of Dunhuang culture, it has become truly necessary to make these research findings—along with the essence of Dunhuang culture—widely known through their translation. In particular, the Belt and Road Initiative has not only strengthened the economic activity between China and the countries along the route, but has also brought closer cultural ties between them. People-to-people exchange must first rely on cultural communication and mutual learning among civilizations so as to uphold the beauty and diversity of civilizations in the world. Dunhuang culture is important, but communication with the international community is even more significant. However, Dunhuang studies, which integrates history, art, and religion, covers a long historical period of time, involves a full range of arts, represents deep religious influences, and reflects a wide range of social developments. It is thus an extremely challenging task to translate the achievements of Dunhuang studies into another language.

It is now gratifying to see that the team led by Professor Jiang Qiuxia of the Gansu Cultural Translation and Interpreting Center has, after six years of hard work, completed the first four volumes of the Chinese-English bilingual *Dunhuang Culture in Translation* series, now being presented to readers at home and abroad. The titles of these four books are *Dunhuang: Pearl of the Silk Road*; *Art Treasures: Murals and Painted Sculptures in Mogao Caves*; *Raiment of Rainbows and Feathers: Music and Dance from Dunhuang Murals*; and *Dunhuang: Its Everlasting Impact*. The publication of this set of books marks the first time that China has introduced the latest Dunhuang culture research in English and Chinese at the same time, and on a planned, large-scale, and systematic basis. The four books use contemporary language to convey the past and present of a Chinese story to an international audience. This translation and publishing project has been a great achievement, and the process has been long and arduous. Translation in general is not an easy job and it is even more difficult to translate Chinese into another language; the difficulty in translating Dunhuang culture lies even beyond all this. For the past six years, Professor Jiang's team has gone through many hardships, for example, expending great effort researching and finding the exact vocabulary and terminology, and considerable time spent on accurately and faithfully conveying each author's point of view. Readers only need to browse through these four books and the difficulties they had to overcome will be made immediately evident.

Since it is so difficult, then why translate? As Professor Jiang said, "Translation is not merely the conversion of language, but also the interpretation of culture. Translating Dunhuang culture is not a simple code conversion, nor is it purely the transmission of information. More importantly, translation reveals and interprets the philosophical thought, humanistic spirit, and values contained in Dunhuang culture and historical relics, which is imbued with the cultural spirit, mind, and confidence of the Chinese nation." Her words convince me that Dunhuang culture translation reflects the translators' deep love for their country and their ideals and determination for communicating with the world at large, as well as their devoted academic scholarship in the face of challenges. Unless translators have firm beliefs, lofty commitment, and a strong work ethic, they may easily pull back from the difficulties of translation work. While congratulating the team of translators, I would also like to express my highest respect for them.

Why does a series of books hold that much significance? Mutual learning between civilizations requires the interchange of cultural information, and doing a good job in communication involves producing works that people from other countries can readily understand. Conveying cultural confidece requires extremely hard and sophisticated work. This book series, the latest achievement in the introduction of Dunhuang culture, is a product of that cultural confidece.

The significance of *Dunhuang Culture in Translation* however is not only in the finished works. The translation of the series also represents a process of continuous maturity of the translation team. *Dunhuang Culture in Translation* marks the first phase of a much larger program—the Silk Road Dunhuang Culture Translation Project. After its launch, the translators found that the work was extremely challenging, especially the translation of cultural concepts. Thus, the translation team began by compiling the Dunhuang Culture Chinese–English Terminology Database, and after the completion of the bilingual *Key Concepts in Dunhuang Culture*, it began to focus on the work of the *Dunhuang Culture in Translation* series. The publication of these four books and their related works of the first series of *Dunhuang Culture in Translation* witnessed the development and growth of a team of young translators starting from scratch, growing from small to large, and from weak to strong. Based at Lanzhou City University, members of this translation team are also teachers who are bringing up even younger translators. Their spirit and experience will inevitably guide them in fostering the next generation of talent for presenting information and culture to the international community.

What is significant is that the *Dunhuang Culture in Translation* series has filled a gap in the promotion of the Belt and Road Initiative. Dunhuang was once an important town on the ancient Silk Road and now holds an important position in promoting the Belt and Road Initiative. This book series provides excellent works for not only Dunhuang but also Gansu Province to conduct exchanges with the world, adding a superb new dimension in cultural communication. Telling China's story and getting China's voice heard is not just a slogan: it needs a series of solid works to help make it happen. *Dunhuang Culture in Translation* not only reveals a glorious history, but also demonstrates the achievements of Chinese cultural confidece and cultural prosperity in our present era. These four works make known not only the formation of culture in Chinese history, but the four facets they introduce also represent four bright stars of China in the process of mutual learning between civilizations. Reflecting the past of China's cultural development and illuminating the heritage of Chinese civilization, they herald the limitless future of Chinese culture.

It is precisely because of this that we now look forward to the next installment in the Silk Road Dunhuang Culture Translation Project.

Huang Youyi

Former Deputy Director-General of China Foreign Languages Publishing Administration

Vice President of Translators Association of China

October 2020

序言二

敦煌文化是丝绸之路文明的精髓，是中外文化交流背景之下形成的哲学思想、人文精神、价值理念、道德规范等，而丝绸之路是连接古代中国与中亚、南亚、东欧的经济文化的交通要道，因其贩运的商品主要是丝绸，所以称之为丝绸之路。同时还因其贩运的物品和使用的货币而被称作为玉石之路、白银之路、香药之路、茶马之路等。

丝绸之路还是一条中外文化交流的重要通道，西方的先进科学技术和文化都是通过这条通道传入中国的，同时中国的先进文化和科学技术也是通过这条国际通道传播到世界各国，中西文化经过这条道路互相碰撞、交融和接纳，促进了汉唐帝国和学术文化的发展。通过这条道路，印度的佛教、欧洲的景教、中亚的祆教和摩尼教进入中国，并在中国迅速传播开来，由于佛教寺院的建造和石窟的开凿，佛教造像的兴盛，犍陀罗佛教艺术流传中国，影响了中国佛教艺术及中国道教艺术的发展。

因景教艺术传入，中亚艺术风格传入中国，并影响了中古时期中国社会生活的方方面面。通过这条道路，产生于印度的天竺乐和中亚的康国乐、安国乐和新疆地区龟兹乐、疏勒乐、高昌乐等的音乐舞蹈相继传入并迅速传播开来，由外来音乐舞蹈和中国古代清乐融合而产生的西凉乐，成为中古中国乐舞的重要组成部分，推进了中国文化艺术的发展。

通过这条道路，中亚西域的物种、医技医籍、饮食、服饰、生活习惯等都进入中国，影响中国古代社会生活的各个方面。汉唐文化就是在对外来文化包容接纳的基础之上产生的。中国古代儒家典籍和道教以及先进的科学技术也是通过这条道路传播到中亚和东欧地区，推动了世界文化和科学技术的发展。古代中国通过这条道路了解世界，而世界也通过这条道路接纳中国。

敦煌文化形成之地的敦煌是丝绸之路东段和中段的交汇之地，也是丝绸之路的必经之地。敦煌最早见载于中国历史典籍《山海经》，《山海经》北山经记载敦薨之山出敦薨之水，敦薨之水西流注入泑泽，是为河源。

敦薨就是敦煌，是历史典籍对敦煌的最早记载。后来张骞出使西域，被匈奴扣押在河西及蒙古高原十余年，对这里的地理地貌非常熟悉，后来又到中亚从大月氏人那里收集到他们在敦煌一带生活的信息，敦煌一词很可能首先是从张骞开始使用，实际上就是敦薨的音译。

根据《汉书》的记载，实际上在汉朝设置敦煌郡之前的元鼎四年，敦煌一词已经开始使用。而敦煌地区的三危山就见载于《尚书·禹贡篇》，记载导黑水经过三危山流入南海，三危山就是敦煌的三危山，而黑水经我们根据《太平广记》和敦煌文书《瓜沙两郡史事编年并序》研究，就是流经敦煌的疏勒河，疏勒河在汉唐间曾称之为冥水，疏勒河上的沼泽湖泊也叫作乌泽，沿着疏勒河修建的军事屏障称之为昆仑障，都与黑有密切关系。

敦煌也是古代中国领导人行经之地，根据《穆天子传》的记载穆天子即位十五年，曾巡游至泑泽，即今天的罗布泊，前往罗布泊必须经过敦煌，因此周穆王十五年就曾来到敦煌。如果这个记载不误的话，公元前962年中国领导人已经来到了敦煌，到了新疆的罗布泊地区或者更远的哈密或者帕米尔高原一带。敦煌的龙勒山就因周时有龙马朝出咸阳，暮至寿昌，遗其衔勒，故名龙勒山。就是说周穆王时中原王朝已经同西域地区进行玉石贸易和马种交换。

汉武帝击败匈奴取得河西地区，置敦煌等河西四郡而拥有二关，玉门关、阳关是汉唐通西域的主要关隘，敦煌是汉唐中央政府经营西域的军事基地，同时也是来往商贾的都会城市。阳关是出敦煌到西域的和亲通使关隘，而与阳关对应的玉门关是出敦煌经营西域的军事关隘，俗称阴关或者凶关，与玉石贸易没有任何关系。

出敦煌西行分别有三条道路，南道至鄯善，中道到高昌，北道经伊吾，总汇敦煌。这三条道路都必须穿越戈壁沙漠地带，“上无飞鸟，下无走兽，复无水草”；“行旅负水担粮，履践沙石，往来困弊”；“西路险恶，人行迷误，沙河阻道，鬼魅热风，遇无免者”。这种情况说明没有充分的准备绝不敢贸然进入沙碛西行。

这样一来，经过沙碛考验的人们才能顺利来到敦煌，他们的精神和灵魂都经过严酷的自然环境的洗礼，有了一个质的升华。汉代李广利征大宛两次都是从敦煌出兵，两汉敦煌太守都参与经营西域，吐蕃占领敦煌之前的唐代，沙州刺史或者敦煌太守，经常参与经营西域的事务。

汉唐的敦煌是一个都会城市，国际化程度非常高。从两汉时期敦煌就居住着很多西域质子和西域商贾，特别是粟特人经常见载于出土文献和典籍中，到唐代更是这样，敦煌的胡人在唐朝中央军队中任职的很多，有的晋升为中央禁军的首领，像曹怀直，祖上帮助唐朝建功立业，被赐姓为曹，历代担任禁军要职。

特别是唐中宗神龙年间石城镇康艳典后裔部落随戍守播仙镇的凉州兵迁居敦煌，唐朝政府为安置这些粟特人在敦煌城周围专门设置了从化乡，从化乡最少有两个里四个村落，粟特人控制敦煌的市场贸易，出任市壁师并管理敦煌市场贸易。直到吐蕃时期敦煌粟特人康秀华仍然担任部落使，而安景旻出任敦煌都督。

张氏归义军时期，安景旻出任归义军节度使副使，而康秀华出任瓜州刺史左威卫将军，到张承奉时期，粟特人安怀恩出任押衙。914 年粟特人曹议金出任归义军节度使，敦煌成了粟特人领导下的归义军政权。除了粟特人，敦煌外来居民很多，有达怛人、回鹘人、突厥人、吐蕃人、波斯人、印度人、鄯善人、于阗人等，他们开店经营商品，经营酒店出卖食品，很多行市的头目都是这些胡人担任，特别是前往各地的商业贸易团体的头目都是由粟特胡人担任，胡商是敦煌市场贸易的主体，因此敦煌市场贸易的商人具有很高程度的国际性。

敦煌市场的商品也具有很高的国际性，敦煌地不产珍，献无奇玩，是一个贫乏的地方。由于敦煌地处交通要道，敦煌市场上商品非常丰富，有西域地区贩运而来的西州布、安西氎，有龟兹出产的胡粉，有中亚来的金青和水银，吐蕃地区的颜料石青、石绿和毛织品，波斯等地出产的胡锦和珠宝，伊州出产的铁器，于阗出产的玉石，东罗马的银器，西域印度的药材和香料，高丽出产的高丽锦，达怛和吐蕃出产的畜牧产品和兵器等，商品来自相邻各个地区或者中亚、南亚和东亚及中国内地各个地方。

作为交换的等价物是银币。金银器皿作为流通货币在晚唐五代的敦煌贸易市场比较常见,有罗马银盏、银盘子、金花银瓶子、银碗等;这些银器标明重量,用于支付物价,其性质显然是货币,不是作为一般意义上的器皿,表明银碗是作为货币流通于敦煌等地的贸易市场中;在对外贸易中还使用丝绸支付物价;在对内或小宗贸易上多用实物特别是粮食支付物价,作为交换的等价物进行交换。因此货币也具有国际性。

敦煌是佛教最早进入的地区。敦煌文献是关于中国佛教最为详细和真实的记载。敦煌汉简中就已经记载了寺院,寺院内的一切均有助于重构中国寺院的面貌。敦煌文献中还保存有最早的汉文景教经典、摩尼教经典,虽然敦煌文献中没有袄教经典,但是作为官府主办袄教祭祀仪式足以看出袄教的影响力。在敦煌佛教、道教、袄教、景教、摩尼教以及儒教之间的和谐共处超过相互排斥和争斗。特别是西域地区的胡腾舞、胡旋舞在敦煌地区非常流行,敦煌人在重大节日都要踏苏幕遮,出现于龟兹的舞蹈成为敦煌的流行舞。这种局面的基础就是敦煌多民族和平共处,互相包容,互相借鉴,共同发展。敦煌作为丝绸之路上的明珠,他的魅力就在于此。

丝绸之路也可称之为科技之路。西域地区的科学技术如医学、医方、天文历法等都是通过这条道路传入中国,中国的科学技术也是通过这条道路传向西域地区。敦煌文献的记载就是很好的见证。我们要交代的是敦煌出产瓜得名称瓜州,传说狐狸吃瓜首尾俱入瓜中,表明敦煌出产的瓜很大。回鹘瓜和大食瓜,名见于敦煌文献中,回鹘瓜,又叫瓤桃,这些地方在晚唐五代时期属于回鹘统治地区,所谓伊州回鹘、西州回鹘,大概称之为回鹘瓜就是出产于回鹘地区。

大食瓜,就是出产在大食地区的瓜,这种瓜是什么瓜呢,我们认为是西瓜,西瓜原产地南非,后来传播到埃及,又从埃及传到中亚,金代陕西同州有个官员出使西域,从中亚引进并在中原地区大量传播开来,当时人对这种瓜没有统一的名称,所以按照以地命名的习惯,称之为西瓜,原意可能是西域的瓜、西方的瓜等。今天陕西大荔的瓜还是很有名的,个大皮厚瓤甜。

医学技术的交流通过丝绸之路也很明显,汉唐时期虽然中医学很发达,但有些医术还没有西域波斯、印度先进,比如眼科中的白内障手术,就是从西域传入，唐史将其作为特殊案例记载。敦煌当地医学家的造诣是学兼中西。

敦煌是丝绸之路上的一颗明珠，敦煌文化是丝绸之路文明精髓所在，而丝绸之路是中西交通文化交流永恒的通途。第一，政治稳定是丝绸之路顺畅的基本要素，这包括历史上中央政权和丝绸之路沿线民族和国家的稳定。先秦时期，由于中原地区文化经济的发展，与周边地区形成很大的社会差异，这种差异导致一种稳定的向心力，加上周边民族对中原政府还不能构成威胁，中原政权虽然没有鼓励也并没阻止中外交往，中西交往属于一种原始状态进行，很多西域地区的特产通过丝绸之路流入中原地区，而中国的产品也经过这条通道进入西域。关于穆天子与西王母的会面，《山海经》关于河源和丝绸之路沿线的地理地貌的记载就是这一背景下的产物。

汉武帝凭借强大的军事实力打败匈奴，重新开启丝绸之路，开始了利用军事政治力量维系丝绸之路安全的时期，汉唐时期都是由国家经营沿线交通设施配置、道路维护和安全保障等，丝绸之路的兴衰几乎与国家政权稳定一致。宋代以后陆路衰落与海路有很大关系，但是沿线政治环境的变化因素起了极大的作用。

第二，经济利益的互惠是丝绸之路发展的基础，维系丝绸之路经久不衰的经济因素是利益的互惠。丝绸之路贸易有几个层面：首先是贡赐贸易，这是一种严重的不对等贸易，中央政府承受非常大的经济压力，贡赐之间的比例 1∶10 到 1∶40 左右，这种贸易是国家政治利益为主的贸易活动。其次是一般性贸易，基本上是由地方政府控制的经济贸易，由政府管理的贸易使团进行的贸易活动，这种贸易活动的利润都在 100%以上，使用等价物以金银丝绸为主，多数进行以物易物贸易，中国的丝绸外销和西域的香料宝物内售，有相当一部分的商人是西域胡人，在中国内地经营。胡商在中国进行的对外贸易和对内贸易，促进了汉唐社会经济繁荣发展，同时由于经济贸易的带动，沿线各地的经济也发展起来。特别是丝绸之路沿线物产并不丰富但地位十分重要的地区，财富经丝绸之路贸易在这些地区得到重新分配。经济上互惠是丝绸之路保持畅通的经济因素。

第三，丝绸之路文化研究是重新发展丝绸之路经济带的先决条件。今天我们研究丝绸之路经济带，更应当重视丝绸之路文化的研究。古代丝绸之路将古代沿线不同地区不同文化连接起来，这些文化通过文物文献等形式在丝绸之路沿线各个地区保存了下来，研究这些文物文献对揭示这一地区古代文明十分重要，研究该地区历史上对丝绸之路经营的经验和教训对今天有十分重要的借鉴作用，只有将其远古文明研究清楚，才有利于丝绸之路的发展。丝绸之路沿线的敦煌、高昌、哈密、库车、于阗等都是丝绸之路上的明珠，因此研究这些地区的历史文化就是丝绸之路的个案研究，是一项十分有意义的工作。

甘肃文化翻译中心组织翻译的“敦煌文化·译丛”，就是响应习近平总书记敦煌讲话精神，弘扬传承敦煌文化，提高文化自信的一个有力举措。

兰州大学敦煌学研究所所长　郑炳林

2020 年 10 月

Foreword Ⅱ

Dunhuang Culture is the essence of Silk Road civilization, with philosophical ideas formed in the context of cultural exchange between China and the outside world. It also represents the spirit of humanism, the concept of values, and the code of ethics. The Silk Road was the major economic and cultural link connecting ancient China, the Central Asia, South Asia and Eastern Europe. The Silk Road is so-called because silk was the main commodity transported along the route. But the Silk Road was also known as the Jade Road, the Silver Road, the Spice Road, and the Tea and Horse Road, among others, because such goods and currencies were also transported and used along the route.

The Silk Road was also an important route for cultural exchange between China and the outside world. This international thoroughfare was the means by which the West's advanced science, technology, and culture reached China, and by which China's advanced culture, science, and technology spread to other nations of the world. Through the Silk Road, Chinese and Western cultures met, mingled, and accepted each other, bringing about developments of the Han and Tang empires as well as academic cultures that have influenced the world. It was via this route that India's Buddhism, Europe's Nestorianism, and Central Asia's Zoroastrianism and Manichaeism entered China and spread quickly. Buddhist temple construction and cave excavation, the rise of Buddhist iconography, and the spread of Gandharan Buddhist art into China all contributed to the proliferation of magnificent Chinese Buddhist art, facilitating the development of the Taoist art.

The presence of Nestorian art and Central Asian art styles in China influenced medieval Chinese society and lifestyles in a multitude of ways. The music and dance originated from Indian music, Central Asia music and music of Xinjiang region entered through the Silk Road and quickly spread. The mingling of foreign music and dance and ancient Chinese *Qingyue* music produced Xiliang music, which became an essential element of medieval Chinese music and dance, and furthered the development of Chinese culture and art.

Through the Silk Road, plant species, medical technology, diet, dress, and everyday habits all entered China, influencing the lifestyle of ancient Chinese society in various ways. The culture of the Han and Tang dynasties emerged on the basis of these outside influences. Ancient Chinese Confucian texts, Taoism and advanced science and technology also passed along the Silk Road on their way to Central Asia and Eastern Europe, promoting the development of culture, science, and technology throughout the world. Through the Silk Road, ancient China was able to understand the world, and the world was able to accept China.

Dunhuang, where Dunhuang culture emerged, is located at the crossroads of the eastern and central sections of the Silk Road; travelers had to pass through Dunhuang on their way. Among Chinese historical texts, Dunhuang was first mentioned in the *Classic of Mountains and Seas*, from which the *North Mountain Classic* records that the Dunhong river flowed down Dunhong Mountain, and then westward into Lop Nur, where it formed the source of the Yellow River.

Dunhong was thus the name for Dunhuang, and was the earliest reference to the site. Later, Zhang Qian had his mission to the Western Regions, but was detained by the Xiongnu for more than ten years in the west of the Hexi Corridor and on the Mongolian plateau, becoming very familiar with the geography and landforms of the area. Then he traveled to the Central Asia to gather information from the Greater Yuezhi people about their life in the Dunhuang area. It is very likely that the name Dunhuang originated with Zhang Qian; he actually transcribed "Dunhong" as Dunhuang.

According to the *Book of Han*, in the fourth year of the Yuanding Era, before the establishment of Dunhuang Prefecture in the Han dynasty, the name Dunhuang was in fact already in use. Moreover, the Sanwei Mountain, recorded in the *Book of Yugong*, through which the Heishui River flowed into the South China Sea was the one situated in Dunhuang, while according to our research into the *Extensive Records of the Taiping Era* and the Dunhuang document *Chronology and Preface of the History of Guazhou and Shazhou*, the Heishui River was the Shule River which flows through Dunhuang. In the Han and Tang dynasties, the Shule River was known as the Mingshui River ("Dark Water"). The marshy lakes on the Shule River were also called the Black Marsh. The military barriers built along the Shule River were called the Kunlun Barrier. All three have implications of "darkness" or "blackness."

In ancient China, Dunhuang was also a place which emperors and high-rank officials passed during their travel to the west. In his 15th year of regin, King Mu, once travelled to present-day Lop Nur according to the *Tale of King Mu*. To reach Lop Nur, one must pass through Dunhuang; that is to say, King Mu had been to Dunhuang. If this account is to be believed, then Chinese leaders had already been to Dunhuang by 962 BC, as well as to present-day Xinjiang's Lop Nur region, or even further to Hami or the Pamir Plateau. Dunhuang's Longle Mountain (*longle* meaning headstall of dragon horse) was so-named because during the Zhou Dynasty, a powerful steed known as "dragon horse" left its headstall there during its trip from Xianyang in the morning to Shouchang (part of Dunhuang) in the evening. That is to say, by the time of King Mu, the Kingdoms in the Central Plains had already exchanged jade and horse breeds with the Western Regions.

Emperor Wu of the Han Dynasty defeated the Xiongnu to gain control of the Hexi Corridor. He set up Dunhuang and three other prefectures on the western side with the Yumen Pass ("Jade Gate") and the Yangguan Pass, which were the main border controls in the western part of the Han and Tang dynasties. Dunhuang was a military base for the central governments of the Han and Tang dynasties, as well as a leading mercantile city. Yangguan Pass was for peace-making envoys from Dunhuang heading west, while Yumen Pass was a protected pass for merchants heading west. It was commonly known as the Yinguan Pass, and actually had nothing to do with the jade trade.

There were three routes heading west from Dunhuang: the southern road to

Shanshan; the central road to Gaochang; and the northern road going via Yiwu. These three routes all crossed the Gobi and desert. These western routes were treacherous: there were no birds above, no animals on the ground, and no succulent plants. Carrying water and grain, walking over sand and rocks, going to and fro, people got lost, and rivers of sand blocked the way while otherworldly hot winds inevitably blew. This indicated that travelers did not dare go to the western side of the moraine without adequate preparation.

Only people who knew the lay of the land were able to get to Dunhuang. Their spirits were baptized by the character–building harshness of such an environment. In the Han Dynasty, Li Guangli conquered Dayuan twice from his base in Dunhuang. The Dunhuang governors of the Eastern and Western Han dynasties were involved in the administration of the Western Regions; likewise, in the Tang dynasty before the occupation of Dunhuang by the Tubo, the Shazhou inspectors or governors were also often involved in running affairs in the Western Regions.

Dunhuang was a burgeoning international metropolis during the Han and Tang dynasties. From the time of the Eastern and Western Han dynasties, Dunhuang was home to descendants of hostages and merchants from the Western Regions. The Sogdians in particular are often mentioned in excavated documents and texts, even more so in those from the Tang Dynasty. Foreigners served in the Tang Imperial Army in large numbers. Some were even promoted to leadership roles, such as Cao Huaizhi, whose ancestors helped build the Tang Dynasty. They were granted the surname Cao, and successive generations of the family served important roles in the Imperial Army.

In particular, during the Shenlong Era of the Emperor Zhongzong in the Tang Dynasty, the descendants of Kang Yandian from the Shicheng Town moved to Dunhuang with the Liangzhou soldiers who guarded the Boxian town; the Tang government set up the Conghua township to house the Sogdians. Conghua was at least two *li* large and contained four villages. The Sogdians controlled and managed Dunhuang's market trade. When the Tubo took over Dunhuang, the Sogdian Kang Xiuhua served as a tribal commissioner, while An Jingmin was appointed governor.

During the *Guiyijun* period under the Zhang clan, An Jingmin served as deputy military commissioner of the *Guiyijun* Force, while Kang Xiuhua served as general of the prefect of Guazhou. In the Zhang Chengfeng period, the Sogdian An Huai'en was appointed to a position equal to the military commissioner. In 914, the Sogdian Cao Yijin was appointed as the *Guiyijun*'s military commissioner, and the Dunhuang *Guiyijun* Force came under Sogdian leadership. Apart from the Sogdians, there were considerable numbers of other foreign residents in Dunhuang, including Tartars, Uyghurs, Turkic people, Tubo people, Persians, Indians, Shanshan people and Khotanese. They set up shops and restaurants, with many business leaders of foreign origin. In particular, commercial and trade groups that traveled to various places were led by Sogdians. Foreign traders made up the majority of Dunhuang market traders. For this reason, Dunhuang's business community was strongly multinational.

The goods for sale in Dunhuang's markets also had a strongly international flavor. Dunhuang itself produced little, with no treasures or exotic goods to offer. But because of the city's location on a major transportation route, its markets offered a rich array of goods. There were textiles from the Western Regions, fine muslin from Anxi, *Hu* powder from Kucha (Qiuci), lapis lazuli and mercury from Central Asia, blue and green mineral pigments as well as woolen fabrics from Tubo, Persian brocade and jewelry, ironware from Yizhou, Khotanese jade, silverware from Byzantium, medicines and spices from western India, brocade from Korea, and livestock products and weapons from Tartary and Tubo. Merchandise arrived here from neighboring regions in Central, South, and East Asia as well as the interior of China.

Silver coins were the currency for trade. Gold and silverware were also used as common circulating currencies in the markets of Dunhuang in the Late Tang era. There were Roman silver chalices, silver plates, gold and silver bottles, silver bowls, and so on. The silverware with marked weight was used when paying for goods, so that its value was as a currency rather than as a functional utensil or vessel in the general sense, revealing that silverware was used as a currency in the markets of Dunhuang and other places. Silk was also used for payment in foreign trade, while in domestic or small-scale trade, goods—especially food or grain—were often paid in-kind. Goods were exchanged for equivalent value, so the currencies themselves were multinational.

Dunhuang was Buddhism's original point of entry into China. The Dunhuang manuscripts themselves offer the most detailed and accurate records of Chinese Buddhism and the monastery is mentioned in Han bamboo slips from Dunhuang. These records are helpful in reconstructing the architecture and appearance of ancient Chinese temples. Among the Dunhuang texts are also the earliest extant Nestorian and Manichaean scriptures in Chinese. Although the Dunhuang manuscripts do not include Zoroastrian classics, the influence of Zoroastrianism can be seen in the fact that Zoroastrian rituals enjoyed official sponsorship. In Dunhuang, the peaceful co-existence of Buddhism, Taoism, Zoroastrianism, Nestorianism, Manichaeism, and Confucianism overcame any mutual exclusion or contention. This is especially true of the *Huteng* dance from the Western Regions, which was extremely popular in Dunhuang. It was enjoyed on important festival days. This dance, which first appeared in Qiuci, became Dunhuang's favorite dance. The basis of this situation was the peaceful co-existence of the many ethnic groups in Dunhuang, as well as their mutual inclusiveness, mutual learning, and common development. Dunhuang was the pearl of the Silk Road, and therein lies its charm.

The Silk Road can also be called the Technology Road. Science and technology from the Western Regions, such as medicine, pharmacology, and the astronomical calendar, entered China via this route; Chinese science and technology, in turn, also flowed westward along the same route. The Dunhuang manuscripts provide historical evidence of this. Dunhuang produced so many melons that it was named Guazhou (land of melons). Legend had it that a fox could eat a Dunhuang melon with its head and tail in it, such was the size of the melons. Uyghur melons and Dashi melons are even mentioned in Dunhuang historical records, where Uyghur melons were also known as "*rangtao*." In the Late Tang period and Five Dynasties, the area was held by Uyghurs. Among the so-called Yizhou and Xizhou Uyghurs, Uyghur melons, as they were probably called, were those produced in Uyghur areas.

Dashi melons were those from Arabia. What type of melons were these? It is believed that they were watermelons, which were originally from South Africa, and later reached Egypt, and from there it was made into Central Asia. In the Jin Dynasty, an official from Tongzhou of Shaanxi travelled west as an envoy, and introduced watermelon, after which it became widespread. The people of the time did not have a uniform name for watermelons, so according to naming conventions, it became the *xigua*. This probably just meant "melon from the Western Regions" or "melon from the West." Today, the melons from the Dali county of Shaanxi are also very well-known, with a thick rind and sweet taste.

The exchange of medical technology along the Silk Road was evident. While traditional Chinese medicine was highly developed by the time of the Han and Tang dynasties, many medical skills were absent. Persia and India, however, was at the forefront in certain skills such as cataract surgery, and this was introduced via the West, with Tang dynasty historical records giving it a special mention. Dunhuang's local medical specialists were accomplished in both Chinese and Western methods.

Dunhuang was the Pearl of the Silk Road, the essence of Silk Road civilization, and an eternal thoroughfare for communication and cultural exchange between China and the West. First, political stability was a basic element for the smooth operation of the route. This included the stability of central political power throughout its history, as well as that of ethnic groups and nations along the route. In the pre-Qin period, owing to cultural and economic development of the Central Plains, great social differences took shape as compared with the surrounding areas. These differences led to a stable centripetal force, with the surrounding ethnic groups not having sufficient strength to threaten the government of the Central Plains. Although the Central Plains government did not encourage Chinese exchanges with foreigners, it is not known to have prevented them, either. Exchanges between China and the West were rudimentary. Many specialty goods from the Western Regions passed into the Central Plains via the Silk Road, and Chinese products also headed west via the same road. According to legend, King Mu and the Queen Mother of the West met in the area extending from the Shule River to Lop Nur; the *Classic of Mountains and Seas* which details the geography and landforms along the Yellow River and the Silk Road is a product of this background.

Emperor Wu of the Han Dynasty defeated the Xiongnu with his powerful military, opened up the Silk Road again, and started using the strength of his military government to sustain a period of peace along the Road. During the Han and Tang dynasties, the state operated transport facilities along the route, maintained roads, and guaranteed safety. The rise and fall of the Silk Road occurred almost in line with the stability of state power. After the Song Dynasty, the decline in overland routes was correlated to the rise of the maritime trade routes, but changes in the political environment along the Silk Road also played a major role.

Second, mutual economic benefit was the basis of development along the Silk Road. The reciprocity of benefits was the factor that sustained the Silk Road economically. There were several dimensions of trade on the Silk Road: foremost was tribute trade, which had serious disparities. The central government withstood enormous economic pressure, with the ratio between tributes roughly somewhere between 1 ∶ 10 to 1 ∶ 40. This kind of trade asserted national political interest above all else. This was followed by general trade, which was basically controlled by regional authorities with government-managed trade envoys conducting trade. Profits from this trading activity exceeded 100%. Gold, silver, and silk were the primary mediums of exchange used, with many traders also engaged in bartering. Quite a few of the merchants engaged in China's silk exports and the sale of the Western Regions' treasured spices within China were foreigners from the West. China's foreign-led exports and domestic trade boosted the economic fortunes of Han and Tang society. Driven by trade, places all along the Silk Road also received an economic boost. For Silk Road areas that were not very productive but were nonetheless in important locations, wealth was distributed thanks to trade along the route. Economic reciprocity was the key factor that kept the Silk Road running smoothly.

Third, research into Silk Road culture is a prerequisite for an economic revival along this route. Today, when we research the Silk Road economic belt, we should pay more attention to the culture that developed there. The ancient Silk Road brought together disparate regions and cultures along the route. These cultures have been preserved in forms of artifacts and other material in different regions along the Silk Road. Researching these artifacts is extremely important if we want to learn more of the ancient civilizations of this area. Researching the historical experiences and lessons from the Silk Road trade is a vital reference point for today. Only careful study of its ancient civilizations will benefit future Silk Road development. Places such as Dunhuang, Gaochang, Hami, Kucha, and Khotan are all "pearls of the Silk Road." For that reason, research into the historical culture of these regions amounts to a special case study. It is an immensely significant work.

The *Dunhuang Culture in Translation* series, organized by the Gansu Cultural Translation and Interpreting Center, is a powerful initiative with which to respond to the spirit of General Secretary Xi Jinping's Dunhuang speech, promoting Dunhuang culture and enhancing cultural confidece.

Zheng Binglin

Head of Institute of Dunhuang Studies of Lanzhou University

October 2020

序言三

翻译，让敦煌文化走向世界

敦煌文化是中华文明几千年不断融会贯通的典范，是中国文化精神的重要代表。曾经，敦煌文化经历"敦煌在中国，敦煌学在国外"的历史。诚然，自20世纪初，敦煌藏经洞的发现、敦煌部分文献流失海外，引发世界各国敦煌学者对敦煌文化的关注，在国外产生了众多敦煌学研究成果。但敦煌文化的"根"在中国，对敦煌文化的认识与理解，源于中国。敦煌学的国际化发展，则需要通过文化的传播与学术的交流形成共识、共知与共享。翻译，无疑是使敦煌文化走向世界、敦煌精神被全人类共享的重要途径。

一、翻译是敦煌文化对外传播的"言说者"

文化对外传播、交流与沟通的重要途径是翻译。翻译敦煌文化，就是对外"言说"敦煌文化，传播敦煌文化的各个方面、各种内容。敦煌文化是包括宗教、艺术、科技、文学、医药、农业、建筑、民俗等内容的综合文化体系。翻译敦煌文化，就是对外讲述敦煌开放交流的文明历史，展示敦煌在中西互学互鉴中形成的艺术，介绍敦煌的科技医药，以及讲述融合发展的宗教文化思想等。通过系统翻译，让世界认识敦煌文化，了解全面的敦煌文化、真正的敦煌文化。

翻译敦煌文化，就是言说和表达最具代表性的、最能体现敦煌文化之源流的优秀文化。就其文化内容而言，一方面转换语言为载体的文化内容，如敦煌文献、敦煌学研究成果、敦煌学术思想等；另一方面转换艺术为载体的文化信息。敦煌文化，就其文化载体而言，具有多元的符号形式。语言载体包含写经、变文、宝卷、简牍等文学与非文学形态；艺术载体包含石窟建筑、雕塑、壁画等。翻译敦煌文化，即对敦煌文化各种载体所蕴含的历史、宗教、文学、艺术等文化内容,及其文化思想和文化精神进行语言转换,精确表达。以翻译言说敦煌文化,既要用语言讲述语言文化,还要用语言讲述非语言文化。一般而言,翻译是语言文本的转换。但在敦煌文化翻译中,除了常规的语际翻译,还存在符际转换方式,即对艺术文化的翻译,运用语言进行“互文性”表达。通过语际与符际双重转换,构建敦煌文化对外传播的系统体系。作为敦煌文化对外传播言说者的翻译,需要注重“言说”的方式,构建有效的话语体系。翻译,在传播文化中,表达文化,沟通文化,协调不同语言之间的文化理解。话语方式、话语风格决定文化元素的显现方式,决定文化内容的接受度,从而决定文化传播的效果和效力,是实现文化传播与交流的基础。翻译敦煌文化,要协调“异化”“归化”转换策略,在尊重文化、名从历史的基础上,运用恰当适切的对外言说话语方式,针对文化内容、受众接受等用国际化语言表达方式,准确言说和表达敦煌文化,构建敦煌文化对外传播的完整叙事。

以翻译言说文化,不仅使敦煌文化充分“走出去”,更使敦煌精神深入“走进去”,有效实现敦煌文化的国际性传播与世界认同。

二、翻译是敦煌文化学术交流的“互动者”

翻译敦煌文化,就是搭建中外敦煌学术交流的互动平台,开展中外敦煌学研究的学术对话。20世纪初以来,国内外学者对敦煌文化的研究,产生了众多研究成果,建树颇丰。通过对中外敦煌学研究成果的互译,对话学术,交流思想,从而深化对敦煌文化的认识。诚然,博大精深的敦煌文化及其精神价值,依旧存在有待认识与研究的极大空间,但交流已有的学术思想,无疑对进一步研究敦煌文化、认识敦煌文化具有重要的意义。互译,为搭建互动机制、建构交互认知,提供必要的路径。

一是开展敦煌文献的互译,通过对各国拥有的敦煌文献进行翻译转换,补充因文献缺省造成的“认识差”,化解研究上的局限。敦煌莫高窟藏经洞发现的文献(包括写本、简牍),涉及佛教经典、道教经典、儒家典籍以及(敦煌)佛教文学、俗文学等文化内容,语言包含除汉文之外的藏文、回鹘文、于阗文、龟兹文、突厥文、粟特文和梵文等。敦煌文献是丝绸之路上中西文明交流的历史书写，是研究敦煌文化，以及其中蕴含的中国文化思想的重要文献资料。但敦煌文献因特殊的历史遭遇，一大部分遗书被劫掠至海外(如英国近万卷，法国五千余卷)，有关同一文化内容的文献资料散藏于中、英、法、日、俄等不同的国家，造成各国对敦煌文化认识的支离破碎，导致敦煌学研究的片面性。通过文献资料的译入、译出，可以搭建国内、国外敦煌学的多维研究平台、系统认识平台，将历史片段缀合起来，将同一文化现象进行综合研究，从而形成世界范围内的“系统敦煌学”。

二是进行敦煌学研究成果的互译，通过互译，使学术思想产生碰撞、比较，从而打开各自封闭的敦煌学，经由“他者”的敦煌学术参照系，关照自身的研究，丰富自身的认识；在与“他者”的交流中、在思想碰撞中深化对敦煌文化的理解。

敦煌文化是在中西方文化交融中形成和发展的，具有综合的文化内容体系、多元的文化思想，以及多样的历史发展形态。它是一个内在结构相互作用的文化体系，存在各系统成分之间的内在关系，如敦煌艺术研究与宗教文化研究的互补，中西方文化交流与文化融合过程的历史关系，文化演变与朝代结构的互动等。对敦煌文化的认识，需要系统地研究，才能构成认识的互补体系；只有互为补充的认识，才能不断完善对敦煌文化认识体系的构建。不同国家、不同时代，基于各自专业领域的研究，难免存在“认识差”。通过中外敦煌学研究思想的双向翻译，进行学术交流与对话，在互动中学习，在交流中互鉴，不仅能够产生新思路和新成果，而且能够使各国学者更深刻地理解敦煌文化，一方面可以减少因文化差异造成的认识误差，减少误读与误解；另一方面通过不同时代、不同文化背景、不同信仰体系的学者对历史文明的学术对话，协调敦煌学研究中的审美心理和文化价值“差”，以便达成共识，形成对敦煌历史文化概念的共同解读，从而提升敦煌文化的交流深度，实现敦煌文化的高层次对话与互动传播。

三、翻译是敦煌文化精神的诠释者和世界传承者

翻译，不仅仅是语言的转换，更是对文化的阐释。翻译敦煌文化，不是简

单的语码转换,也不是单纯的信息传递,更重要的是揭示和阐释敦煌文化和历史遗存所蕴含的哲学思想、人文精神、价值理念、道德规范;弘扬和传承蕴含其中的中华民族的文化精神、文化胸怀和文化自信。敦煌文化是中西文化交流融合的典范,敦煌石窟建筑、壁画,以中原文化为基础,充分吸收了中亚、西亚佛教艺术思想内容,体现了多元文化交融互鉴的内在精神,是中华文明开放体系的重要代表。在综合、系统的翻译过程中,深刻阐释其文明历程、文化精髓,阐释敦煌文化文明交流融合的思想方法,诠释中华文明海纳百川、兼容并蓄、博采众长的文化精髓,挖掘世界文明共同的存在根源,以及人类共同的理想目标。

翻译是一种诠释,具有文化"阐释力"。翻译敦煌文化,就是在研究敦煌文化的前提下,诠释敦煌文化的深刻含义。翻译敦煌文化,是译者与敦煌文化思想、文化精神的交流和互动,是现代视域与历史精髓的互文。作为敦煌文化"诠释者"的翻译,是某种意义上的敦煌文化研究,是敦煌学的一种组成部分。但诠释不是自创性解读,正如孔子所言,文化的传承,要遵循"述而不作,信而好古"。真正的敦煌文化翻译,就是在精准理解与充分诠释的基础上向世界传播敦煌文化思想,传承敦煌文化精神。

敦煌文化是在中西文明的相遇、相识、相融中形成和发展的,是各种文明交流融汇的结晶,蕴含开放包容、互学互鉴的文化精神。翻译是文化的交流、思想的对话,其本身就是敦煌文化精神的"外显"形式。敦煌学研究成果的翻译,是学术思想的互学与互鉴,尤其建立在中外学者"中西合璧"方式上的合译,更是在互动的理解过程中实践敦煌精神,是传承与弘扬敦煌文化的又一种深化、物化、具象化的方式。敦煌文化翻译,以其特有的文化交流与对话方式,向世界讲述敦煌故事,传播敦煌思想,弘扬敦煌精神,让敦煌文化在交流中成为世界的文化,敦煌学研究成为"世界的敦煌学",敦煌精神成为人类的思想精神。

兰州城市学院副校长　教授
甘肃文化翻译中心　主任　姜秋霞

2020 年 10 月

Foreword Ⅲ

Translation Connects Dunhuang Culture with the World

Dunhuang culture is a model of the continuous amalgamation of Chinese civilization over a span of thousands of years, and an important representation of the essence of Chinese culture. There was a time when Dunhuang culture experienced a historical reality of "Dunhuang itself is in China, yet Dunhuang studies is in the West." Of course, the discovery of the Dunhuang manuscripts at the beginning of the 20th century—with many of them taken overseas—brought the attention of scholars from all over the world to Dunhuang culture, and produced a large corpus of research from Dunhuang studies abroad. But Dunhuang culture is rooted in China, and the knowledge and understanding of Dunhuang culture originated in China. The international development of Dunhuang studies requires consensus, common knowledge, and sharing through cultural dissemination and academic exchange. Thus, translation is undoubtedly an important way to bring Dunhuang culture out to the world and for the spirit of Dunhuang to be shared by all humankind.

1. Translation is the voice of Dunhuang culture for the world community

Translation is an important method of cultural dissemination and communication. To translate Dunhuang culture is to introduce Dunhuang to the outside world, in other words, to share all aspects and content of Dunhuang culture. Dunhuang culture is a comprehensive cultural system that integrates religion, art, technology, literature, medicine, agriculture, architecture, and folk customs. Translating Dunhuang culture informs the public about the history of Dunhuang's civilization and its open exchanges, reveals the art of Dunhuang as a reflection of the mutual learning between China and the West, introduces Dunhuang's science, technology, and medicine, and explains the integration and development of its religious culture. Thus, systematic translation allows the world to not only know about Dunhuang, but also understand the true, comprehensive culture of Dunhuang.

Translating Dunhuang culture is to relate and express that which is most quintessential, reflecting the pinnacle of culture emanating from its source in Dunhuang itself. As far as cultural content is concerned, on the one hand, Dunhuang translation converts language—that of the Dunhuang manuscripts, Dunhuang studies, and Dunhuang academic theories—as a carrier of cultural content; on the other hand, it converts art as a carrier of cultural information. Dunhuang culture is embodied in multiple symbolic and semiotic forms. Language carriers include literary and non-literary forms such as scripture, *bianwen* (transformation texts), *baojuan* (prosimetric narratives), and bamboo slip archives; artistic carriers include rock-cut architecture, sculpture, and murals. Translating Dunhuang culture entails language conversion and the precise expression of its historical, religious, literary, artistic, and other cultural content contained in various carriers, as well as its cultural values and cultural spirit. The expression of Dunhuang culture through translation requires the use of both linguistic and non-linguistic conversion. Generally speaking, translation is the conversion of language text. However, in Dunhuang culture translation, in addition to the conventional interlingual translation, there is also an intersemiotic transformation method, which is to say that translation of art and culture uses language to express intertextuality. Through this interlingual and intersemiotic conversion, a systematic method for the communication of Dunhuang culture can be constructed. When we translate as the "voice" of Dunhuang culture, it is necessary to pay attention to the manner of "speaking," in order to construct an effective discourse system. Translation, in disseminating, expressing, and communicating culture, must coordinate cultural understanding between different languages. The style and mode of discourse—the foundation for achieving cultural dissemination and communication—determine how cultural elements appear, determine the acceptability of cultural content, and thus determine the effect as well as effectiveness of cultural transmission. When translating Dunhuang culture, it is necessary to closely coordinate both foreignization and domestication conversion strategies, and, on the basis of respecting culture and history, use appropriate foreign language expressions as well as international expressions for cultural content and audience acceptance. To accurately express Dunhuang culture, a complete narrative must be constructed for communicating Dunhuang culture to the world outside China.

Speaking through the language of translation not only enables Dunhuang culture to fully "go forth" into the world, but also enables the essence of Dunhuang to "go in" deeply as well, effectively realizing the international spread and world recognition of Dunhuang culture.

2. Translation is the liaison for Dunhuang cultural and academic exchange

Translating Dunhuang culture creates an interactive platform for academic exchange between China and the rest of the international community, facilitating academic dialogue between Chinese and overseas Dunhuang scholars. Since the beginning of the 20th century, academics both within China and abroad have produced much research on Dunhuang culture, making considerable achievements in the field. The understanding of Dunhuang culture can be deepened through the mutual translation of research findings in Dunhuang studies both within China and overseas, as well as through academic dialogue and the exchanging of ideas. It is true that there is still a great deal to be learned about Dunhuang with its extensive, profound culture and spiritual value, but the exchange of existing academic theories is undoubtedly of great significance for the further research and understanding of Dunhuang. Mutual translation provides a necessary pathway for constructing an interactive mechanism for the field and for the interchange of expertise.

The first task is to carry out the mutual translation of Dunhuang documents. The translation and conversion of Dunhuang documents owned by various countries can help supplement the deficiencies in understanding caused by dispersed and fragmented manuscripts, and thus resolving the limitations of research. The documents, manuscripts, and bamboo slip found in the Dunhuang Mogao Caves include Buddhist, Taoist, and Confucian classics, Buddhist scriptures unique to Dunhuang, popular literature, and other cultural content. In addition to Chinese, the languages include Tibetan, Uyghur, Khotanese, Kuchean, Turkic, Sogdian, Sanskrit, and more. The Dunhuang manuscripts constitute historical written records of the cultural exchanges between China and the West along the Silk Road. They are important documents for studying Dunhuang culture and the Chinese cultural thought contained therein. However, due to the special history of the Dunhuang documents, a large part of the manuscripts was unlawfully removed overseas, including nearly 10,000 manuscripts now located in the United Kingdom, and more than 5,000 in France. As a result, various countries have a fragmented interpretation of Dunhuang culture, leading to one-sidedness in research. Through the translation of documents and materials, a multi-dimensional research platform and a systematic understanding for Dunhuang studies at home and abroad can be developed, with historical manuscript fragments recombined to allow comprehensive research on the same cultural phenomena, thereby forming a worldwide system for Dunhuang studies.

The second task is to carry out the mutual translation of research findings in Dunhuang studies. Through mutual translation, academic theories can interact and undergo comparison, thereby broadening researchers' own closed-off Dunhuang research. Through "other" Dunhuang research and reference, scholars can reflect on their own research, enrich their own expertise, exchange ideas with the "other," and deepen the understanding of Dunhuang culture through the interaction of different theories.

Dunhuang culture was formed and developed as a fusion of Chinese and Western cultures. It comprises a comprehensive system of cultural content, ideology, and historical development. It is a cultural system with interactive structures, and there are internal relationships between the components of the system, as well. For example, Dunhuang art research and religious cultural studies complement one another; there has been a historical connection between the exchange of Chinese and Western cultures and the process of cultural diffusion; and there has been an interrelationship between cultural evolution and dynastic structures. The understanding of Dunhuang culture requires systematic research in order to form an interrelated branch of knowledge; only when mutual understanding is complementary, can the knowledge of Dunhuang culture be continuously improved. Differences in interpretation have been inevitable amongst different countries and throughout different eras, based on research in their respective professional fields. The Sino–Western translation of Chinese and international Dunhuang research findings and theories, academic exchange and dialogue, and interchange of ideas can not only generate new ideas and new results, but can also enable scholars from all over the world to have a deeper understanding of Dunhuang culture. On the one hand, this can reduce errors from misreading as well as misunderstandings caused by cultural differences. On the other hand, academic dialogue between scholars from different eras, cultural backgrounds, and religious viewpoints on historical civilizations can redress the gaps in Dunhuang research regarding its artistic and cultural value. This will better form a consensus and a common interpretation of Dunhuang historical and cultural concepts, thereby enhancing the depth of Dunhuang cultural exchange as well as enabling high–level dialogue and interactive communication on Dunhuang culture.

3. Translation is the interpreter and world inheritor of the spirit of Dunhuang culture.

Translation is not merely the conversion of language, but also the interpretation of culture. Translating Dunhuang culture is not simple code conversion, nor is it purely the transmission of information. More importantly, translation reveals and interprets the philosophical thought, humanistic spirit, and values contained in Dunhuang culture and historical relics, which is imbued with the cultural spirit, mind, and confidence of the Chinese nation. Dunhuang culture stands as a model of Chinese and Western cultural exchange and diffusion. Dunhuang cave temple architecture and murals are based on the Central Plains culture, which also absorbed the content of Central and Western Asian Buddhist art aesthetics and ideals, reflecting the inherent spirit of multicultural synthesis and mutual learning. Dunhuang is an important representation of the openness and inclusiveness of Chinese civilization. Comprehensive, systematic translation can profoundly explain Dunhuang's historical development and its cultural essence, reveal the thinking behind Dunhuang cultural exchange and integration, interpret the cultural essence of Chinese civilization, explore the common roots of world civilizations, and even tap into the common ideals of the human race.

Translation is a type of interpretation, with cultural interpretative power. Translating Dunhuang culture is to interpret the profound meaning of Dunhuang culture under the auspices of researching it. The translation of Dunhuang culture is the exchange and interaction between the translator and Dunhuang cultural ideology and spirit, as well as the intertextuality of modern vision and historical essence. To engage in translation as the "interpreter" of Dunhuang culture is indeed the study of Dunhuang culture in a certain sense, and is a component of Dunhuang studies in and of itself. However, interpretation is never self-generated. As Confucius said, the inheritance of culture must follow the principle of "transmitting but not innovating, loving antiquity and having faith in it." Dunhuang culture translation means sharing and inheriting the essence of Dunhuang culture on the basis of accurate understanding and full interpretation.

We can conclude that Dunhuang culture has formed and developed from the encounter, acquaintance, and fusion of Chinese and Western civilizations. It is the crystallization of the exchange and synthesis of various civilizations, and contains a cultural spirit of openness, inclusiveness, and mutual learning. Translation is cultural exchange, a dialogue of ideas, and itself is the "external" form of Dunhuang's cultural essence. The translation of Dunhuang studies involves the interchange and mutual appraisal of academic ideas. In particular, co-translations based on the Sino-Western cooperation by Chinese and foreign scholars put the spirit of Dunhuang culture into action. Through the process of interactive understanding, the inheritance and promotion of Dunhuang culture is further deepened and substantiated. Dunhuang culture translation brings the story of Dunhuang to the world, shares Dunhuang thought, and promotes the essence of Dunhuang via its unique cultural exchange and methods of communication. Thus Dunhuang culture becomes the world's culture in the exchange, Dunhuang studies becomes the world's Dunhuang studies, and the spirit of Dunhuang culture becomes humankind's ideological spirit.

Jiang Qiuxia
Professor and Vice President of Lanzhou City University
Head of Gansu Cultural Translation and Interpreting Center
October 2020

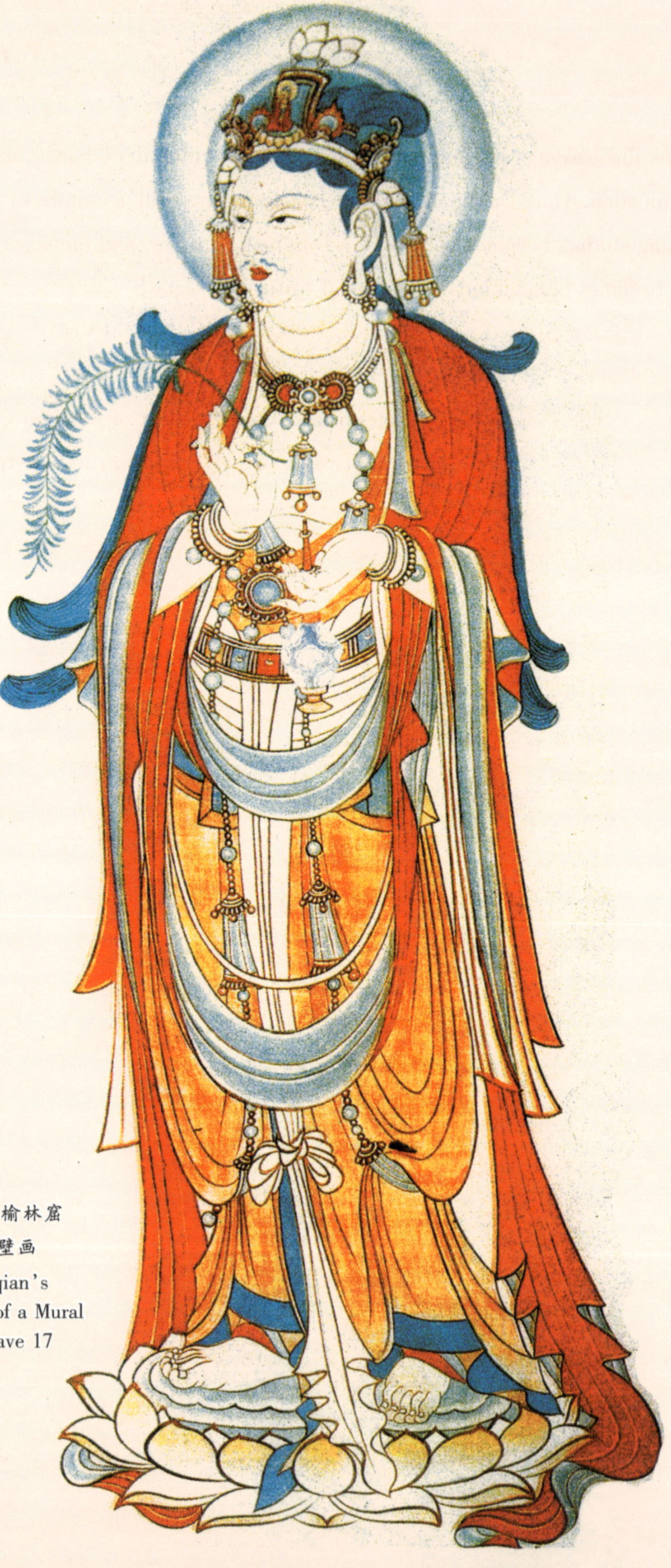

张大千临摹榆林窟
第 17 窟壁画
Zhang Daqian's
Reproduction of a Mural
in Yulin Cave 17

引言——世界的敦煌学

Introduction: Dunhuang Studies Around the World

1900 年，敦煌藏经洞遗书的发现，震动了国内外学术界，引起了国内外学者的关注与研究，从而在世界上兴起了一门新的学科——敦煌学。

所有的学科都一样，资料是研究的基础与前提，这正如陈寅恪先生在《陈垣敦煌劫余录序》中所指出："一时代之学术，必有其新材料与新问题，取用此材料以研求问题，则为此时代学术之新潮流。"对于敦煌学来说，这一点显得更为重要。

虽然敦煌文书发现于 1900 年，但敦煌学界一般都将 1909 年定为敦煌学之始，这主要是因为：第一，任

First discovered in 1900, the ancient manuscripts hidden in the Library Cave at Dunhuang sent shock waves within a few short years throughout academic circles both in China and overseas, attracting wide attention and setting off research in this field. Accordingly, a new discipline—Dunhuang studies—entered the scene.

First-hand sources and materials are the foundation of all field research. Similar to what Chen Yinque, a noted scholar in the 20th century, said in his preface to the *First Catalogue of Dunhuang Manuscripts*, "Academic research in each era must have new materials and new questions. The utilization of these materials for questions and exploration is the new academic trend in this era." This is particularly true of Dunhuang studies.

Although the Library Cave manuscripts were

何一门学问都要有一定的资料。敦煌文书虽然早就被发现，但在1909年伯希和在北京展示之前，只有个别学人见到过个别文书。第二，要有一定的研究规模。1909年前，虽然叶昌炽等人曾对敦煌文书有所关注，但引起学界的重视及有规模的研究还是从1909年开始的。第三，对继续研究的引导。1909年伯希和与罗振玉等中国学者相遇后，罗振玉即根据从伯希和处抄录的资料进行刊布，最早的就是发表在1909年9月25日出版的《东方杂志》第六卷第十期上的《敦煌石室书目及发见之原始》，这就是第一批公开的敦煌文献，随后又有同年9月王仁俊的《敦煌石室真迹录》、同年11月罗振玉和蒋斧的《敦煌石室遗书》等第一批敦煌学研究著作的问世。

伯希和在北京时，接待的不单纯是中国学者，当时在北京由日本人开办的文

discovered in 1900, Dunhuang scholars generally consider 1909 as the beginning of Dunhuang studies as a discipline for several reasons. First, any discipline needs a certain amount of materials as its foundation. Only a few of the manuscripts had been seen by scholars before Paul Pelliot showed them to others in 1909. Also, every discipline needs a scope. Although Ye Changchi and other Chinese scholars knew of the Dunhuang manuscripts before 1909, it was only after 1909 that scholars attached importance to this field and engaged in relevant research on a large scale. Finally, every discipline needs some direction for future research. After Paul Pelliot met Chinese scholar Luo Zhenyu in 1909, Luo began writing articles based on the manuscripts. The earliest academic article, "A List of Manuscripts from the Dunhuang Caves with a Description of their Recovery" was published in Vol.6. No.10 of *The Eastern Miscellany* on September 25, 1909. Then, the first wave of monographs on the Dunhuang Caves, such as *Records of Dunhuang Cave Manuscripts* by Wang Renjun and *Dunhuang Cave Manuscripts* by Luo Zhenyu and Jiang Fu, were published in late 1909.

In Beijing, Paul Pelliot not only met with Chinese scholars, but with those from other countries as well. Tanaka Keitaro from Japan,

求堂书店的主人田中庆太郎也曾访问过伯希和，他在1909年11月1日出版的《燕尘》杂志上，以《敦煌石室中的典籍》为题介绍拜访伯希和的见闻，还全面介绍了罗振玉的《敦煌石室书目及发见之原始》一文。与此同时，罗振玉也将敦煌发现古代文书的信息，写信告诉了日本学者内藤湖南等人，从而引发了日本的敦煌热。

1909年开始的敦煌研究，逐渐形成为一门国际性的学问——敦煌学。

敦煌学的含义非常广泛，但经过科学的归纳、分类，其研究对象可以概括为以下几个方面：

第一，敦煌遗书。敦煌发现的遗书，总数达5万卷（编号超过6万）之多，其中绝大部分是写本。这些写本文献当然主要是用

the storekeeper of Bunkyudo in Beijing, was one of them. In his article "Classics from Dunhuang Caves" originally published in Vol. 2. No. 11 of *Enjin*[①] on November 1, 1909, Tanaka Keitaro described his meeting with Paul Pelliot and the article "A List of Manuscripts from the Dunhuang Caves with a Description of their Recovery" written by Luo Zhenyu in great detail. Meanwhile, Luo also wrote to Japanese scholar Naitō Konan about the discovery of ancient manuscripts in Dunhuang, which ushered in a tide of Dunhuang studies in Japan.

Thus, from 1909 on, the research on Dunhuang has gradually developed into an international academic discipline in its own right: Dunhuang studies.

Dunhuang research encompasses a broad range of disciplines. However, the subjects can generally be summarized as follows:

I. Dunhuang manuscripts

The number of Dunhuang manuscripts is almost 50,000 items (its accession numbers reach more than 60,000), among which most are transcripted copies. The major language is Chinese, although there are writings in other

① *Enjin* is a Japanese monthly journal started in Beijing on January 20, 1908, with its Japanese name《燕塵》.

汉文书写的，之外还有藏文、梵文、回鹘文、于阗文、龟兹文、突厥文、粟特文、西夏文、叙利亚文、八思巴文等文字的写本。敦煌作为曾经的佛教圣地，文书的内容自然也以佛教文献为多，此外还有道教、祆教、摩尼教等宗教典籍；中国传统的经、史、子、集四部书；诗、词、曲、赋以及变文等通俗文学；图经、方志、医药、历书、社会经济资料等也是应有尽有。另外还有寺院的账簿、契约、户籍、信札等经济历史资料。

敦煌遗书所反映的时代，主要是从魏晋到北宋初，而这一阶段的官府档案早已经不存在了，敦煌文书就成了留存下来的有关这一时期的唯一档案，而且都是出自当时人之手，没有经过后人的加工改造，是当时社会政治、经济、文化生活的原始记录，是研究这一阶段社会生活的真实资料，因此被称为“学术的海洋”和

languages, including Tibetan, Sanskrit, Uyghur, Khotanese, Tocharian, Turkic, Sogdian, Tangut, Syriac, and Phags-pa. The major content of the manuscripts are Buddhist-related, owing to Dunhuang's unique position as an ancient sacred site of Buddhism, but there are writings relating to other religions as well, such as Taoism (Daoism), Zoroastrianism, and Manichaeism. They also include four categories of Chinese classics, including *jing* (classics), *shi* (histories), *zi* (philosophers), and *ji* (belles-lettres), as well as popular literature including poems, lyrics, and narrative literature. Furthermore, there are many other mundane materials, including letters, maps, records, medical texts, almanacs, account books, contracts, and household registration records.

The period reflected in the Dunhuang manuscripts mainly ranges from the Wei and Jin to the early Northern Song dynasties, but there are no remaining official archives from this period. Therefore, the Dunhuang manuscripts, original records of social, political, economic, and cultural life at the time and authentic source materials for modern research into that period, remain the only materials found from a local area without any modification whatsoever. For this reason they are considered the "ancient academic ocean" as well as the "encyclopedia of

我国中古时期社会生活的“百科全书”。

第二，敦煌石窟艺术。我们所说的敦煌石窟，包括以莫高窟为主体的古敦煌郡境内的所有石窟，如莫高窟、榆林窟、西千佛洞、五个庙石窟等，共计有洞窟 800 多个，壁画约 5 万平方米。在这些大大小小的石窟中，以莫高窟的规模最大，内容最丰富。这些石窟的时代上起十六国，下止清代，绵延 1600 多年，其规模之大，举世无双。仅就壁画的内容而言，它描绘了我国各民族、各阶层的活动，如生产劳动、风俗礼仪、帝王将相、贵族妇女、商旅往来、使者朝会、民族关系、音乐舞蹈、衣冠服饰、天文地理、医疗卫生等等。因此有的学者将敦煌壁画称为“墙

Medieval China①.”

II. Dunhuang cave art

The Dunhuang caves actually encompass various types of rock-cut architecture in the area surrounding ancient Dunhuang Prefecture, including the Mogao Caves, the Yulin Caves, the Western Thousand Buddha Caves, and the Five Temple Caves. There are more than 800 caves and nearly 50,000 square meters of murals in total. The Mogao Caves are the most well-known for both their number and dazzling content. The time period of these caves ranges from the Sixteen Kingdoms (304–439) until the era of the Qing Dynasty (1636–1912), although the majority was created during the Tang Dynasty (618–907). It is a time period stretching more than 1,600 years and is unmatched in size anywhere else in the world. In terms of content, the murals depict a wide range of subjects and themes from different ethnic groups and classes, including emperors and noble ladies, manual laborers and messengers, customs and etiquette, travel and processionals, music and dance, health and medicine, astronomy and geography, and so forth. Because of this wide range of images, some scholars consider the Dunhuang

① Medieval China refers to the period of the Wei, Jin, Northern and Southern, Sui and Tang dynasties, ranging from AD 221 to AD 960.

壁上的图书馆”。

以上所述敦煌遗书和敦煌石窟艺术，是敦煌学研究最主要的内容。这两类宝藏加在一起，真可谓包罗万象、博大精深。内容如此丰富的敦煌文化既不单纯是西来的，也不是东去的，而是中国古老的传统文化在敦煌这个特殊的地理环境中与外来文化相结合的产物。魏晋南北朝时，除了本土文化外，主要从西域接受了佛教文化，同时也从东面传来了中原和宋齐梁陈时期的儒学与写经。隋唐时期，主要从长安传来了大量写经、文献、诗词和画稿。晚唐五代宋初归义军政权时期，敦煌已成为一个独立的“藩镇”，它亦有自己的根植于本土的政治、经济、军事、文化体系。

第三，敦煌史地。这里所说的敦煌史地，就

murals “a library on walls.”

Dunhuang manuscripts and cave art constitute the main branches of Dunhuang studies. These treasures are both extensive and invaluable. What the rich content of Dunhuang culture represents is not purely a Western tradition, nor something entirely from the East, but the integration and synthesis of traditional Chinese culture with outside cultures, thanks to its unique geographical location as an international crossroads. During the period of the Wei (220–265), Jin (265–420), and Northern and Southern Dynasties (420–589), ancient China absorbed Buddhist culture from India and the Western Regions, integrating it with the local and regional cultures as well as Confucianism and Buddhist scriptures from China's interior, known as the Central Plains. During the Sui (581–618) and the Tang Dynasty (618–907), a large number of Buddhist scriptures, manuscripts, poetry, and paintings mainly from Chang'an (present-day Xi'an) were brought into Dunhuang. During the *Guiyijun* regime from the Late Tang period (836–907) to the beginning of the Song Dynasty (960–1279), an independent military vassal state in Dunhuang was formed with its own comprehensive system of politics, economics, military, and culture of that region.

III. The history and geography of Dunhuang

What is mentioned here about the history and

是指中古时代敦煌的历史和历史地理。因为敦煌艺术,乃是东传的佛教在一个具有成熟封建文化的区域内与汉地文化相结合的特有产物,也是华夏各民族传统文化受外来宗教刺激下出现的新形态,所以敦煌艺术的特点，就在于其地理条件的特殊，使它具有鲜明的个性差异。因此,作为敦煌学研究对象的敦煌史地，就是与敦煌艺术的产生、发展等有密切关系的敦煌历史和敦煌历史地理。另外还包括古敦煌郡境内的城址、关址、长城遗址、烽燧遗址、墓葬等和发现的汉晋简牍。

第四,敦煌学理论。敦煌学是一门发展中的学科,其理论建设还不够完备,仍在不断深化和探讨中。敦煌学理论主要包括敦煌学的概念、范围、特点、研究对象，敦煌学在学术研究上的价值,目前研究敦煌学的作用和意义,敦煌学史,等等。

geography of Dunhuang refers to that of Medieval China. Dunhuang art is a special historical synthesis of Buddhism spreading eastward from India and the Western Regions, a mature feudal culture from China, and new forms of Chinese culture influenced by outside religions. The special characteristics of Dunhuang art also lie in its unique geography as a desert oasis and frontier trading crossroads. In addition, as a subject of study, the history and geography of Dunhuang also comprises the sites of towns and passes, ruins of the Han Great Wall, remains of ancient beacon towers, graves, and unearthed bamboo and wooden slips from the Han Dynasty and the Jin Dynasty.

IV. Theories on Dunhuang studies

As a developing discipline, theories related to Dunhuang studies are still in their infancy. They mainly include the concepts, scope, features, and objects of study, as well as the value, role, and significance of Dunhuang studies in academic research.

菩萨　莫高窟第 159 窟西壁龛内北侧　中唐

Bodhisattva. Northern Section in the Niche of the West Wall, Cave 159 at Mogao. Middle Tang Period

遗响千年：敦煌的影响

Dunhuang: Its Everlasting Impact

四海茫茫寻国宝

The Worldwide Search for China's National Treasures

众所周知，敦煌文献从发现之始,就遭到了各国探险家的欺骗掠夺,绝大部分被劫往世界各地，目前被收藏在十几个国家的几十个博物馆、图书馆中。

由于斯坦因、伯希和等盗足先登，把藏经洞整个翻了一遍，将大部分完整的和重要的文献都劫走了，劫余部分才被送到了北京，并且在运送途中和到北京后又一次遭到了某些人的劫掠,因此,早期的敦煌学家，都是利用各种机会前往世界各国阅读、抄写、复制敦煌文献,如刘复、胡适、向达、王重民、于道泉、潘重规、姜亮夫、王庆菽等,都曾通过各种途径,赴海外搜寻国宝。

After the discovery of the Library Cave by Wang Yuanlu in 1900, a vast number of Dunhuang manuscripts were soon removed by explorers from different countries and dispersed to the four corners of the world. They are now exhibited in dozens of museums and libraries in various countries, with the large part housed in Britain, France, Japan, and Russia.

Aurel Stein, a Hungarian-British archaeologist, and Paul Pelliot, a French sinologist, were the first to remove items from the Library Cave, where they had their pick of the most important and valuable manuscripts. Making matters worse, many of the remaining manuscripts disappeared as they made their way to Beijing, and yet more went missing after their arrival in Beijing. As a result, early scholars in Dunhuang studies, including Liu Fu, Hu Shi, Xiang Da, Wang Zhongmin, Yu Daoquan, Pan Chonggui, Jiang Liangfu, and Wang Qingshu, went to great lengths to go to countries around the world in search of these removed Chinese treasures, so that they could read, transcribe, and copy the lost Dunhuang manuscripts.

避难京都的敦煌学家

Dunhuang Experts in Kyoto, Japan

王国维和罗振玉可以说是中国学术史上非常奇特的两个人，他们不仅学术兴趣、爱好相同，共同作出了许多贡献，而且个人关系也非常不一般，有一段时间还是儿女亲家。

Wang Guowei and Luo Zhenyu were special among scholars in the academic history of China. They were close, personal friends with common academic interests; they were even in-laws for a period of time. During their stay in Kyoto, they were both devoted to sinology, with part of their work including the study of the Dunhuang manuscripts. In 1916, Wang came back to China and was offered a

图1　罗振玉(右)与王国维(1916年春摄于日本京都净土寺町"永慕园")

Fig.1　Luo Zhenyu (Right) and Wang Guowei (Left), Shinshōgokuraku-ji Temple, Kyoto, 1916

在京都期间，他们专心从事于包括敦煌文书在内的国学研究。1916 年，王国维先行回国，到上海出任英国人哈同所办《学术杂志》的编辑，主管《学术丛编》。

在此之前，当劫余敦煌文献被运到北京，中国的敦煌学研究正方兴未艾，也就在此时，中国爆发了辛亥革命。当革命将清王朝埋葬之时，对清王朝忠贞不贰的罗振玉，就想找一个地方“洁身引退”。

恰在此时，日本西本愿寺门主大谷光瑞派来的一个僧侣来到了罗的门前，劝他去日本避难。由于罗振玉和大谷光瑞素不相识，对其邀请也感到十分惊诧，因此罗犹豫后并没有立即给予答复。紧接着(1911 年 10 月下旬至 11 月中上旬之间）京都大学的内藤湖南、狩野直喜和富冈谦藏等敦煌派诸教授联名邀请罗振玉至京都避难，并继续从事他的研究工作。收到内藤等人的邀请信后，罗振玉还是态度犹豫，但随着革命浪潮迅速席卷全国，罗振玉看到清廷大势已去，便与王国维、刘大绅(刘鹗之子、罗振玉女婿）三家共 20 多人从

position as editor of *Academic Journal*, a Shanghai publication sponsored by a British businessman Silas Aaron Hardoon, and he was in charge of *Academic Journal Series*.

Even before the Dunhuang remnants were transported to Beijing, researchers showed a keen interest in the content of these documents. Shortly after that, China witnessed the outbreak of the Revolution of 1911, after which the Qing Dynasty was overthrown. Because of these circumstances, Luo Zhenyu, unswervingly loyal to the Qing Dynasty, decided to go into hiding.

Just as he was preparing to flee, a monk dispatched by Count Ōtani Kōzui, the 22nd Abbot of Nishi Honganji Temple, came to Luo's house and advised him to seek refuge in Japan. This invitation came as a great surprise to Luo, who did not even know Ōtani Kōzui. Hesitating, Luo did not give an immediate reply. Then between late October and mid-November of 1911, faculty members at Kyoto University, including Naitō Konan, Kano Naoki and Kenzo Tomioka who were engaged in Dunhuang studies, sent out an invitation, asking Luo to come to Kyoto and continue his research there. Luo still hesitated. However, with a wave of revolution sweeping the whole country, Luo understood that the Qing Dynasty was in a hopeless situation. Luo Zhenyu, Wang Guowei, and Liu Dashen (son of Liu E, Luo Zhenyu's son-in-law), together with a total of more than 20 people from three families, boarded a

图 2　罗振玉 60 岁时像(1925 年)

Fig.2　Luo Zhenyu at the Age of 60, 1925

天津搭乘日本货船到神户，藤田丰八等日本学者在港口迎接。随后乘车前往京都，入住田中村。

罗振玉东渡日本，将其多年搜集的书籍古董几乎都带上了，暂且寄存在京都大学图书馆，其中图书就有 50 万册，另外还有许多甲骨、碑铭拓片和青铜器等文物。

罗振玉等在田中村住了

Japanese cargo ship, taking them from Tianjin to Kobe. When they arrived, Japanese scholars such as Fujita Toyohachi welcomed them at the port. They then set out for Kyoto and settled down in a village called Tanaka.

When Luo went to Japan, he took almost all the books and antiquities he had collected over the years with him and temporarily deposited them in the Kyoto University Library. In addition to 500,000 books, there were also oracle bones, rubbings of inscription, and bronze artifacts.

The three families lived in Tanaka Village for a year. Luo's residence was not large enough

一年，由于田中村的居所狭小，其寄存在京都大学的图书取读不便，尤其是当时国内秩序混乱，恐怕一时难以回国，因此，罗就与藤田剑峰商量，借他的名义在市内京都大学旁的净土寺町购地数百坪以建设宅院。1913 年春，罗振玉寓所“永慕园”落成，其中书屋之名大而醒目，曰：“大云书库”，概因他曾藏有北朝初年写本《大云无想经》的缘故。

由于罗振玉带到日本的图书资料很多，基本上能够满足学术研究的需要，因此，到京都后，罗振玉、王国维在“大云书库”里，除了与京都大学的内藤湖南、狩野直喜等学者有文字交往外，主要从事甲骨文、敦煌文献和简牍的整理研究。罗振玉和王国维的许多重要学术著作都是在京都完成的，也正是在这个时候，形成了他们学术上的一个高峰。

1913 年，罗振玉将伯希和陆续寄他的 18 种敦煌文献照片经过悉心整理后，编成了其寓日期间的第一部敦煌学著作——《鸣沙石室佚书》。

to store his books, and he found it inconvenient to travel back and forth to Kyoto University to read the books he was keeping there. It was also impossible for him to return to China due to the ongoing political turmoil at the time. He asked Fujita Toyohachi to help purchase some land in Fujita's name near Kyoto University with the purpose of building a house on the site. Luo's house—which he named Yongmuyuan—was completed in the spring of 1913. He wrote the name "Dayun Book Repository" in bold, eye-catching characters for his study inside the house. The name was taken from *Dayun wuxiang jing* (*Great Cloud Sutra*) that he possessed, a rare manuscript from the Northern Dynasties (386–581).

The huge number of books and materials Luo took to Japan could well meet his demands for academic research. After their arrival in Kyoto, apart from corresponding with Naitō Konan, Kano Naoki and other scholars, Luo and Wang Guowei were mainly engaged in organizing and studying oracle bone scripts, Dunhuang manuscripts, and bamboo and wooden slips at the Dayun Book Repository. Much of their important academic research was completed during their stay in Kyoto, which had been considered the zenith of their academic careers.

In 1913, Luo carefully sorted out 18 categories of Dunhuang manuscript photographs which had been sent to him in succession by Paul Pelliot. He then integrated these pictures into the *Lost Manuscripts from the Dunhuang*

由于斯坦因将在新疆、敦煌所获的汉晋简牍交由巴黎法兰西学院的沙畹考释研究，1912 年，罗振玉致函沙畹，希望能得到这批材料的影印件，1913 年冬，沙畹的著作已交付出版，就将其手头的稿本(即“手校之本”)寄给罗振玉。因该书系用西文撰写，经罗振玉之子罗福苌翻译后才能通读。得到译文的罗振玉、王国维如获至宝，但经反复阅读，仍觉其

Caves, his first book on Dunhuang studies written during his stay in Japan.

As Aurel Stein had given the inscribed bamboo and wooden slips he obtained in Xinjiang and Dunhuang from the Han and Jin dynasties to Émmanuel-Édouard Chavannes from L'Institut de France for further study, Luo wrote a letter in 1912 to Chavannes in the hope that he could get copies of these slips. In the winter of 1913, Chavannes published his book on the bamboo and wooden slips and mailed a copy to Luo. The manuscript was in French, which meant it had to be translated into Chinese before Luo Zhenyu and Wang Guowei could use it for research, and Luo Fuchang (Luo Zhenyu's son) was assigned to translate it. When they received the translated version, Luo Zhenyu and Wang Guowei were very excited, but found the book still left much to be desired after repeated reading. They

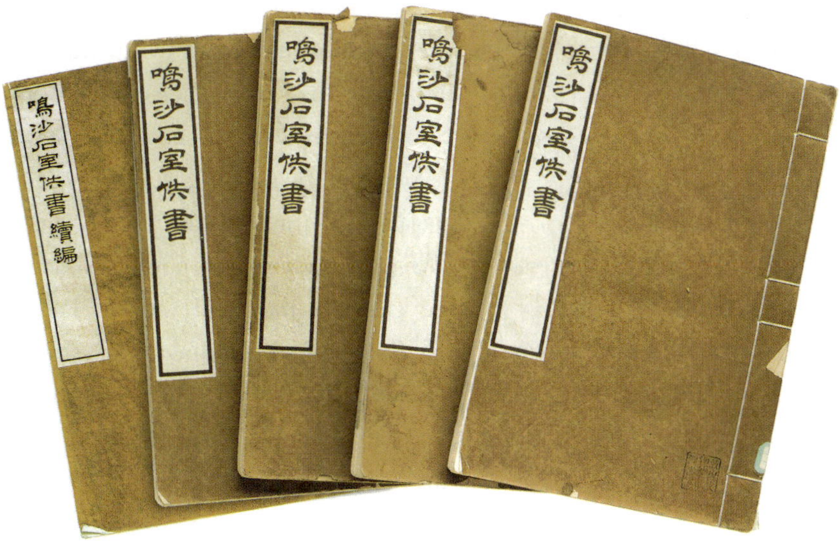

图 3 《鸣沙石室佚书》及《鸣沙石室佚书续编》

Fig.3 *Lost Manuscripts from the Dunhuang Caves* and *More Lost Manuscripts from the Dunhuang Caves*

中还有许多不尽如人意之处，两人便分工合作，将敦煌、罗布泊、尼雅等地发掘的简牍重新进行分类考释，于 1914 年出版了《流沙坠简》。

《流沙坠简》是罗振玉、王国维合作的第一部大著作，也是我国学者整理研究汉晋简牍的开山之作，具有很高的学术价值。鲁迅在 1922 年所写《不懂的音译》中曾这样评价该书和王国维:"中国有一部《流沙坠简》，印了将有十年了。要谈国学，那才可以算一种研究国学的书。开首有一篇长序，是王国维先生做的，要谈国学，他才可以算一个研究国学的人物。"(《鲁迅全集》第一卷第 398 页）平心而论，鲁迅一生所推崇的人和书不多，《流沙坠简》能够得其青睐，自然是有原因的。

《流沙坠简》在署名问题上也很有意思。在本书的书名之下没有任何署名，而在书中的各个部分，则根据每人的工作各自署名，如第一册的第一部分《小学术数方技书》，是由罗振玉分类排列的，便署“罗振

then collaborated with each other to reclassify and study the bamboo and wooden slips discovered in Dunhuang, Lop Nur, and the Niya ruins. They published their own book, *Records of Lost Bamboo and Wooden Slips in the Desert*, in 1914.

It is the first major work resulting from the cooperation between Luo Zhenyu and Wang Guowei. It is also a groundbreaking study of Han and Jin inscribed bamboo and wooden slips by Chinese scholars, with great academic value. Lu Xun, who admired few people and recommended few books in his life, commented in his article "Inexplicable Transliteration" in 1922, "The book, *Records of Lost Bamboo and Wooden Slips in the Desert*, having been in publication for over 10 years, is genuine research in sinology. Wang Guowei, the writer of its preface, is indeed one of the few great masters in this field." This rare compliment offered by Lu Xun in a sense testifies to the significance of this work.

The credit for the book's authorship was carried out in an interesting way. Instead of clarifying the authorship directly on the book cover, the authors were identified according to the chapters they had written. For example, Luo Zhenyu had classified the first chapter "A Book of Chinese Linguistics, Astrology, and Medical Skills," thus his name was signed in this chapter. The second chapter "On Watchtowers and Garrison Soldiers" was credited to Wang Guowei since he had made textual criticisms and explanations for it. This

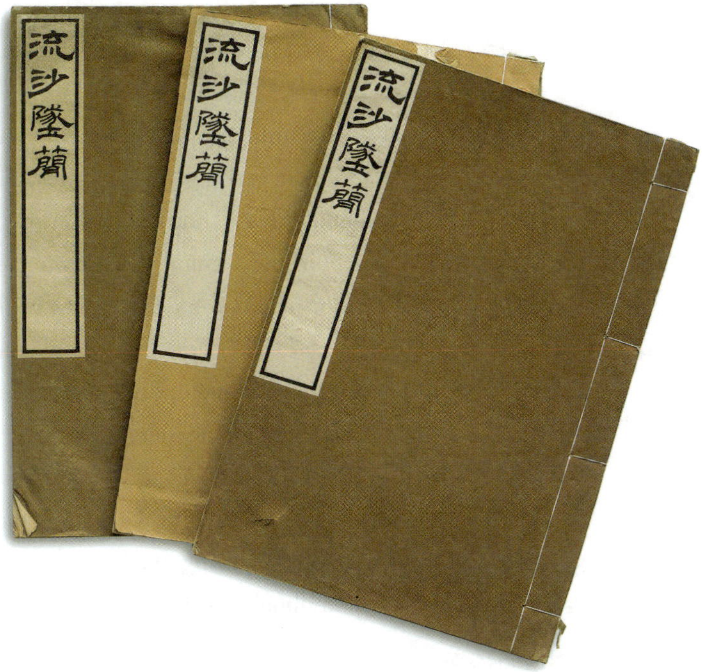

图 4 《流沙坠简》

Fig.4 Records of Lost Bamboo and Wooden Slips in the Desert

玉排类";第二册第二部分是王国维逐条考释的《屯戍丛残》，就署名"王国维考释"。这种客观公平、各负其责的署名方式，也是值得我们今天借鉴学习的。

1914 年 2 月，罗振玉将其收藏的西域和敦煌碑刻拓片 15 种编为《西陲石刻录》，8 月，他又赴大谷光瑞所居的二乐庄，获得大谷探险队所获高昌墓砖

equitable and responsible way of crediting work is worth imitating by scholars today.

In February 1914, Luo Zhenyu edited *Records of Stone Inscriptions from the Western Regions of China*, in which 15 types of Dunhuang inscriptions and rubbings were recorded. In August, he visited Ōtani Kōzui in Villa Niraku and obtained copies of inscriptions of tomb bricks from Gaochang, which had been discovered by the Ōtani expedition. To get a better understanding of the scripts, he then personally visited Yoshikawa Koichirō for proofreading. Eventually, *A Sequel to the Records of Stone Inscriptions from the Western Regions of China* was completed.

That same year, Luo visited the "Western

录文，不清楚之处又亲自到吉川小一郎处校录，编为《西陲石刻后录》。

同年，罗振玉还在武库参观了“西陲古物展览会”，并与橘瑞超相见。当罗振玉从橘瑞超处看到大谷探险队所获敦煌文书的目录后，立即借回参阅，并据此编成《日本橘氏敦煌将来藏经目录》刊布，使学界对其概貌有了较多的了解。

罗振玉居日 8 年（1911—1919），王国维居日 5 年（1911—1916），其有关敦煌研究的论著，除以上所介绍者外，还有《鸣沙

Frontier Antiquities Exhibition” held in an arsenal of Japan and met Tachibana Zuichō. After Tachibana showed Luo the catalogue of the Dunhuang documents obtained by the Ōtani expedition to northwestern China, Luo immediately borrowed it for reading and accordingly compiled *Catalogue of Chinese Manuscripts from Dunhuang in the Tachibana Zuichō Collection*. This catalogue presented a better understanding of the Dunhuang documents to academic circles.

Luo Zhenyu stayed in Japan from 1911 to 1919 and Wang Guowei stayed from 1911 to 1916. During that period, they published many books on Dunhuang studies. Apart from those mentioned above, there were *More Lost Manuscripts from the Dunhuang Caves, Fragments of Classics from the Dunhuang*

图 5　1919 年罗振玉返国前与日本友人合影（左起为长尾甲、犬养毅、罗振玉、富冈百炼、内藤湖南）
Fig.5　Luo Zhenyu with Japanese Friends, 1919 (from Left to Right: Kou Nagao, Ki Inukai, Luo Zhenyu, Hyakuren Tomioka, Naitō Konan)

石室佚书续编》《鸣沙石室古籍丛残》《高昌壁画菁华》等。他们不仅自己对敦煌文献进行深入研究，取得了一系列重要成果，而且还推动了日本的敦煌学发展，这正如石滨纯太郎 1925 年在一次演讲中所说："最后，可算是中国敦煌派领袖人物的罗叔言（罗振玉，字叔言）和王静安（王国维，字静安）两先生流亡到日本来，诸位先生在同时蜂拥而上，又是写论文，又是著书，又是开展览会，甚嚣尘上，气势大振，敦煌派的势力确实也因此而兴盛到了极点。"

另外，值得一书的是，居日期间正是王国维学术转移的重要时期。王国维是中国近代著名的历史学家，他在甲骨文、金文、敦煌文献、先秦史、古代文学和西北史地方面都有举世公认的成就。他将近代西方的实证论思想方法与中国传统的乾嘉考据方法融会贯通，提倡著名的"二重证据法"，即"取地下之实物与纸上之遗文互证"。这种方法，不仅使他在中国古代历史的研究

Caves, and *Quintessential Gaochang Murals*. They not only studied Dunhuang manuscripts, but also promoted the development of Dunhuang studies in Japan. Ishihama Juntarō commented during his speech in 1925, "Fortunately, two leading scholars, Luo Zhenyu and Wang Guowei, came to Japan and published numerous articles and books. They held exhibitions as well. Dunhuang studies thrived thanks to their efforts."

It is worth noting that the stay in Japan was a critical period of transition for Wang Guowei in his academic life. He was a prominent historian in China, globally recognized for his great contributions to research on oracle bone scripts, Chinese bronze inscriptions, Dunhuang manuscripts, pre-Qin history, ancient literature, and the history and geography of northwestern China. In addition, he integrated the modern empiricism of the West with traditional Chinese textual research theory of the Qianjia School to put forward his "double evidence method." This method involved combining unearthed artifacts with written records for study, which not only helped him make great achievements in studying ancient Chinese history, but also set a model for future scholars interested in exploring different methods of study. His method is a milestone for the modernization of Chinese historical research. As a result, Wang Guowei was honored as a "pioneer of new historical research methodologies" by Guo Moruo, a leading intellectual in China.

During Wang Guowei's stay in Japan,

图 6　1925 年的王国维，当时他刚担任清华研究院导师
Fig.6　Wang Guowei, Supervisor at the Tsinghua Research Institute, 1925

上取得了巨大的成就，而且对当时和后世学者的治学思路有着极大的示范作用，是中国历史研究走向近代化的重要标志，因而被郭沫若誉为中国“新史学的开山”。

在日本期间，罗振玉“大云书库”中丰富的藏书，以及为数不少的甲骨文、金石拓片等，基本上能够满足王国维学术研究所需。另外，他生活上有保障，无须为衣食所奔波，还能与罗振玉及一批

Luo's book collection, oracle bone scripts, and bronze inscriptions met his academic research needs. Financially well off with no need to worry about his livelihood, he spent considerable time exchanging ideas with Luo Zhenyu and Japanese scholars, as well as learning from them, which enabled him to make great progress in academic research, and ultimately earn remarkable achievements during his four years and three months in Japan.

Apart from Luo Zhenyu and Wang

日本学者相互切磋，取长补短。因此，王国维在日本短短的四年零三个月的时间中，学术上的进步日新月异，取得的成果也令世人瞩目。

还有一位董康先生，在避居日本期间也与敦煌文献甚有关系，不能不说。

董康(1867—1947)，字授经，又字绶经、绶金，号诵芬室主人，生于清同治六年，光绪进士。他是一位很特殊的人物，曾任法律馆提调、刑部主事、大理院推事。入民国后历任大理院院长、司法总长、财政总长等职，晚年任上海法科大学、东吴大学法学院、北京大学教授，就是这样一个政治人物，却与敦煌文献有很密切的关系。

当年伯希和得到敦煌文书后，从其内心讲并不想很快让别人，尤其是中国人知道。最先得到这一消息的是两江总督端方，然后端方将此消息告诉了与其交往密切的董康，再由董康传播开来。1909 年到伯希和寓所观看敦煌文书、在六国饭店招待伯希和，董康都

Guowei, another important figure staying in Japan, Dong Kang, the self-titled "Master of Songfenshi" should be mentioned for his dedication to the Dunhuang manuscripts.

Dong Kang (1867–1947) was a *jinshi* (a successful imperial examination candidate) during the reign of Emperor Guangxu (1871–1908). During the Qing Dynasty, he was offered several governmental posts in judicial and legal system, including supervisor of the Bureau of the Compilation of Law, director of the Ministry of Corrections, and judge of the Supreme Judicial Court. Throughout the 37 years of the Republic of China (1912–1949), he was appointed president of the Supreme Judicial Court, attorney-general and finance minister. In his later career, he taught at Peking University, Shanghai College of Law, and College of Law in Soochow University. What is interesting is that such an active political figure was closely associated with Dunhuang manuscript studies.

Meanwhile, Paul Pelliot did not intend to let anyone else, especially the Chinese, know that he had taken manuscripts from Dunhuang. Duan Fang, the governor-general of Liangjiang (present-day Jiangsu Province, Anhui Province, Jiangxi Province, and Shanghai), however, was the first person within the Chinese government to find it out. He shared this information with his close friend Dong Kang, who then spread it to others. Dong Kang visited Paul Pelliot for a look at the Dunhuang manuscripts and invited

是积极的参与者。我国敦煌文献的第一部重要著作——罗振玉根据伯希和携至北京的部分敦煌文献所编《敦煌石室遗书》，就是 1909 年 12 月在董康的诵芬室刊行的。

当 1911 年辛亥革命爆发后，董康也与罗振玉、王国维一样避往日本京都，但不同的是，罗、王对清朝的灭亡有

Pelliot to dinner at the Grand Hotel des Wagons-Lits in Beijing. The first important work on Dunhuang studies in China, *Dunhuang Cave Manuscripts*, edited by Luo Zhenyu, was published by Dong's Songfenshi Press in December of 1909.

When the Revolution of 1911 broke out, Dong Kang went to Kyoto for refuge, just as Luo Zhenyu and Wang Guowei had done. However, they were in entirely different circumstances. Luo and Wang supported the Qing Dynasty and at the same time were able to live a comfortable life in Japan. As a result, they stayed in Kyoto for several years, focusing on academic research and utilizing the precious resources in their possession. Dong, by contrast, lived in straitened circumstances in Japan, and was forced

图 7　董康

Fig.7　Dong Kang

"失君之痛"，且生活安定又能坐拥"大云书库"，故能一住多年并安心学术。而董康只是避乱且生活无着，甚至于以出售自己所携藏书维持生活。因此董康于1913年10月即返回国内，很快就活跃于北京的政坛。

1922年，董康辞去财政总长的职务后，率一实业考察团赴欧美考察。在巴黎，他又见到了十多年前见过的伯希和，并亲眼看见了由伯希和劫往法国的敦煌文献。董康利用这一难得的机会，在巴黎图书馆中待了30天，抄录敦煌文书中有关法制方面的资料。随后，董康还前往伦敦，观看斯坦因劫往英国的敦煌文献，并幸运地抄到了《云谣集》等文学方面的珍贵资料。

1926年底，作为上海法科大学校长的董康，由于被别人冒名发通电而遭孙传芳的通缉，便于12月30日化名前往日本避难。在船上，董康为"受政治之影响"而深感寂寞惆怅。但当1927年元旦下午到达日本京都，其友人示以珍籍，并邀他"往读其中秘本"时，他又立即觉得"可谓不虚此行矣"。

to sell his book collection in order to support himself. Because of financial hardship, Dong soon returned to China in October of 1913. After returning to China, he once again entered the political field in Beijing.

In 1922, Dong resigned from his position of minister of finance and led a delegation to visit Europe and the United States. In Paris, he met Paul Pelliot once again, and personally had a look at the Dunhuang manuscripts which had been taken out of China. Seizing upon this opportunity, Dong spent 30 days in la Bibliothèque nationale de France copying those parts of the manuscripts relating to law. Later, he went to London to read the manuscripts taken to Great Britain by Aurel Stein. Fortunately, he also had the chance to copy various precious records of literature, such as *An Anthology of Folk Poetry from the Tang Dynasty*.

In late 1926, Dong Kang, then president of the Shanghai College of Law, was involved in a political scandal when somebody else, falsely assuming his name, published a controversial open telegram to the nation. A warrant was issued for his arrest. He fled to Japan for refuge on December 30 of the same year. Extremely frustrated by this political imbroglio, Dong felt depressed throughout the entire journey. However, upon his arrival on January 1, 1927, his friend showed him

董康这次在日四月(1927年元月1日至4月30日),他往来于东京、京都之间,搜访古籍珍本,记其版式,存其题识,完成了以访书为主要内容的《书舶庸谭》。

本书记载了许多日本的敦煌学家,如内藤湖南、狩野直喜、羽田亨等,董康与这些敦煌

some rare ancient books and invited him to read a few, which made him immediately regard the trip to Japan as worthwhile.

During his stay in Japan from January 1, 1927 to April 30, 1927, Dong travelled between Tokyo and Kyoto in order to locate and copy ancient literature. He did this to complete a book he was working on called *Diaries of Four Trips to Japan.*

This book recorded his communication

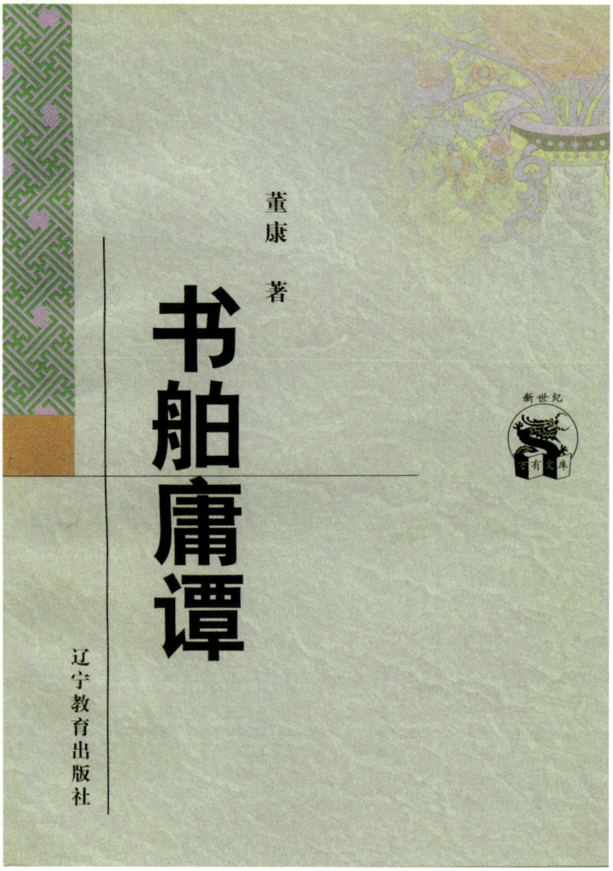

图 8 《书舶庸谭》

Fig.8 Diaries of Four Trips to Japan

学者及其他学者有着广泛的联系与交流。

董康在《书舶庸谭》一书中还记载了许多有关敦煌文献的信息，如他见到了许多日本公私收藏的敦煌文书，还看到了一些日本学者从巴黎和伦敦拍摄的敦煌文献照片；抄录了许多流散到日本的敦煌文献，如《王绩集》《尔雅》《王梵志诗》《秦妇吟》《舜子变》《新修本草》《珠英集》《古文尚书》，等等。内中还有日本学者赠送其羽田亨与伯希和合编之《敦煌遗书》影印及活字本各一册之事；从狩野直喜处借阅罗振玉《敦煌零拾》等。还记狩野“喜谈清朝旧闻”，1900年狩野正在北京留学，当义和团攻打使馆时，“日使署警卫不及廿，曾充兵役”等等。

and exchange with many Japanese scholars interested in Dunhuang studies, including Naitō Konan, Kano Naoki, and Haneda Tōru.

Diaries of Four Trips to Japan included considerable information about the Dunhuang manuscripts. For example, Dong found documents in both public and private collections, as well as photos of manuscripts taken by Japanese scholars in Paris or London. He also copied certain Dunhuang manuscripts that had been brought to Japan, including *Collected Works of Wang Ji, Erya,* the earliest Chinese dictionary, *Wang Fangzhi's Poetry Anthology, The Lament of Qinfu, Narrative on Emperor Shun's Filial Piety, Tang Materia Medica, An Anthology of Chinese Classical Poetry,* and *Classics of History in Small Seal Style*. He mentioned that a Japanese scholar presented him with one photocopy and one movable-typed book of *Dunhuang Manuscripts*—the book that had been coauthored by Haneda Tōru and Paul Pelliot—and that he had also borrowed Luo Zhenyu's book *A Collection of Miscellanous Literary Works from Dunhuang* from Kano Naoki. Also included in his book were some depictions of Kano Naoki, who "likes to talk about the history of the Qing Dynasty," and who "served as a soldier since there were no more than 20 policemen" when the rebels of the Boxer Uprising attacked the Japanese Embassy.

巴黎图书馆中的王重民

Wang Zhongmin in la Bibliothèque nationale de France

王重民（1903—1975）先生，字有三，号冷庐。1929 年于北京高等师范学校（今北京师范大学）国文系毕业后，任教于河北大学，后出任北平图书馆编纂委员兼索引组组长。1934 年—1939 年奉派前往法国国家图书馆工作；1939

Wang Zhongmin (1903-1975) graduated from the Chinese Department of Beijing Higher Normal School (present-day Beijing Normal University) in 1929. After graduation he taught at Hebei University. He later worked as a member of the cataloguing committee of the Peking Library and served as the head of the indexing group. From 1934 to 1939, he was assigned to work in la Bibliothèque

图 9　王重民(1936 年秋摄于巴黎法国国家图书馆敦煌写本书库)
Fig.9　Wang Zhongmin in the Dunhuang Manuscripts Stack Room of la Bibliothèque nationale de France, Fall of 1936

年—1947年应美国国会图书馆和普林斯顿大学葛斯德图书馆的邀请，在美国整理鉴定中国善本古籍。1947年2月回国后，任北平图书馆参考组主任、代理馆长。1949年任北京图书馆副馆长。1952年起任北京大学教授、图书馆学系主任。

王重民先生能在敦煌学等方面取得突出的成就，与他的工作环境和工作性质有着非常密切的关系，可以说，他的工作环境和性质影响着他的学术成就，其中最关键的当是1934年—1939年的巴黎之行。正如白化文先生在《冷庐文薮》序中所述："以敦煌学而言，1934年夏，王先生奉派去法国与英国工作，直至1939年欧战开始后撤离。这五年多时间里，大量地接触了伯希和与斯坦因盗去的遗书材料，所得甚丰，从材料搜集等方面奠定了以后研究的基础。这段时间，不但对王先生个人，即便对于国际和我国敦煌学界来说，都可说是一个高潮时期、黄金时代。"

nationale de France. From 1939 to 1947, he worked on the identification and descriptive cataloguing of Chinese historical manuscripts in the United States at the invitation of the Library of Congress and the Gest Library of Princeton University. After returning to China in February 1947, he served as director of the National Library of Beiping (present-day National Library of China) Reference Department, as well as acting director of the library and in 1949, he became assistant director of the Beijing Library (present-day National Library of China). He was appointed professor and dean of the Department of Library Science at Peking University in 1952.

Wang's outstanding achievements in Dunhuang studies can be greatly attributed to his work environment. In a sense, the nature of his work had a direct impact on his academic achievements. For example, his trip to Paris from 1934 to 1939 was crucial to his academic life. As Bai Huawen wrote in the preface to the *Collected Works of Wang Zhongmin*, "Wang was sent to work in France and Britain in the summer of 1934 and had to evacuate after the outbreak of the war in Europc in 1939. During those years, in terms of Dunhuang studies, he had access to a large number of manuscripts removed by Paul Pelliot and Aurel Stein. That benefited him greatly and laid a good foundation for future research with much material collected. This period was a golden age not only for Wang himself, but for international and domestic Dunhuang studies as well."

谈到王重民先生的巴黎之行，不能不说到袁同礼先生。

袁同礼(1895—1965)，字守和，祖籍河北，本人出生在北京。他是我国最早完整地受过图书馆学专业教育的人士之一。当他刚刚接触西学的时候，恰遇美国传教士韦棣华女士在武汉创办文华大学“公书林”，发起中国现代图书馆运动。受其影响，袁同礼立志专攻图书目录学，并与图书馆事业结下了终身之缘。

When talking about Wang's trip to Paris, it is necessary to mention another figure, Yuan Tongli.

Yuan Tongli (1895-1965) was born in Beijing, with his ancestral home in Hebei. He was among the earliest to receive a professional library science education in China. When he was first introduced to Western studies, he met an American missionary whose Chinese name was Wei Dihua. She was leading the modern library movement in China by establishing a "public book collection" at Wenhua University. Inspired by her, Yuan determined to specialize in cataloguing and thus began his lifelong career as a librarian.

After graduating from the preparatory

图 10　袁同礼
Fig.10　Yuan Tongli

袁同礼在1916年北大预科毕业后即在清华大学图书馆参考部工作，1920年赴美国哥伦比亚大学学习两年，获历史学学士后即转入纽约州立图书馆专科学校学习，紧接着就赴欧考察各国图书馆和博物馆，并在伦敦历史研究院从事研究，1924年回国，任广东大学图书馆馆长，次年回到北京大学任图书馆馆长和目录学教授。

北京图书馆的前身是1926年由中华教育基金会建立的“北平北海图书馆”，当时的正副馆长分别是梁启超和李四光，袁为图书部主任。1929年正式创建“国立北平图书馆”时，蔡元培任馆长，袁为副馆长。梁、李、蔡诸位都是以名望而就此位，他们的主要职务都不在图书馆，因此，实际担当创业重任的自然就是袁同礼了。

袁同礼先生任北平图书馆副馆长并主持馆务时，一方面使图书馆发挥了其公共职能，更重要的是将图书馆办成了一个学术研究机构。

program of Peking University in 1916, Yuan worked in the Reference Department of the Tsinghua University Library. In 1920, he went to study at Columbia University and received a bachelor's degree in history two years later. He then transferred to the New York State Library School for further study. After that, he immediately went to Europe for an investigation of libraries and museums and began doing research at the Institute of Historical Research in London. Returning to China in 1924, he was appointed director of Guangdong University Library. The following year he went back to Peking University and served as director of the library and professor of Bibliography.

The Beijing Library, formerly known as the Beiping Beihai Library, was established by the Chinese Education Foundation in 1926. At the time of its founding, Liang Qichao served as director, and Li Siguang as deputy director. Yuan was director of the Materials and Acquisitions Department. When the National Library of Beiping was formally established in 1929, Cai Yuanpei was appointed director and Yuan deputy director. In fact, Liang, Li, and Cai received these job appointments mainly on the basis of their prestige in academic circles, yet their major duties were not actually in library administration. Thus, Yuan was the one who actually undertook the operational management of the library.

When Yuan was in charge of the National Library of Beiping as deputy director, apart from developing its public services, he attempted to

为此目的，他网罗了一大批卓有成就的学者，如徐鸿宝（森玉）、叶渭清、向达、王重民、孙楷第、贺昌群、谢国祯、刘节、赵万里、谭其骧、王庸、于道泉先生等。这些学者皆发挥各自所长，撰写论文专著，出版中英文馆刊，不仅使北京图书馆一跃而成为世界有名的国家图书馆之一，而且还成为学术研究的重镇。

当时的北平图书馆和欧美各大图书馆都订有学术交流的协议，1934 年，袁同礼先生就派王重民、向达先生赴法国、英国进行学术考察。在巴黎的一年多时间，王先生就写成《巴黎敦煌残卷叙录》，并在天津《大公报·图书副刊》陆续发表 41 篇。

王重民先生赴巴黎后，就将主要精力用于搜集、研究敦煌遗书。尤其难能可贵的是，在当时那样艰难困苦的条件下，他不仅阅读敦煌卷子，而且还把伯希和劫去的卷子，选出较为重要的摄制成照片，为我国的敦煌学研究提供了宝贵的第一手材料。

王重民先生拍摄的这些照片目录，袁同礼先生在 1940 年曾以《国立北平图书馆现藏海外

forge the library into an academic research institution. To achieve the aim, he recruited a large number of leading scholars, including Xu Hongbao (Sen Yu), Ye Weiqing, Xiang Da, Wang Zhongmin, Sun Kaidi, He Changqun, Xie Guozhen, Liu Jie, Zhao Wanli, Tan Qixiang, Wang Yong and Yu Daoquan, all scholars were excelled in writing articles and books. Additionally, they published library journals in both Chinese and English, which not only made the library renowned but made it a center of academic research.

Based on an academic sharing agreement between the National Library of Beiping and several prominent European and American libraries, in 1934, Yuan sent Wang Zhongmin and Xiang Da to France and Britain for academic study. It was during the one-year stay in Paris that Wang wrote *Records of Dunhuang Manuscript Fragments in the Paris Collection* and published 41 articles in the newspaper supplement of *Ta Kung Pao* in Tianjin.

While in Paris, Wang set about collecting Dunhuang manuscripts and doing related research. Under difficult conditions, he not only read but also took photos of manuscripts that had been taken out of China by Paul Pelliot, providing invaluable first-hand materials for the study of Dunhuang in China.

In 1940, Yuan published 402 categories of photographs that had been taken by

敦煌遗籍照片总目》为题，在《国学季刊》新二卷第四期上发表过一部分，刊布了 402 种。袁同礼先生还在文后特别写明了目录不全的原因：“摄取伯希和、斯坦因二氏携去敦煌古经影片，随摄随寄。迨卢沟桥变起，遂将继续所摄者，暂存巴黎东方语言学校，旋又在欧战爆发前，运往美国国会图书馆寄存。总数约在万

Wang Zhongmin with the title *Catalogue of Photographs of Overseas Dunhuang Manuscripts in the National Library of Beiping* in Vol.2, No. 4 of *Journal of Sinological Studies*. Yuan also explained the incompleteness of the catalogue, “Since the photos were taken from ancient Dunhuang sutras removed by Pelliot and Stein, they were sent to China once taken. After the July 7th Incident of 1937 (Lugou Bridge Incident), the photos taken later had to be kept temporarily in the Paris Oriental Language School. Before the outbreak of the war in Europe, they were shipped to the Library of

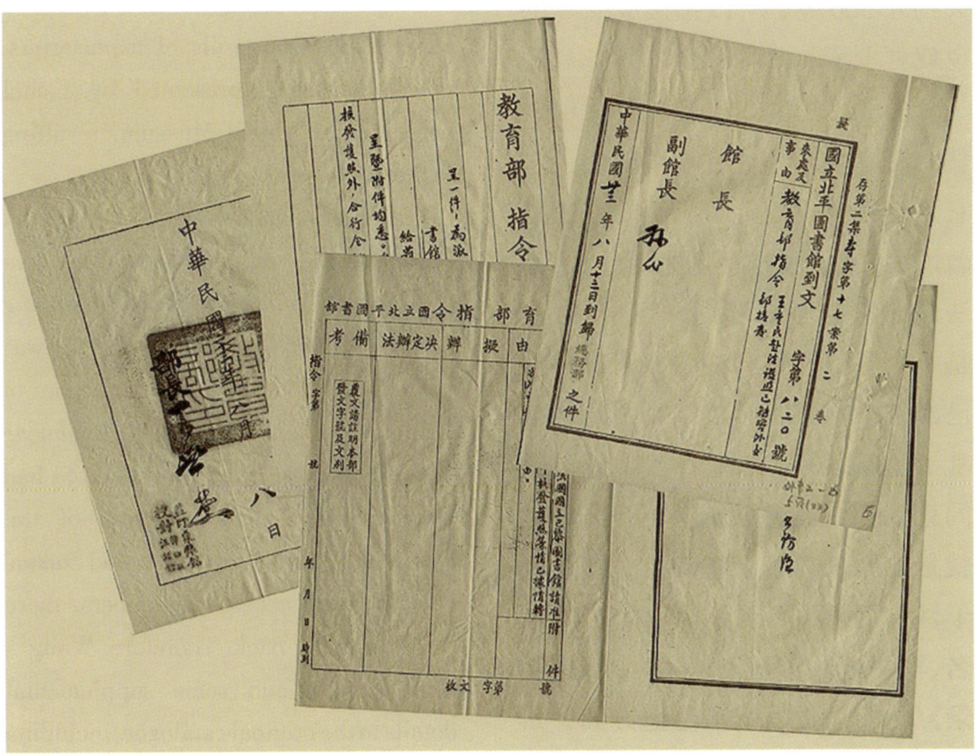

图 11　王重民赴法护照

Fig.11　Wang Zhongmin’s French Passport Papers

片，正在编目中。兹先将卢沟桥事变前收到者，编成简目，披露如右。”可见在二次大战的艰难困境中，得到并保存这些照片是多么的艰辛。

目前存放在中国国家图书馆敦煌吐鲁番学资料中心的13000余张敦煌遗书照片，其主体部分就是王重民先生当年在巴黎拍摄的。而同时期的向达先生，在伦敦博物馆检阅敦煌遗书时，由于受到小翟理斯的刁难，看到的卷子比较少，一共大约才500卷，所以拍摄成照片的也就更少了。

王重民先生在巴黎的另一项成就，就是编写了《伯希和劫经录》，它是王先生代伯希和所编的《法藏敦煌汉文写卷》的“注记目录”。因为法国的伯希和先编了一个目录，这是一个“财产账”式的登录号，并且已经登录上架，形成定局，如果打乱了重新编写，原主管者大概不会同意。所以，王重民先生的工作，也就是在原来的目录基础上，增加若干注释性质的记录，即为原卷定名、写注记。实际上，《伯希和劫经录》的最大贡献就在注记方面，如卷子的大致归类及现存形式、首尾题记的抄录、对卷子内容的提示，

Congress. The photos, about 10,000 in total, are being catalogued now. And those taken before the July 7th Incident of 1937 were catalogued first and displayed here.” His words clearly revealed the great difficulty in obtaining and keeping the photos given the hardships of World War II.

Currently, more than 13,000 photos are stored in the Dunhuang and Turfan Studies Document Center in the National Library of China, among which, the majority were taken by Wang during his stay in Paris. During the same period, Xiang Da had access to only about 500 scrolls of manuscripts, due to obstacles presented by Lionel Giles of the British Museum, resulting in fewer photos.

Wang’s another achievement in Paris was the compilation of *Catalogue of Chinese Manuscripts from Dunhuang in the Pelliot Collection*, which was created as a descriptive catalogue of Pelliot’s *French Collection of Dunhuang Chinese Manuscripts*. As Pelliot had already compiled a catalogue of the Dunhuang manuscripts he had taken, complete with accession numbers, there was no turning back. Therefore, Wang’s work was to add some supplemental details to the original catalogue, including naming manuscripts, adding descriptive notes, classifying the manuscripts,

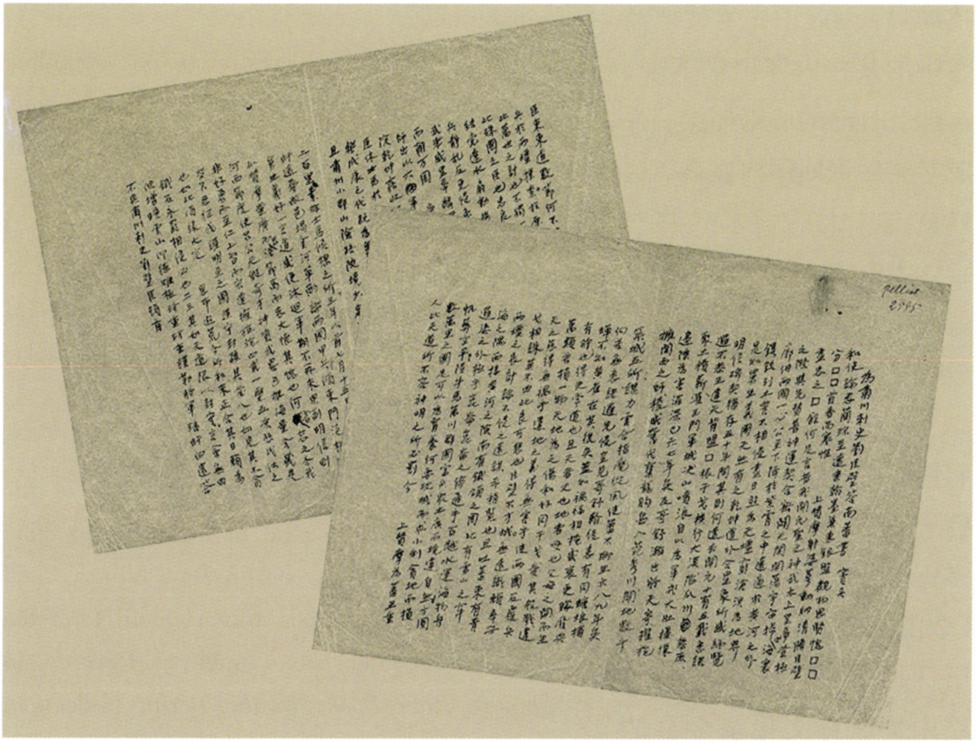

图 12　王重民先生手抄伯希和 2555 号《为肃州刺史刘臣壁答南蕃书》

Fig.12　Wang Zhongmin's Writings on Paul Pelliot's No. 25555: "A Reply to Tubo on Behalf of Suzhou Governor Liu Chenbi"

等等。另外，用"V"指卷子背面，也是王先生推广使用的。对于背面内容的介绍，在法文登录中，是用 V 下另作一条附录的方式解决的，注记方式与正面的相同。王先生则采用在卷内加"V"的方式处理。这一注记方式，为以后的敦煌文献编目和研究者所完全采纳。

正是由于王重民先生在编写《伯希和劫经录》时有上

copying the foreword and afterword, and writing a reader's guide for each manuscript. These annotated supplements to the catalogue could be considered the highlight of the book. In addition, he was the first to employ the letter "V" (for verso) to indicate the reverse or back side of the manuscripts. This method was different from Pelliot's way of marking scripts in the French catalogue. In the French system, there was no simple method to differentiate the front from the back of manuscripts. Wang's annotation approach was adopted by later researchers in cataloguing the Dunhuang

述局限，因此王先生就把经卷中的某些内容记录下来，再加上自己的心得体会，写成专文后寄回国内发表，这样就与广大的学术界共享了学术资源。其中的一部分就成了后来出版的《敦煌古籍叙录》的主要内容。

另外，1935年，王先生利用休假的机会，在柏林普鲁士图书馆看书，搜集了许多资料，写成《柏林访书记》《金山国坠事零拾》《敦煌本历日研究》等论著；1938年，受中华教育文化基金会的资助，王重民与向达先生一同赴英国伦敦，阅读英国图书馆所藏的敦煌卷子，后来写成了《伦敦所见敦煌卷子群书叙录》。

正是由于20世纪30年代的欧洲之行，奠定了王重民先生敦煌学研究的基础，从而使王先生成为我国第二代敦煌学的代表人物之一。其敦煌学方面的著作有《敦煌曲子词集》《敦煌古籍叙录》《敦煌遗书论文集》等，并合著有《敦煌变文集》

manuscripts.

In view of such restraints on compiling *Catalogue of Chinese Manuscripts from Dunhuang in the Pelliot Collection*, Wang recorded content of these Buddhist sutras and wrote articles on the basis of his own views and experiences. The articles were then published in China as a way of sharing academic resources with domestic scholars. Some of these articles later became the main section of *Compilation of Dunhuang Classics*.

In addition, Wang made full use of his vacation in 1935 to read in the Prussian State Library (present-day Berlin State Library) and thus collected materials which would form the basis of his later books, such as *Records on Chinese Rare Books in the Berlin Collection*, *Research on the History of Jinshan State*, and *Research on the Calendar Day in Dunhuang Manuscripts*. In 1938, sponsored by the Education and Culture Foundation of China, Wang and Xiang Da went to London, where they read the collections of Dunhuang manuscripts housed in the British Library. Later, *Catalogue of Dunhuang Manuscripts in the London Collection* was published.

It was the trip to Europe in the 1930s that laid the foundation for Wang's research on Dunhuang and made him one of the leading figures among the second generation of Chinese scholars involved in Dunhuang studies. His works on Dunhuang include *A Collection of Dunhuang Quzi Ci*, *Compilation of Dunhuang Classics*, and *Collected Papers on Dunhuang*

《敦煌遗书总目索引》等。

王重民先生在“文革”中遭迫害，于1975年4月16日逝世，其有关敦煌学的许多手稿都有待整理。如关于P.2555号“敦煌唐人诗集残卷”的整理出版就很费周折。1973年，于道泉先生带王尧去见王先生时，王先生就将其在巴黎抄录的有关唐与吐蕃关系的敦煌文书交给了王尧。1976年“四人帮”被粉

Manuscripts. In addition, he coauthored *An Anthology of Dunhuang Bianwen* and *General Index of Dunhuang Manuscripts*.

Wang died on April 16, 1975, as a result of persecution during the Cultural Revolution, leaving his reputation unjustly tarnished. He left behind many manuscripts on Dunhuang studies to be collated, which was a tremendous task. For example, the editing and publishing of manuscript P.2555, “An Anthology of Tang Poetry Fragments” was by itself a difficult job. When Yu Daoquan introduced Wang Zhongmin and Wang Yao to each other in 1973, Zhongmin gave Yao the Dunhuang manuscript copies he had made in Paris. The manuscripts involved the relationship between the

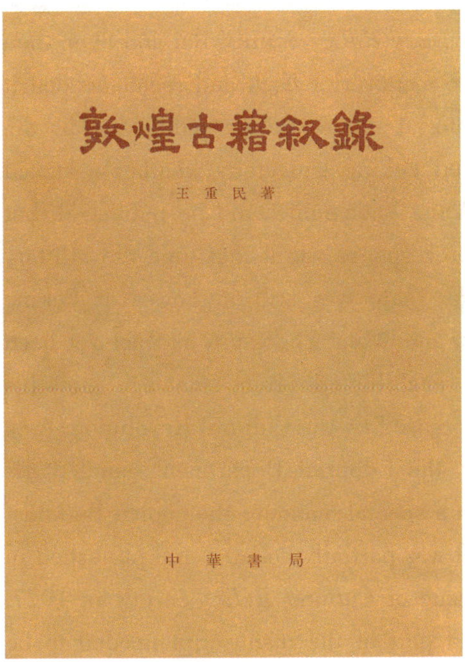

图13 《敦煌古籍叙录》
Fig.13 Compilation of Dunhuang Classics

图14 《敦煌遗书总目索引》
Fig.14 General Index of Dunhuang Manuscripts

碎后不久，在文物出版社《文物》编辑部帮忙的白化文、沈玉成，为了有关敦煌藏文卷子的问题，去中央民族学院见王尧教授。王尧主动出示了王重民先生的一篇稿子，其中第一部分就是王先生当年在巴黎抄录的P.2555号卷子中两位作者的诗作72首，第二部分是有关考释。此稿已经有几位学者看过并提出了意见，其中也包括王尧教授的贡献。当时《文物》编辑部正准备编《文物资料丛刊》，王尧教授就推荐此稿，白化文与沈玉成先生遂将此稿带回并向编辑部推荐。当编辑部准备刊载此稿后，就多次向王先生的原工作单位——北京大学有关部门征求能否发表署名稿的意见，但一直得不到答复。由于当时军宣队还在北大掌权，王重民先生还未获平反，在不得已的情况下，编辑部遂采取了特殊的处理：将录文部分经过整理后，

Tang Dynasty and the Tubo regime. The Gang of Four fell from power and were arrested in 1976, officially bringing the Cultural Revolution to a close. Shortly after, Bai Huawen and Shen Yucheng, who had been assisting in the editorial office of *Cultural Relics* in the Cultural Relics Publishing House, called on Professor Wang Yao in the Minzu University of China, inquiring about the Dunhuang Tibetan manuscripts. Wang Yao showed them a manuscript compiled by Wang Zhongmin. It consisted of two parts: the first part was 72 poems by the two authors from manuscript P.2555; the second was relevant interpretations and commentaries on the poems. The draft had been reviewed by several scholars including Wang Yao himself. He recommended this draft when the editorial office of *Cultural Relics* was preparing to compile *Cultural Relics Serials*. Bai and Shen then brought the manuscript back and recommended it to the editorial office. Before publishing it, the editor asked Peking University whether a signed draft by Wang Zhongmin could be published, but received no response, as at that time the Military Propaganda Team was still in power at Peking University, and Wang Zhongmin had not yet been formally rehabilitated from damage to his reputation caused by the Cultural Revolution. As a last resort, the Editorial Department handled the problem in a special manner: the copied Buddhist manuscript was partially collated and published in the first issue of *Cultural Relics Serials* in 1977. The second part of the manuscript needed to be rewritten due to various factors such as the difficulty in getting the authorship's credit

发表于1977年出版的《文物资料丛刊》第一辑；考释部分因各种因素，如署名难办、不合《文物资料丛刊》的体例等不好发表，就由白化文先生将其精粹也就是结论部分改写为“前言”。这里既不能埋没王重民先生的业绩，又要避免因出现“王重民”而不能出版，白化文先生就提出在“前言”中用王先生的字“有三”来代替。“前言”中说：

> 这些诗虽算不得文学上的好作品，内容上也有一些糟粕，但在历史上是很宝贵的纪行诗，也是研究这段历史的有用的参考材料。新中国成立前，有三先生曾从巴黎图书馆将这一残卷全文录出，以后又做过整理加工，惜未最后完稿。现在我们在王先生原来录文的基础上，又据北京图书馆所藏照片做了一次校对整理，在这里发表，供有关研究工作者参考。

文章定名为《敦煌唐人诗集残卷》，作者署名为“舒学”。这里的“舒学”是一笔名，是取了“初学”的谐音。按照当时编辑部的惯例，凡发表经编辑人员大修大改的文

approved as well as its mismatched style with the journal. Bai then adapted the original conclusion to the preface of the article. To give credit to Wang while avoiding mention of his name—doing so might revoke permission for the article to be published—Bai suggested using Wang's courtesy name "You San" to take the place of his real name. The preface states:

> These poems are both historically valuable as travel poetry and useful as references for the research of this period, even though some defects in the content kept them from being fine works of literature. Before 1949, You San had the complete record of these scripts from la Bibliothèque nationale de France, and later collated them. Unfortunately, he failed to finish its compilation. Now, on the basis of Wang's work, and according to photographs archived in the Beijing Library, we have made a collation and are ready to publish this article, with the aim of providing references for future study.

The article was named "An Anthology of Tang Poetry Fragments" with "Shu Xue," a homophone on the word "Chu Xue" meaning "beginner" as its signature. According to the rules of the Editorial Department at that time, whenever there was an article to which major changes had been made by the

章时，在征求作者同意的前提下，可以用编辑部自定的某一笔名。某一编辑或编辑组人员经常固定使用一个乃至几个笔名，内部人员一看就知道是谁，这样既有利于联系，也便于分清责任。因此，“舒学”与其说是笔名，不如说是一个代号。“舒学”代号的出现与白化文、沈玉成、王尧等先生有关，但又不是他们中哪一个人的笔名。

王重民先生去世后，除整理出版了《敦煌遗书论文集》《冷庐文薮》《中国目录学史论丛》《中国善本书提要》外，还有许多手稿资料尚需整理，其中有关敦煌学方面的资料，受其夫人刘修业先生的委托，由柴剑虹先生于1984 年 2 月带到敦煌，赠送给敦煌研究院，现在正由敦煌研究院李永宁、程亮先生整理。

这些资料中，既有王重民先生亲笔做的伯希和劫经录卡片 2700 余张、敦煌写本分类卡片近 2000 张，也有王先生与刘修业先生抄录整理的敦煌写卷录文 50 多种、王先生的《敦煌

editor, the editor could employ a pseudonym for authorship provided the original author gave his permission. Usually one or more particular pseudonyms were used by an editor or within a certain editorial team, either for organizing projects within the department more easily or for distinguishing responsibility. In this sense, “Shu Xue” was more symbol than pseudonym. Its use was related to Bai Huawen, Shen Yucheng, and Wang Yao, but it was the individual pseudonym of none of them.

After Wang Zhongmin’s death, besides editing and publishing *Collected Papers on Dunhuang Manuscripts*, *Collected Works of Wang Zhongmin*, *Collected Essays on China’s Bibliographic History*, and *An Anthology of Rare Books in China*, there were still many manuscripts that needed to be collated. Under these circumstances, Wang’s wife, Liu Xiuye, asked another scholar named Chai Jianhong to take the materials on Dunhuang studies back to Dunhuang in February, 1984 and to donate them to the Dunhuang Academy. They are currently being managed by Li Yongning and Cheng Liang, who are responsible for continuing Wang’s unfinished work.

These archives include more than 2,700 cards on records of sutras removed by Paul Pelliot and nearly 2,000 catalogue cards on Dunhuang manuscripts, which were all made by Wang Zhongmin personally; over 50 kinds of manuscript records transcribed and

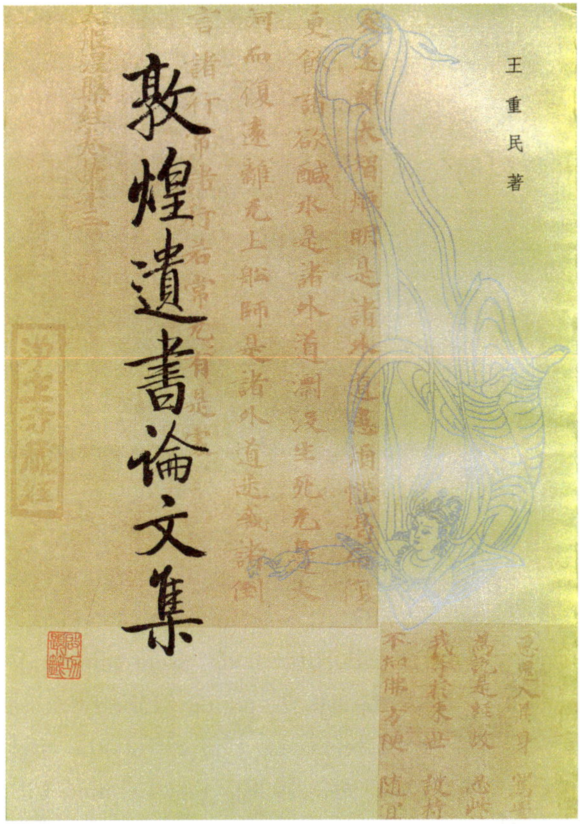

图 15 《敦煌遗书论文集》

Fig.15 Collected Papers on Dunhuang Manuscripts

古籍叙录》和《补全唐诗》的原稿，还有王先生与姜亮夫先生的通信及马叙伦、张政烺、孙楷第等先生的文章等。

除了在巴黎进行的敦煌学研究外，王重民先生在美国保存中国善本书的行动，也值得一记。1939 年，应华盛顿国会图书馆远东

organized by Wang Zhongmin and Liu Xiuye; as well as Wang Zhongmin's manuscripts of *Compilation of Dunhuang Classics* and *Supplement to The Complete Collection of Tang Poems*. The letters between Wang and Jiang Liangfu and the articles written by Ma Xulun, Zhang Zhenglang, and Sun Kaidi are also part of the materials.

Apart from his research on Dunhuang studies in Paris, Wang Zhongmin's preservation of Chinese rare books in the United States is also worth noting. In 1939, at the invitation of the

部主任的邀请，王重民先生赴美国鉴定其所收藏的中国善本书。在美期间，王重民先生曾想回国参加抗日战争，后在袁同礼先生的劝说下，他便留在美国从事中国善本书的著录工作，撰写了 1600 多篇提要，取名《美国国会图书馆所藏善本书录》。

王重民先生参与北图善本书的保存，也是值得一提的。北图成立之始所继承的古物来源依次上溯为：京师图书馆（北洋政府）→内阁大库（清）→文渊阁（明），实际上是宋、金、元、明、清所遗中国古籍之精华。九一八事变后，蒋介石政府决定将故宫国宝南迁，其中也包括北图的一部分藏书，分别寄放在上海的租界和南京，这样就有了北图非正式的上海分馆和南京分馆。卢沟桥事变后，袁同礼先生率北图随北大、清华等校

director of the Far East Department of the Library of Congress in Washington, D.C., Wang went to the United States to identify the library's collection of Chinese rare books. During his stay there, Wang expected to return to China to participate in the War of Resistance Against Japanese Aggression. However, he was persuaded by Yuan Tongli to stay there to catalogue the Chinese rare book collections. During this time, he wrote more than 1,600 summaries for the books and compiled them into a book titled *Catalogue of the Collection of Rare Books in the Library of Congress*.

Wang also participated in preserving rare books in the National Library of China. When the library was initially founded, the antique and collectible books were inherited successively from the Metro-politan Library (present-day National Library of China) of the Beiyang Government (1912-1928), the Cabinet Library of the Qing Dynasty (1636-1912), and Wenyuan Pavilion of the Ming Dynasty (1368-1644), which were all antique books representing the quintessence of Chinese culture in the historical periods of the Song, Jin, Yuan, Ming, and Qing dynasties. After the September 18th Incident (Mukden Incident) in 1931, the National government under Chiang Kai-shek decided to transfer the treasures of the National Palace Museum to southern China, including part of the book collections of the National Library of China, which were kept in the foreign concession areas in Shanghai and Nanjing. As a result, two informal branches came into being, one in Shanghai and the other in Nanjing. After the July 7th Incident of 1937, Yuan Tongli helped the

南迁，而派其助手钱存训到上海主持分馆业务。上海沦陷后，袁即与当时的驻美大使胡适取得美国政府和国会图书馆的同意，将一批善本书运往美国保管，并说好待和平恢复后即物归原主。

为此，袁先生于1940年冒险从内地秘密到沪，王重民先生也从美国返回上海，他们从北平图书馆存放在上海的300箱善本书中，选出了2720种约3万册，装为102箱，并作了防水处理。当时上海海关已被日军占领，检查非常严，好几种运送方案都无法行得通。最后，通过钱存训夫人的间接关系，由一位在海关负责检查的张先生帮忙，在他值夜班时秘密运送，交一张假的发货单，由他签字放行。这102箱书共分10批交运，最后一批是1941年12月5日。两天后，珍珠港事件爆发，日军立即进占了租界。秘密运往美国的这批善本书，藏于美国国会图书馆远东部。后于1965年由美国运

National Library of China move southwards, together with Peking University and Tsinghua University. His assistant, Qian Cunxun, was assigned to be in charge of the Shanghai branch. After the fall of Shanghai to the Japanese, with the consent of the U.S. government and the Library of Congress, Yuan and Hu Shi, the Chinese ambassador to the USA, escorted a number of rare books to the United States for preservation, with both sides agreeing that the books would be delivered to China once peace was restored.

For the safety of the rare books, Yuan and Wang Zhongmin ventured to Shanghai in 1940. They selected approximately 30,000 scrolls comprising 2,720 subjects from the 300 boxes of ancient rare books stored in the Shanghai branch, packing them in 102 waterproof boxes. At that time, the Customs Office in Shanghai was being tightly controlled by the Japanese army. Although Yuan and Wang tried various ways to get the scrolls to pass through the customs, they ultimately failed. Finally, Yuan and Wang turned to Qian Cunxun's wife for help. Qian's wife knew the officer, Mr. Zhang, who was in charge of customs inspections, and the latter agreed to help. During the night shift, the boxes were secretly transported with a fake invoice signed by Zhang. The 102 boxes were divided into 10 batches for delivery and the last batch was delivered on December 5, 1941. Two days later, the Japanese attacked Pearl Harbor; the Japanese army simultaneously invaded and occupied the foreign concession areas in

往台湾，现存于台湾“中央图书馆”。

这期间，具有远见卓识的袁同礼馆长，为了保存北图的善本书，欲将存放在美国的这102箱的善本书拍摄成缩微胶卷。这一意愿得到了美方的同意，于是双方达成协议：由美国提供资金和技术，中国方面由王重民先生负责，撰写提要。这一工作费时四五年。

在抗日战争的艰难环境中，王重民先生除协助有关方面将此100余箱珍贵图书转移到美国保管，并制成缩微胶卷加以保存外，还撰写了提要，为保存中国的文化典籍作出了贡献。

Shanghai. The rare books secretly shipped to the United States were preserved in the Far East Department of the Library of Congress. In 1965, they were transported to Taiwan and have been deposited in Taiwan's National Central Library ever since.

During this period, Yuan Tongli, a visionary director, intended to microfilm the 102 boxes of rare books stored in the United States, which was approved by the United States, with the two sides reaching an agreement: the United States provided funds and technology, and the Chinese side, led by Wang Zhongmin, was responsible for writing summaries for the rare books. This time-consuming work lasted four to five years.

Under the harsh circumstances of the War of Resistance Against Japanese Aggression, Wang Zhongmin not only assisted in transferring more than 100 boxes of rare books to the United States and microfilming them for preservation, he also wrote the summary for each. It is fair to say that Wang made great contributions toward the preservation of Chinese classics.

敦煌藏学研究的开拓者——于道泉

Yu Daoquan: Pioneer of Dunhuang Tibetan Studies

敦煌文献中约有七八千卷的古藏文文书，绝大多数都被窃运海外，分别收藏在巴黎的法国国家图书馆和伦敦的印度事务部图书馆，其中法国国家图书馆中就藏有3358号。

所谓敦煌古藏文文献，就是指吐蕃时期的藏文文献。藏族原无文字，松赞干布曾派屯米桑布扎赴天竺学习梵文和佛法，他学成返回吐蕃后，就依据梵文创立了藏文。吐蕃灭亡以后，其经籍文献全部被毁，现在所见大多是宋元以后集结起来的。敦煌藏经洞发现的古藏文文献，是藏民族最早的文字记录，它对于全面了解西藏历史，诠释藏族文化，认识藏汉文化的双向交流，具有举足轻重的意义。

20世纪30年代初，于道泉先生就致力于藏学研究，在巴黎大学师从巴考教授，

Ancient Tibetan manuscripts account for about 7,000 to 8,000 scrolls of the Dunhuang manuscripts, but the majority of them have been removed and shipped overseas. Today, they are preserved in la Bibliothèque nationale de France and the India Office of the British Library, with a total of 3,358 scrolls in the former alone.

Dunhuang ancient Tibetan manuscripts refer to the manuscripts of the Tubo period. There was no written language in Tibet before Songtsen Gampo sent Thonmi Sambhota to India to study Sanskrit and Buddhism. Thonmi Sambhota later created the Tibetan language on the basis of Sanskrit. Unfortunately, all the Buddhist classics were destroyed when the Tubo regime fell. Those that remained were mostly collected after the Song and Yuan dynasties. As the ancient Tibetan manuscripts discovered in the Library Cave are the earliest written records of the Tibetans, they are of great value for a comprehensive understanding of Tibetan history and culture, and for the mutual communication between Tibetan and Han cultures.

In the early 1930s, Yu Daoquan was devoted to Tibetan studies at the Université de Paris. During this time, he studied ancient Tibetan manuscripts under Professor Jacques

考察这些古藏文文书。今天，当我国学者与世界有关国家的图书馆、研究机构合作，编辑出版敦煌藏文文献时，我们更加怀念为此作出巨大贡献的于道泉先生。

于道泉（1901—1992）教授是山东临淄人，青少年时期就学于山东济南，1920年考入当时的齐鲁大学（今山东大学的前身），在社会

Bacot. His contributions in this field still exert great influence on Chinese scholars who continue to edit and publish these Tibetan manuscripts in cooperation with foreign libraries and research institutions.

Yu Daoquan (1901–1992) was born in Linzi, Shandong Province and as a teenager, he studied in Jinan. He was admitted to Qilu University (present-day Shandong University) in 1920, majoring in sociology and Western history. He also audited mathematics and other courses. With only about 20 students, the Sociology Department at Qilu University was one of the

图 16 于道泉 1982 年留影
Fig.16 Yu Daoquan, 1982

学系专修社会学和西洋史，同时旁听数学等课程。当时齐鲁大学的社会学系是我国最早设立的社会学系之一。该系只有二十来个学生，所有课程全系美国教师担任，用英语讲授。班里英语水平较高，能完全听懂所授内容的学生只有四五个，年轻的于道泉就是其中之一。

于道泉走上藏学之路，其转折点是泰戈尔访华。1924年，印度诗人泰戈尔访问中国，在从南京去北京时路经济南。当时，年轻的于道泉怀着崇敬的心情前往火车站欢迎这位诺贝尔奖获得者。在去车站的路上，济南各中学的校长推荐他为泰戈尔一行的英语翻译，由他带着印度客人观光济南。当参观至济南佛经流通处时，泰戈尔发现这位年仅二十来岁的青年不但会说一口流利的英语，而且还能认识梵文，并对佛经也有一定的了解，这使泰戈尔非常惊讶，就对于道泉说："你是我们来中国见到的第一个对印度语言和文化发生兴趣的人。"并建

earliest of its kind in China. All the courses were taught in English by American teachers, which demanded proficiency in English from the students; Yu was one of only a handful of students who could follow the lectures.

It was the Indian poet Rabindranath Tagore's visit to China in 1924 that inspired Yu to switch majors to Tibetan studies. Tagore was travelling from Nanjing to Beijing, with a stop in Jinan. Young Yu Daoquan, having great respect for the poet, went to the railway station to welcome the Nobel Prize winner. Once there, a group of Jinan secondary school principals recommended Yu as the English interpreter for Tagore's delegation, and to be their sightseeing guide around Jinan as well. During their visit to the circulation of Buddhist sutras, Tagore was greatly impressed by this 23-year-old young man who not only could speak fluent English but also had a certain knowledge of Sanskrit and Buddhist sutras. He said to Yu, "You're the first person we have met in China who is interested in Indian language and culture." Appreciating Yu's talents, Tagore advised him to study at the Visva-Bharati University established by Tagore himself. Tagore highly commended Yu to the Chinese government. At that time, Yu had already been enrolled in an American program on a Shandong government scholarship, but he gave it up without any hesitation and went to Beijing with Tagore in order to prepare for future studies in India. Unfortunately, Tagore's proposal of an

图 17　1924 年泰戈尔(中)访华时，　于道泉(第二排左一)任翻译

Fig.17　Yu Daoquan (Far Left, Second Row) as an Interpreter During Tagore's (Center, First Row) Visit to China, 1924

议于道泉去北京，由他们向中国政府推荐到泰戈尔自己创建的印度国际大学去留学。当时，于道泉已经考取了山东官费留美生，但他为了学习梵文，从事佛经研究，毅然放弃了这个留美的机会，而决定随

exchange program with 20 to 30 students from Peking University failed to receive approval because of civil unrest and internecine fighting between warlords. Consequently, Yu's desire to study in India came to a premature end. Before his departure, Tagore introduced Yu to Gang Hetai, a Sanskrit professor at Peking University and told him,

泰戈尔去北京，准备到印度国际大学深造。由于当时军阀混战，泰戈尔向北京大学提出交换二三十名留学生的建议没有得到采纳。于道泉来到北京后，没有实现留印的愿望。泰戈尔在离京前，就把时任北京大学梵文教授的钢和泰教授介绍给于道泉，并对他说："这位爵士可以教你梵文、藏文，可以满足你探索生命秘密的要求。"于是他就学于北京大学，跟随钢和泰教授，并住在他家，一面学习梵文和藏文，一面研究佛经，同时还担任钢和泰的课堂英语翻译。

"钢和泰"这一姓名的原文是 Alexander von Stael-Holstein，"钢"是 stael 的意译，"和泰"则是 Holstein 的音译。他 1877 年 1 月 1 日出生在当时隶属于沙皇俄国的爱沙尼亚专区，家庭是世袭的贵族——男爵，因此，他自幼就受到了良好的教育。后来，钢和泰到了德国，在柏林大学和其他学校学习梵文和东方学。20 世纪初，钢和泰在德国学成返回俄国后，即受到了当时俄国著名东方学家谢尔巴茨科依和奥登堡的器重，并曾问学于奥登堡。

由于钢和泰曾去过印度进行学

"This gentleman can teach you Sanskrit and Tibetan and can satisfy your desire to explore the secret of life." Thanks to Tagore's recommendation, Yu followed Professor Gang, studying at Peking University while living in the professor's home. During that period, Yu learned Sanskrit and Tibetan and also studied Buddhist religious texts while serving as an English interpreter in Professor Gang's class.

In fact, Gang Hetai was the Chinese name of Baron Alexander von Stael-Holstein. "Gang" was the Chinese translation of "steel" and "Hetai" was the transliteration of "Holstein." The professor was born on January 1, 1877, in Estonia, while the country was under control of the Russian Empire. He received an excellent childhood education, being from an aristocratic family. Later, he went to Germany and studied Sanskrit and Oriental studies at the University of Berlin and other universities. He went back to Russia in the early 1900s and won the appreciation of renowned scholars in Oriental studies including Sher Batz Coy and Sergey Fyodorovich Oldenburg; he was later taught by Oldenburg as well.

Gang's previous academic research in India led to his interest in studying Xuanzang (Hsuan Tsang), an eminent monk from the Tang Dynasty in China.

术考察，增加了对中国唐代高僧玄奘的兴趣。1916年，他途经西伯利亚来到北京，一方面搜集有关玄奘的资料，另一方面还查阅蒙文和藏文的资料，因为当时的北京是中国文化和学术的中心。1917年俄国爆发了革命，因为钢和泰是贵族，就没有返回俄国的可能了，而他的经济来源也随之中断。经当时英国驻西伯利亚高级专员义理和的推荐，北大校长胡适就聘请钢和泰在北大任教，讲授梵文、藏文和印度古代宗教史。其间除1928年—1929年到美国哈佛大学做访问学者外，一直在北大授课与研究，直到1937年初去世。当1924年于道泉到北京时，钢和泰正在北大任教，这样才就有了向钢和泰学习梵文的机会。

从那个时候起，于道泉先生对藏文发生了极大的兴趣。为了进一步掌握藏语言，来京一年以后，他设法认识了雍和宫的几位藏族喇嘛，住进了雍和宫。在那里，经过两年的刻苦学习，他不仅完全掌握了藏语言，而且还向寺里的蒙古族喇嘛学会了蒙古文。季羡林先生在《平凡而伟大的学者——于道泉》中写道：“他曾经为了学习西藏文和蒙古文，干脆搬进了雍和宫，同蒙藏喇

In 1916, he headed from Siberia to Beijing—the cultural and academic center of China—to collect information on Xuanzang and to look up Mongolian and Tibetan manuscripts. The October Revolution in 1917 deprived him of the chance to return to Russia because of his aristocratic status; naturally, his financial support was cut off as well. With the recommendation of Yi Lihe, British High Commissioner in Sikeria, Hu Shi, president of Peking University, hired Gang to teach Sanskrit, Tibetan, and ancient Indian religious history. Gang worked there giving lectures and doing research until his death in early 1937. He was also a visiting scholar at Harvard University from 1928 to 1929. Yu Daoquan went to Beijing in 1924 when Gang Hetai was teaching at Peking University and thus Yu had the opportunity to learn Sanskrit from Gang.

Meanwhile, Yu also made an effort to learn Tibetan. In order to learn the language, he managed to meet several Tibetan lamas at Lama Temple (Yonghe Palace) and also moved into it. After two years of hard work, he not only mastered Tibetan but learned Mongolian from the lamas living there. In the book *Ordinary but Great Scholar*: *Yu Daoquan*, Ji Xianlin wrote, “Yu once moved to Yonghe Temple and

嘛住在一起，因此得绰号‘于喇嘛’。”

就在钢和泰在北京大学授课的时候，陈寅恪先生从德国学成归国，并任清华国学研究院的导师。由于陈寅恪与钢和泰都学习梵文，并都有在德国长期学习的背景，在治学上都具有彻底性和缜密性的特点，因此，在陈寅恪回国后的四五年内，几乎每周都要与钢和泰共同探讨梵学一次。正是这种机缘，陈寅恪认识了于道泉，同时也鼓励于道泉学好藏、梵两种文字。

1927年，经袁同礼先生推荐，于道泉来到当时的北海图书馆担任满蒙藏文书的采访编目工作，同时还给中央研究院历史语言研究所历史组组长陈寅恪先生做助理研究员。当时于道泉的待遇比较低，看到生活颇为困苦却毫无怨言，仍孜孜治学的于道泉，陈寅恪心为所动，曾三次向傅斯年推荐于道泉。他说：“于君甚精藏语，又兼治蒙文，实不可多得之人才。现在北海图书馆，月仅三十元，甚不敷用；前年弟每月借钱与之。他时历史语言所北平分所中似可以用，此人断不至为羊公不舞之

lived with Tibetan and Mongolian lamas to learn Tibetan and Mongolian, and so he earned the nickname‘Lama Yu.’”

While Gang Hetai was teaching at Peking University, Chen Yinque returned to China from Germany and served as a supervisor at Institute of Guoxue Studies at Tsinghua University. Thanks to the similar experiences—they both had learned Sanskrit while studying in Germany—and their similar meticulous teaching styles, Chen and Gang would have discussions on Sanskrit studies once a week for four or five years after his return. Also in that period, Chen got to know Yu Daoquan and encouraged him to gain a strong command of Tibetan and Sanskrit.

In 1927, with the recommendation of Yuan Tongli, Yu Daoquan went to work in the Beihai Library, undertaking acquisitions and cataloguing work in Manchurian, Mongolian, and Tibetan languages. He also served as an assistant researcher for Chen Yinque who was then the leader of the history team at the History and Language Institute of the Academia Sinica. At the time, Yu had a relatively low income, but he never complained about hardship. Instead, he devoted himself to his work. Chen Yinque was impressed by his dedication, recommending him to Fu Sinian three times with praise, which read, “Mr. Yu is

鹤，请放心用。”“羊公不舞之鹤”，取“羊叔子有鹤善舞，尝向客称之，客试使驱来，不肯舞”的典故。

正是由于陈寅恪的推荐，1928 年，于道泉到新成立的中央研究院历史语言研究所历史组担任助理研究员的职务，同时继续兼任北海图书馆的工作。1930 年，他发表了《第六代达赖喇嘛仓央嘉措情歌》一书，作为国立中央研究院历史语言研究所单刊甲种之五。该书出版以后，在国际藏学界引起了很大的反响。书中不仅附以汉英两种文字的情歌译词和注释，而且还有著名语言学家赵元任先生为歌词所配的藏语拉萨话记音。

1934 年，他被中央研究院派往法国留学，到巴黎大学攻读藏文和土耳其语。同时兼为北图与国外交换资料，与袁同礼馆长书信往返，为北图带回许多敦煌藏文卷子胶片。两年以后，他去德国进行考

a rare talent indeed. He is proficient in Tibetan and is good at Mongolian. As his low income at the Beihai Library cannot make ends meet, I've been lending him some money every month for the past two years. I'm sure he'll never be 'Old Yang's crane which does not dance,' and I believe he is capable of working in the Beiping branch of the History and Language Institute. Please feel free to employ him." The reference to "Old Yang's crane which does not dance" is taken from an old story, which means a talent that proves useless.

Yu Daoquan was offered the post of assistant researcher at the History and Language Institute of the Academia Sinica in 1928, thanks to the recommendation of Chen Yinque. Meanwhile, he still kept his job at the Beiping Beihai Library. In 1930, he published *Love Poems by Tsangyang Gyatso, the Sixth Dalai Lama,* which turned out to be a highly regarded publication by the institute, generating great impact in international Tibetan academic circles. The book included not only translation and annotation of the verses in both English and Chinese, but also phonetic notations in the Lhasa dialect by the well-known linguist Zhao Yuanren.

In 1934, Yu was sent by the Academia Sinica to France where he majored in Tibetan and Turkish at the Université de Paris. In the meantime, he was in charge of exchanging resources between National Library of Beiping and foreign libraries, maintaining regular correspondence with Yuan Tongli, director of National Library of Beiping. Yu brought back

察，并在那儿很快学会德语。

1938 年，他由德国藏学家西门华德（Simon Walter）介绍到英国伦敦大学东方非洲研究院执教，在那里，他先后给该院的高级讲师、研究生和大学生讲授过藏、蒙古、汉等语言课程，历时十年。

1949 年中华人民共和国成立后，于道泉回到祖国，就任北京大学东方语文

many rolls of film taken of the Dunhuang Tibetan manuscripts. Two years later, he went to study in Germany, mastering the language in a short time.

In 1938, Yu went to teach at the Oriental and African Research Institute of the University of London, on the recommendation of Simon Walter, a German Tibetologist. He stayed there for 10 years during which time he gave courses on Tibetan, Mongolian, and Mandarin to senior lecturers, graduate students, and undergraduates.

After the founding of the People's Republic of China in 1949, Yu returned to China, where he worked as a professor of Tibetology in the Oriental Languages Department of Peking University. Not long after, he was transferred to

图 18　于道泉在巴黎大学文学院留学时的学生证

Fig.18　Student ID Card of Yu Daoquan at the Faculté des Lettres, Université de Paris

图 19　1939 年—1945 年间摄于英国,时在伦敦大学任教
Fig.19　Yu Daoquan During his Time as a Teacher at the University of London, 1939-1945

系藏学教授。不久，调至中央民族学院少数民族语文系，直到 1992 年去世。

中华人民共和国成立后的四十多年，于道泉先生在藏学方面的贡献主要是：

第一，为藏文和拉萨话方言制定了一整套具有较高学术水平的拉丁转写和拉丁注音符号系统。在 1951 年的第一期藏语班的教学中，他充分利用了 26 个拉丁字母，没有再附加其他任何符号，进行了上述工作，从而给藏文转写和注音的打字、排版印刷以

the Minority Language Department at Minzu University of China and stayed there until his death in 1992.

In his long career, Yu Daoquan made many significant contributions to Tibetan studies.

First, he devised complete transcription and phonetic systems for the Tibetan and Lhasa vernacular. Beginning with the first Tibetan language class he taught in 1951, he made full use of the 26 letters of the Latin alphabet to establish a system using no other symbols, which greatly simplified and streamlined typing,

及现代的电子计算机文字信息处理等方面，带来了极大的方便。

第二，筹办中央人民广播电台藏语广播。胡乔木是我国第一任新闻总署署长，他在担任署长初，就听说了于道泉先生的逸闻故事，也知道他通晓多种语言，而且还是留学欧洲多年的专家，因此，就将筹办藏语广播的工作交给了于道泉，请他协助中央人民广播电台设立藏语翻译和播音小组。于道泉从 1950 年 4 月 10 日开始筹办，经过努力，中央人民广播电台于 5 月 22 日晚上正式用藏语播音。

第三，编纂《藏汉对照拉萨口语词典》。1951 年，于道泉到中央民族学院后，即担任了藏语专业的教研组组长。他在组内建立了字典编写小组，开始了主编《藏汉对照拉萨口语词典》的工作。这部词典收集了二万九千多条藏语拉萨口语词汇，逐条加以拉萨话注音。这对藏语方言、藏语口语、藏语历史比较等方面的研究提供了宝贵的资料，从而填补了藏学教学和研究的一个空白。

typesetting, printing and computer processing in Tibetan.

Second, Yu initiated the Tibetan Broadcasting Service at China National Radio. Hu Qiaomu, the first director of the General Press Administration, had heard anecdotes about Yu Daoquan, his proficiency in several languages, and his experience of overseas studies in Europe. As a result, he assigned the organization of a Tibetan Broadcasting Service to Yu and asked him to assist in establishing a Tibetan translation and broadcasting group. On April 10, 1950, Yu began work on the project. Thanks to his efforts, on the evening of May 22 of that year, China National Radio made its first broadcast in Tibetan.

Moreover, he compiled *Tibetan-Chinese Lhasa Vernacular Dictionary*. In 1951, Yu served as the leader of the teaching team for Tibetan majors at Minzu University of China. He organized a special team to compile *Tibetan-Chinese Lhasa Vernacular Dictionary* in which more than 29,000 entries of Tibetan colloquial words and phrases were included with phonetic notations in Lhasa vernacular. This dictionary has proved an invaluable resource for studying Tibetan vernacular and Tibetan colloquial expressions and for a comparative study of Tibetan history.

潘重规与《列宁格勒十日记》

Pan Chonggui and his *Record of Ten Days in Leningrad*

1973年，当中国大陆正在进行“文革”，敦煌学家或被批斗，或蹲“牛棚”，敦煌学研究已经停顿之时，却有一位中国的敦煌学家，只身前往列宁格勒(今圣彼得堡)，阅读收藏在列宁格勒东方学研究所的敦煌文献。他，就是国际著名的敦煌学家、当时任职于香港中文大学新亚书院的潘重规先生。

潘重规先生，安徽省婺源县人。1908年生。本名崇奎，小名梦祥。章太炎先生为之易名为重规，黄季刚先生易其字为袭善，而先生则自号石禅。1924年入国立东南大学(后改名中央大学）中文系，师从黄季刚先生。中央大学中文系毕业后，曾先

In 1973, when the Cultural Revolution was still running riot in mainland of China, Dunhuang studies were forced into hiatus, with researchers either denounced or sent to rural areas for labor reform. However, there was a Chinese researcher who went to Leningrad (St. Petersburg) during this time to study the Dunhuang manuscripts held at the Institute of Oriental Studies of the USSR Academy of Sciences (presen-day Institute of Oriental Manuscripts of the Russian Academy of Sciences). He was Pan Chonggui (P'an Chung-kuei), one of the most prestigious Dunhuang scholars in the world, then working for the New Asia College at the Chinese University of Hong Kong (CUHK).

Born in 1908 in Anhui Province, Pan was originally named Pan Chongkui. Later, his name was changed to Pan Chonggui. In 1924, he was admitted to the Chinese Department of National Southeast University (present-day Nanjing University), where he studied under Huang Jigang. After graduation, he served as a professor at National Northeast University and then professor and dean of the Chinese Department at National Sichuan University. He held various positions after the War of Resistance Against Japanese Aggression, including professor at National Chi Nan University, professor and dean at National Anhui University, dean and institute director of the Chinese Department at National Taiwan Normal University, professor of the Chinese Department at

图 20　潘重规(1908—2003)
Fig.20　Pan Chonggui (1908-2003)

后担任国立东北大学教授，国立四川大学中文系教授兼系主任。抗战胜利后，任国立暨南大学教授，国立安徽大学教授兼主任，国立台湾师范大学国文系主任兼研究所所长，新加坡南洋大学中文系教授，香港中文大学新亚书院中文系主任兼文学院院长。1973 年，自香港中文大学退休，应聘为法国巴黎第三大学博士班客座教授，次年返台，先后担任中国文化大学中文研究所主任兼文学院院长，东吴大学讲座

Nanyang University in Singapore, and dean of both the Chinese Department and the College of Literature at the Chinese University of Hong Kong (CUHK). Pan retired from CUHK in 1973 and was hired as a returning visiting professor for the PhD program at Université Sorbonne Nouvelle-Paris 3. He worked there for one year before returning to Taiwan where he acted as director of the Institute of Chinese and dean of the College of Literature at Chinese Culture University, visiting professor at Soochow University, and

教授，台湾师范大学、中国文化大学兼任教授。2003年4月在台北去世，享年96岁。

潘重规先生赴列宁格勒阅读敦煌文献，既是偶然的，又是必然的。说是必然，那是因为潘先生早就致力于敦煌学研究，到1973年时，已出版了《唐写文心雕龙残本合校》《敦煌诗经卷子研究论文集》《瀛涯敦煌韵书新编》和《瀛涯敦煌韵辑别录》等敦煌学著作，并发表了十多篇敦煌学方面的论文。

偶然的是，潘重规和俄罗斯的孟列夫先生兴趣一致，他们既喜好和研究《红楼梦》，又对敦煌文献情有独钟。因此，孟列夫看到潘先生研究敦煌文献和《红楼梦》的论文时，颇有同调之感，遂写信欢迎潘先生到列宁格勒参观他研究的资料。

正因为有孟列夫的邀请，1973年8月，潘重规先生在巴黎参加第29届国际

professor at both Taiwan Normal University and Chinese Culture University. In April 2003, he passed away in Taipei at the age of 96.

His trip to Leningrad to study the Dunhuang manuscripts seemed both coincidental and inevitable. It was inevitable because Pan had dedicated his career to Dunhuang studies for so long that he could not afford to miss seeing such a valuable collection. By 1973, apart from writing 10 more academic articles on Dunhuang studies, he had already published several related works, including: *Proofread Edition of the Literary Mind and Dragon Carvings of the Tang Dynasty*, *Theories on The Book of Songs Found in Dunhuang*, *Compilation of Dunhuang Rhyming Manuscripts from Overseas Collections*, and *Compilation of Additional Dunhuang Rhyming Manuscripts from Overseas Collections*.

It was serendipitous that Pan Chonggui and Lev N. Menshikov, a professor in Leningrad, shared common research goals. Both of them showed keen interest in both *A Dream of Red Mansions* and Dunhuang studies. When Menshikov learned that they cherished the same goals, he immediately wrote a letter inviting Pan to study his collections in Leningrad.

Thanks to this invitation, Pan headed for Leningrad soon after the conclusion of the 29th International Orientalist Conference in Paris in August, 1973. He described the situation then in his *Record of Ten Days in Leningrad*, "After the closing of the conference, I wrote to Menshikov and informed him of my arrival in Leningrad on August 8, but there was no reply before my

东方学家大会后，即赴列宁格勒阅读敦煌文献。据潘先生《列宁格勒十日记》载："我在东方学会闭幕之后，写信给他，告诉将乘八月八日班机飞列宁格勒，临到起飞前夕，没有得到一字回音。巴黎到列城，只需四小时航程，去信两星期，竟然杳无消息，不能不绕室彷徨。许多可能的坏结果，不断地在脑海冲击。我茫然、怅然，最后抱着不顾一切的决心闯向前去。这是我启程前夕时的心情。"

俄藏敦煌文献是最具神秘感的收藏品。孟列夫教授在《俄藏敦煌文献》前言中说：1929年前称为亚洲博物馆的现俄罗斯科学院东方研究所圣彼得堡分所敦煌藏品，绝大部分是奥登堡院士率领的俄国西域考察团1914年—1915年间所搜集的写卷。还有一部分同类型汉文写卷，则分别是当时俄国驻乌鲁木齐领事克罗特科夫，1906年—1909年间前往和阗的马洛夫考察团以及1909年—1910年间前往吐鲁番的奥登堡考察团所搜集。就总体而言，所有这些文献，我们将它们都称之为

departure. The four-hour short flight from Paris to Leningrad was full of uncertainties which made me more anxious about my visit; I became rather frustrated at the possible disappointing result. But finally I made up my mind to go ahead and give it a try. That was exactly what I thought before I set off."

The Dunhuang manuscripts collected in Russia proved to be the most mysterious ones. As Menshikov wrote in the preface to *Dunhuang Documents Held in Russia*, prior to 1929 most of the Dunhuang collections in the Institute of Oriental Studies of the USSR Academy of Sciences were manuscripts gathered by the second Russian expedition to Turkestan headed by orientalist Sergei Fyodorovich Oldenburg in 1914 and 1915. Other Chinese manuscripts of the same category were collected by Nikolai Nikolaevich Krotkov who was then the Russia Consul in Urumchi, the Sergei Efimovich Malov expedition to Khotan during 1906 and 1909, and the Oldenburg expedition to Turfan during 1909 and 1910. Later, all the scrolls discovered by the Russian expedition were generally referred to as "Dunhuang Manuscript Collections."

The Oldenburg expedition arrived at Dunhuang in August of 1914. Although the outbreak of World War I put an early end to the archaeological work, the Russians were impressed by their findings there. Oldenburg located a total of 350 bundles of manuscripts

敦煌藏卷。

奥登堡考察团于1914年8月赴敦煌，到1915年1月考察工作因第一次世界大战爆发而被迫结束，但是考察工作却给人留下深刻的印象。奥登堡深入到当地居民之中寻觅写卷，最终搜集到三百五十件。此外，还在石窟底部沙土之中，发掘出大量残卷。目前，这些卷子经过沃尔科娃、丘古耶夫斯基和诺索娃等完整登记编目后，已达一万八千余件。

俄藏敦煌文献中有一些黑水城和吐鲁番的资料，对此，孟列夫曾对潘先生说明了原因："当初黑水城资料用箱装好，存入书库时，偶有从箱里跌出，管理人员没注意，有二十件左右放置在敦煌抄本中。以前我编的两册敦煌目录，其中掺杂有少数黑水城资料，未曾剔除。但在索引中注明哈拉火陀的，即是黑水城资料。现在我已将黑水城资料全部分辨清楚，编成完整的目录。"

可以说，在20世纪60年代以前，苏联已开始了有计划的敦煌学

by going into local residences. In addition, they unearthed many manuscript fragments buried under the sand in the Buddhist cave temples. The number of the fragments and scrolls totaled approximately 18,000 after being completely catalogued by M. P. Volkova, Leonid Chuguevsky, and N. Nosova, among others.

Included among these manuscripts were documents from Khara-Khoto① and Turfan. As Menshikov explained to Pan, "The documents from Khara-Khoto were originally packed into one box but about 20 fell out from the box in carrying them into the stack room. When the librarian noticed the documents, he mistakenly placed them together with the Dunhuang manuscripts. Two Dunhuang catalogues I compiled before actually contained some entries about Khara-Khoto, and I labeled them as Kholodko. Now I've sorted out all the documents from Khara-Khoto and made a complete catalogue of them."

It can be safely said that the Soviet Union had started systematic research on Dunhuang before the 1960s, but few foreign scholars had read these manuscripts and even fewer had any understanding of them. In 1960, the

① Khara-Khoto is also known as "Black City" or "Heishui City."

研究，但看过苏藏敦煌文献的外国人很少，了解其详情者更没有。1960 年，在莫斯科举行第 25 届国际东方学家大会期间，苏联才宣布了其拥有敦煌文献的消息，并由列宁格勒分所陈列了敦煌文书若干件，供与会各国学者参观。个别学者也曾到列宁格勒观看敦煌文献。当时的情景，正如法国学者戴密微在《列宁格勒所藏敦煌汉文写本简介》中所说："1960 年 8 月 14 日，来自欧亚大陆两端的两位多年研究敦煌写本的汉学家，一个日本人，一个法国人，共同登上位于涅瓦河畔豪华建筑的巨大楼梯。苏联科学院亚洲民族研究所(前东方学研究所)就设在那里。当他们在一张桌子上发现了一大堆特意为他们准备的敦煌写本时，显得多么惊讶而不知所措啊！因为他们不仅根本就不知道此处还存在有这类写本，而且半个多世纪以来，所有的汉学家们实际上都对这批写本一无所知。""一个日本人"就是吉川幸次郎，"一个法国人"就是戴密微自己。此后，关于苏藏敦煌文献的消息逐渐为国际学术界所知，再加上 1963 年和 1967 年，苏联出版了

Soviet Union announced its collection of Dunhuang manuscripts during the 25th Conference of Orientalists held in Moscow and exhibited some manuscripts in Leningrad for scholars from around the world to look at. In pursuit of these manuscripts, some scholars did indeed go to Leningrad. The French scholar Paul Demiéville depicted the scene in *Dunhuang Chinese Manuscripts at Leningrad*: "Two sinologists from both ends of Eurasia—Japan and France—climbed up the long stairs inside the luxurious building on the banks of the Neva River, where the Institute of Asian Ethnology of the USSR Academy of Science (the former Institute of Oriental Studies) is located. They were pleasantly surprised and bewildered at the first sight of the Dunhuang manuscripts piled up high on a table, since for more than half a century so many sinologists, including themselves, had no idea of the existence of these manuscripts." The above-mentioned Japanese sinologist was Yoshikawa Kojiro; the French onc was Demiéville himself. Thereafter, the news that the Soviet Union had obtained some of the manuscripts became gradually known throughout the academic world. In addition, two catalogues by Lev N. Menshikov were published in 1963 and 1967 in the Soviet Union. These catalogues lifted the veil on the previously unknown

孟列夫主编的两册目录，苏藏敦煌文献的真相也就被揭开了。潘重规先生正是在这种背景下去苏联阅读敦煌文献的。

8 月 8 日，潘先生从巴黎出发到达列宁格勒。第二天，即 8 月 9 日上午，潘先生拿着一份地图，从旅馆找到东方研究所。“才知道孟希科夫（即孟列夫）教授本星期刚刚离开列城去度假。我虽然失望，但在巴黎旅馆斗室中彷徨的时候，早有许多不佳的预感，这只是不佳的预感中的一种罢了。……好不容易，才请到东方院一位秘书。据说：东方院的敦煌卷子和《红楼梦》抄本必须通过孟希科夫教授才能看到。终于他介绍一位所果洛夫教授，设法和孟希科夫教授联络，并约我明日中午再到东方院和所果洛夫教授见面。”

8 月 10 日中午，潘先生到东方所见到左义林女士时，“才知道孟希科夫教授没有接到我巴黎的来信，以为我在东方学会会议完毕后，打消了访苏之行，所以他离开东方院度假去了。”后在左义林女士的努力

manuscripts. It was under this background that Pan Chonggui made his trip to the Soviet Union.

On August 8, Pan left Paris for Leningrad and the next morning found his way from the hotel to the Institute of Oriental Studies. “I didn't know Professor Menshikov had just gone on vacation when I arrived there. Disappointed as I was, I did have some awful premonitions when I was struggling in the hotel room in Paris... I finally met a secretary of the institute and learned that only with the permission of Professor Menshikov could I gain access to those Dunhuang manuscripts and handwritten copies of *A Dream of Red Mansions*. In order to contact Professor Menshikov, the secretary introduced me to Professor Sokolov who invited me to meet him in the institute at noon the next day,” said Pan in his *Record of Ten Days in Leningrad*.

At noon on August 10, Pan met Ms. Zorin who finally helped him get in contact with Professor Menshikov. Pan recalled, “Professor Menshikov hadn't received my letter, so he thought I had cancelled my trip to the Soviet Union and left on vacation. When he returned to Leningrad after 6:00 p. m., he immediately came to meet me. I was expecting an elderly scholar. However, I was greeted by a handsome, smart, and cheerful man who was not only able to speak fluent Chinese but able to write in Chinese as well. What impressed me most was that he

下，找到了孟列夫教授，下午六点多，孟列夫教授赶回列宁格勒后，“便赶来旅馆和我见面。我本来以为他可能年纪相当大，但出现在我面前的竟是一位英俊、聪明、爽朗的学者。他不但能用中文写文章，而且中国话也说得相当流利。以一个没有离开苏联一步的学者，居然中国语文能达到如此高深的水准，颇令人十分诧异。我们一见如故，从敦煌卷子谈到抄本《红楼梦》，从考古队谈到黑水城文物的发现，谈了差不多两个钟点”。

8月11日、12日是星期六、星期天，东方所停止办公。潘先生就游览列宁格勒和涅瓦河。

8月13日是星期一，潘先生上午到东方所，由孟列夫教授陪同到图书馆善本藏书室，介绍两位善本室的正副主任。“然后引导我参观敦煌卷子和黑水城发现文物。以前看见两册目录和西方学者传说，始终不能确知敦煌卷子的数量。这次亲见藏书，才知道敦煌抄本编目虽有一万二千个号码，实

could be so proficient in Chinese without having ever studied in China. That was the first time we met each other, but we had a truly enjoyable talk like two old friends for almost two hours. Our topics ranged from the Dunhuang manuscripts to handwritten copies of *A Dream of Red Mansions* and to the relics discovered in Khara-Khoto."

Since the next two days—August 11 and 12—were Saturday and Sunday, Pan visited Leningrad and the Neva River during the weekend break.

On the morning of Monday, August 13, Pan went to the Institute of Oriental Studies. Accompanied by Professor Menshikov, Pan visited the room for rare books and was introduced to the director and the assistant director of the room. "After that, Professor Menshikov showed me the Dunhuang manuscripts and relics from Khara-Khoto. I had read two Dunhuang catalogues and the biographies of some Western scholars before, but I failed to understand the exact number of the manuscripts. When I finally saw these catalogued documents, it dawned on me that although there were about 12,000 accession numbers in the catalogue, only some 300 of them could be called 'books' since even one or two pages from scroll fragments were also numbered. Number 1517 of *The Book of Songs* I once copied from Professor Ogawa turned out to be a fragment of a page. I pored over it and corrected a wrongly written character in my paper. All those bundles of

际成卷的只有三百余轴，其余无论是一叶、半叶都算是一个号码。我往年从小川教授处抄来的一五一七号诗经卷子，实际上只是半纸残书。我亲自披览之后，校正了我论文中一个错字。这些卷子庋藏在大书橱中，果然成卷的不算多。孟希科夫教授又把他近年描写的黑水城发现的汉文资料卡片给我看。据说，全部汉文资料达五六百种。最后，取出《红楼梦》抄本三十五册给我过目。”

8 月 16 日，“我独自上楼，借书阅览。承善本室主任告知，今日阅览室提早于下午三时关闭。我提高警惕，更加快速度进行工作。中午孟先生来阅览室邀我去食堂，我婉言早餐多食过饱，加以推辞。我想，人生吃饭的机会太多，异域阅读异书的机会太少。千辛万苦换来十几小时的阅读机会，岂肯为了吃饭而耽误。”

8 月 17 日，是潘先生阅读敦煌文献的最后一天，

scrolls, large quantity of pages and fragments, and a comparatively small number of books, were collected in a huge bookcase. Later, Professor Menshikov showed me the Chinese bibliographies he had written in recent years, which introduced the 500 to 600 kinds of Chinese documents discovered in Khara-Khoto. At last, he took out 35 handwritten copies of *A Dream of Red Mansions* from the shelves for me."

On August 16, he recalled, "When I went to read by myself in the room for rare books, I was informed by the director that the reading room would be closed early at 3 p. m. that day. I had no choice but to hurry up. Professor Menshikov came to invite me for lunch at noon, but I declined with the excuse that I had eaten a large breakfast in the morning. I thought to myself that compared with the rare opportunity of reading such valuable documents abroad, some routine event like dining seemed so trivial. How was it possible for me to spare some time for lunch with such limited time for reading?"

The reading room was not open on August 17 which was the last day for Pan's reading. "I had to read at the private desk of Professor Menshikov in the Rare Books Room. He selected some important manuscripts of Khara-Khoto and Dunhuang for my studying and copying, and I kept reading until 6 p.m. without any break," wrote Pan.

Altogether Pan's trip to Leningrad lasted for ten days. Such a short period was insufficient for reading a large number of Dunhuang manuscripts. Inspired by the trip, he wrote a book called

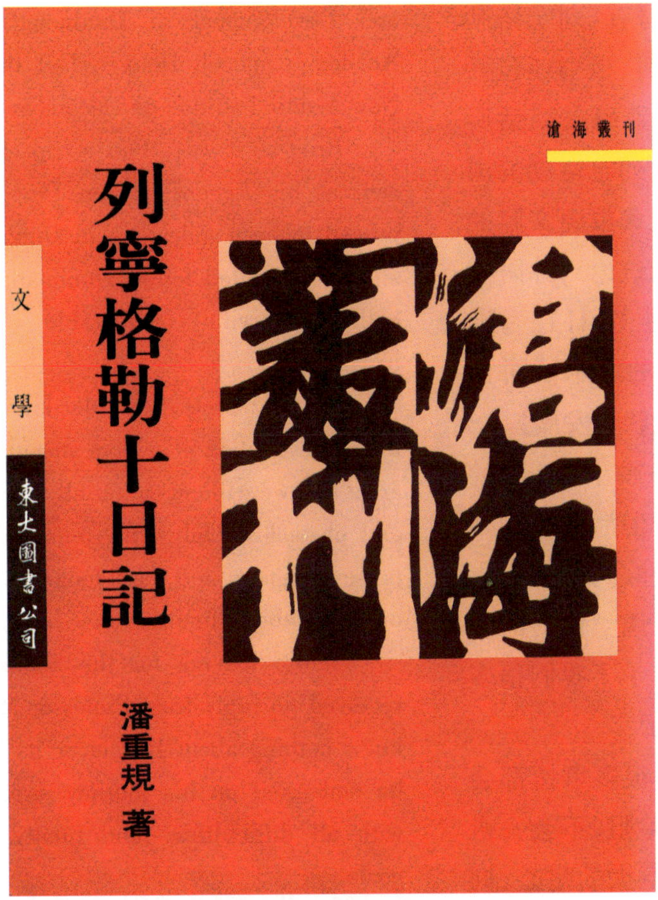

图 21 《列宁格勒十日记》

Fig.21 Record of Ten Days in Leningrad

而“今天阅览室又关门，必须在孟先生特设在藏书室的工作桌上阅读。”孟先生“把黑水城和敦煌的卷子，择要的给我阅览和抄写。我一直披读到下午六时”。

综观潘重规先生的列宁格勒之行，一共只有十天，真正看敦煌卷子的时间也有限。关于这次在列城的经

Record of Ten Days in Leningrad. The book includes several articles: “The Chinese National Treasury Collection in Leningrad” which is based on Pan’s interview with Menshikov; “On the ‘Gratitude Sutra’ Bianwen” which records the studies of the Dunhuang manuscripts held in Russia; and “The Status Quo

历，潘先生写有《列宁格勒十日记》，同时，该书还包括潘先生根据孟列夫谈话所写的《我国在列宁格勒的国宝》、研究俄藏敦煌文献的《变文双恩记试论》，并附有1972年12月16日在香港新亚研究所的学术演讲词《敦煌学的现状和发展》。

《列宁格勒十日记》的篇幅也不长，但潘先生的列宁格勒之行和《列宁格勒十日记》却是敦煌学史上的一件大事，它给予了我们很多的思考和启示：

第一，做很多事情都会有许多艰难险阻，不会一帆风顺。要有巨大的耐心、韧劲和锲而不舍的钻研精神，才可能克服所遇到的困难。

潘先生去苏联前，未接到孟列夫教授的回信，而他又不懂俄语，但他仍坚定地按照计划前往，从而克服了种种困难，终于达到了目的。

不知是历史的偶然，还是上天的安排，同样的境况、同样的行程，20年后又

and Development of Dunhuang Studies: An Academic Speech Delivered at the Hong Kong New Asiatic Institute on December 16, 1972."

Brief as it was, Pan's trip to Leningrad as well as his *Record of Ten Days in Leningrad* proved to be a milestone in Dunhuang studies, since it provided fellow Dunhuang scholars and enthusiasts with considerable reflections and insights.

Firstly, he lets the reader know that the path to our destination is seldom smooth; chances are great that we will encounter all kinds of hardships and obstacles. Only with remarkable patience, perseverance, and assiduous work can we overcome the difficulties ahead.

Before leaving for the Soviet Union, Pan received no reply from Professor Menshikov and knew nothing about Russia or its language. Yet he embarked on his journey as planned, dealt with all difficulties, and finally achieved his goals.

By coincidence or destiny, another journey under similar circumstances occurred two decades later. In August of 1993, Li Weiguo, the associate editor-in-chief of Shanghai Classics Publishing House, and the Chinese associate editor of *Dunhuang Documents Held in Russia* was working in Paris on the editing of *Dunhuang and Western Region Manuscripts Held in France* with his colleague Fu Xianzhan. He received a message from Leningrad (St. Petersburg) that the curator of the State Hermitage Museum was interested in talking to Shanghai Classics Publishing House about

一次重现。1993年8月，当时的上海古籍出版社副总编、《俄藏敦煌文献》中方副主编李伟国先生与其同事府宪展先生在巴黎从事《法藏敦煌西域文献》的编辑工作时，得到了从俄罗斯圣彼得堡传来的信息，俄罗斯冬宫博物馆愿意与上海古籍出版社商谈冬宫所藏敦煌艺术品的出版问题。“消息传来，我们认为事不宜迟，应立即设法前往圣彼得堡与之谈判。经与大本营联系，魏同贤社长赞同我们的建议，并发来一个文件，委派我为上海古籍出版社社长全权代表，前往圣彼得堡与冬宫博物馆馆长彼奥特罗夫斯基先生谈判。接着，冬宫方面的邀请函也到了。在匆匆准备以后，我买了一张俄罗斯航空公司由巴黎到莫斯科再到上海的机票，由一位中国驻法国大使馆秘书陪同来到了戴高乐机场。那时候苏联已经解体，我国与俄罗斯尚无互免签证条约，但我按照过去的惯例没有去签证。俄罗斯航空公司的工作人员要求检查签证，而这时如果我再回头去办签证，就需要等几天时间。不行，还是

publishing its Dunhuang artwork collections. Li later recalled, “Upon receiving the message, we knew this negotiation needed to be conducted right away and immediately reported to our director, Wei Tongxian. He approved our plan and sent a letter of authorization, entrusting me to negotiate on behalf of Shanghai Classics Publishing House with Mikhail Piotrovsky, curator of the State Hermitage Museum. Having received their invitation, I reserved a flight from Paris to Moscow to Shanghai with little preparation, and then with a secretary from the Chinese Embassy in France flew directly to the Paris Charles de Gaulle airport. Everything on my way to Russia seemed orderly until my schedule was disrupted by the visa. After the dissolution of the Soviet Union, Russia did not grant visa-free access to the Chinese, and I had not applied for a visa based on the visa-free policy previously enjoyed between China and the Soviet Union. However, the staff of Aeroflot wanted to see my visa. It would take several days for me to get one! Since I could not delay this trip, I had no choice but to explain the causes to them. I could speak a little Russian but I was too anxious to speak at that moment. The embassy secretary also helped to negotiate in French. Finally, the staff of Aeroflot permitted my boarding. I arrived in Moscow late at night. As expected, I was asked to show my visa upon entering customs. At that moment my potential

跟他们磨磨看吧。秘书也帮助交涉，他用的是法语，我能讲一点俄语，但这时急得一句也讲不出来。最后俄航终于放行了。”深夜到了莫斯科，“进关时，果然要看签证。这时，我的俄语突然涌出来了，我告诉莫斯科机场边检人员，我们正在同贵国学术界进行着一项重要的文化合作，我是贵国一个重要的学术机构邀请的客人，我曾经为此事多次来贵国访问，与贵国的著名学者共同工作。边检终于被打动了，一挥手让我进了关。走进楼下大厅，找到了焦灼等待的张惠明博士，驱车进入莫斯科市区。”（李伟国《敦煌话语》）

深夜 12 点后，李伟国先生等登上了开往列宁格勒的列车，凌晨时分到达了列宁格勒。然后经过非常艰巨的谈判，终于签订了出版合同。这样就有了 6 册《俄藏敦煌艺术品》和 11 册《俄藏黑水城文献》的出版。

第二，中国学者应为敦煌学的发展作出自己的贡献。

在《列宁格勒十日记》所

suddenly came out and some Russian sentences came flying out of my mouth. I told the customs officer, ‘Since China is conducting a cultural cooperation of far-reaching significance with the Russian academic community, I’ve been invited by an important academic institution and I’ve already visited Russia several times for this purpose.’ The customs officer was eventually convinced by my explanation and permitted my entry. When I went downstairs, Dr. Zhang Huiming was waiting anxiously in the arrivals hall and we drove to downtown Moscow.” (Li Weiguo, *Dunhuang Discourses*)

It was after midnight when Li got on the train to Leningrad and he arrived early that same morning. After a long and arduous negotiation, the contract for publication was signed: the results were the publication of the six-volume *Dunhuang Artworks Collected in Russia* and the eleven-volume *Documents from Khara-Khoto Collected in Russia.*

In addition, Pan Chonggui believed that Chinese scholars should strive to make a contribution to the research on Dunhuang.

In “The Status Quo of Development of Dunhuang Studies: An Academic Speech Delivered at the Hongkong New Asiatic Institute on December 16, 1972” which is included in *Record of Ten Days in Leningrad*, Pan proposed, “Every piece of Dunhuang manuscripts collected throughout the world ought to be preserved by photography, for it is the best way to prolong their vitality. With the

附《敦煌学的现状和发展——一九七二年十二月十六日新亚研究所学术演讲词》中，潘重规先生就提出："应将全世界保存的敦煌卷子全部摄影。因为摄影，才能延续推广它的生命。" 20 年后，经过中俄双方学者的共同努力，"中俄两国的专家和出版者已决定毫无保留地以影印方式合作出版全部珍藏在俄罗斯圣彼得堡的敦煌写卷。该项工作已作周密策划，其宗旨在于向世界各国的学者直接展示敦煌写卷的真实面貌，排除其他任何出版方式可能造成的失真现象。"

潘重规先生还一再强调："敦煌遗书是中国人的文化遗产，如何使支离破碎的遗产恢复完整、发扬光大，这主要是我们中国人的责任。我希望中国学人抱着恢复国土的心情，来从事阐扬绝学的工作。"

在潘先生"新亚"演讲和赴列宁格勒阅读敦煌文献 30 年

joint efforts of China and Russia, two decades on, experts and publishers of both countries have determined to co-publish all the facsimiles of Dunhuang manuscripts collected in St. Petersburg without conditions. This carefully planned project excludes all the possible distortions from any other way of publishing and aims to present to scholars all over the world an authentic version of the Dunhuang manuscripts."

Pan constantly emphasized, "Dunhuang manuscripts are the cultural heritage of China and it is the due obligation of the Chinese to both restore its fragmented heritage and increasingly spur its development. My sincere hope is that Chinese scholars can carry forward this lost knowledge in the spirit of reacquiring the lost cultural heritage."

Thirty years have passed since Pan Chonggui's speech at the Hong Kong New Asiatic Institute and his trip to Leningrad. Today ①, the major parts of the Dunhuang manuscripts collected in Russia, Britain, France, and other countries have been published, photographed, and digitized. This fact reflects the tremendous contributions made by Chinese scholars to international Dunhuang studies and is a model of friendly cooperation in international academic circle.

① Today refers to the year 2007 when the Chinese version of the book—《遗响千年——敦煌的影响》was published.

图 22 庆祝潘重规先生九五嵩寿暨从事敦煌学研究一甲子国际学术研讨会现场剪影

Fig.22 International Symposium Celebrating the 95th Birthday of Pan Chonggui and his Sixty-year Research on Dunhuang Studies

后的今天，俄、英、法等国所藏敦煌文献的主体，已基本摄影公布完毕。这是中国学人对国际敦煌学的巨大贡献，也是国际学界友好合作的典范。

1973 年的列宁格勒之行，是潘重规先生敦煌学研究的一大转折。从此以后，他将主要精力都投身于敦煌学研究，并取得了举世瞩目的成绩。1974 年，法国法兰西学术院有见于潘先生在敦煌学

The trip to Leningrad in 1973 was the turning point in Pan's Dunhuang studies. Afterwards, he dedicated himself to Dunhuang studies and made remarkable achievements in the field. In honor of his decades of painstaking devotion and contributions, and in recognition of his outstanding achievements in Dunhuang studies, Pan Chonggui garnered many awards and honors such as the Prix Stanislas Julien—the crowning glory in French sinology circles—awarded by the French Academy

研究方面的卓越成就，特主动颁予代表法国汉学最高成就的茹莲奖（Julian Price）；法国科学院敦煌学研究会也聘潘先生为名誉会员。1976 年，韩国岭南大学授予潘先生名誉文学博士学位。1992 年，敦煌研究院为推崇先生数十年来在倡导敦煌学研究方面所投注的心力及其在研究上的贡献，特由院长段文杰先生率团赴台颁赠该院荣誉院士头衔。1995 年，台湾“行政院”为表彰先生发扬中华文化的卓著贡献，及在敦煌学研究方面所取得的辉煌成就与倡导敦煌学的不遗余力，特

in 1974, Honorary Member awarded by the Dunhuang Studies Institute of the French Academy of Science in 1974, and an Honorary Doctor's Degree of Literature granted by Yeungnam University in 1976. In 1992, the Dunhuang Academy dispatched a senior delegation headed by Duan Wenjie, the then president of the Dunhuang Academy, to Taiwan to confer the title of Honorary Academician on him. In 1995, the Government Information Office of Taiwan presented him with the Chinese Culture Award. In July of 2000, Pan was bestowed the Special Contribution Award for the Study and

图 23　潘重规先生接受敦煌研究院荣誉院士

Fig.23　Pan Chonggui Receiving an Honorary Academician Certificate from the Dunhuang Academy

颁赠中华文化奖。2000 年 7 月,国家文物局、甘肃省人民政府为庆祝敦煌藏经洞发现 100 周年,表彰先生的成就与贡献,特授予"敦煌文物保护研究特殊贡献奖"。

Preservation of Dunhuang Relics by the State Cultural Relics Bureau and the Gansu Provincial Government during the celebration of the centennial anniversary of the discovery of the Mogao Library Cave.

敦煌文献的整理刊布

Compilation and Publication of Dunhuang Documents

资料是一切学术研究的基础，对于敦煌学来说，这一点显得更为重要，因为敦煌文书的绝大部分已被劫往国外，就是藏在国内各图书馆、博物馆中的敦煌文献，也首先是将其作为文物而收藏的，并不是作为图书资料而利用的。因此，对于绝大多数的研究者来说，根本不可能亲自阅读敦煌文献，而作为文物保存的敦煌文献，由于年代久远，纸张碎破，也不允许被多次翻阅。根据原件照相拍摄，然后影印出版，就成了最好的刊布方式，这样既可以保存原状，又可以满足绝大多数研究者的需要。

另外，敦煌文献是在西北边远的一个小县城的石窟中发现的，其中虽然也有许多中原的或全国性的东西，但不可否认，它被打上了当时当地的许多烙印，文书上也就有了一些当地的方言方音；当时的一些俗字俗语，对于今天的学者来说，也是不容易搞懂的；一些写经人或其他的作者，由于文化水平较低，还出现了不少的错字和别字。正是由于这些原因，敦煌文献仅仅靠影印出版还是不够的，还需要有像二十四史和《资治通鉴》那样的整理本，供学者们使用。

As the foundation of all academic research in the field, primary sources play a particularly essential role in Dunhuang studies. It is a fact that the majority of the Dunhuang manuscripts were removed from China and taken abroad. Even those still remaining in Chinese libraries or museums were initially preserved as a kind of cultural relics rather than as research materials in archives. Therefore, for the vast majority of researchers, it is impossible to read Dunhuang manuscripts in person. Even if there is access, it is usually not permitted to consult these sources multiple times, as the pages are fragile, with some crumbling or disintegrating from old age. To preserve the original materials as well as meet the needs of numerous scholars, the best solution is to photograph them and then publish the facsimiles in illustrated books and catalogues.

In addition, as most Dunhuang manuscripts were discovered in a cave temple at a remote town in the northwest of China, it is little wonder that they bear the defining characteristics from that time and place. The local vernacular recorded in the manuscripts is a prime example. It is challenging for today's scholars to understand the common sayings from these time periods. To make matters worse, some scribes or authors even wrote characters incorrectly because of their low level of literacy. Considering these factors, it is not sufficient to publish only photographic plates or reproductions alone. Comprehensive annotated editions, similar to the *Twenty-Four Histories* or *Comprehensive Mirror for Aid in Government*, fulfill a great need.

《敦煌宝藏》及其他

***The Treasures of Dunhuang* and Other Documents**

《敦煌宝藏》是出版界出版的最早、最全面的敦煌图版照片，在敦煌学研究中曾发挥了重大的作用。

《敦煌宝藏》从1980年开始编辑，由黄永武先生主编，台北新文丰出版公司于1982年—1986年陆续出版。它收入了从世界各地当时已经公布的敦煌遗书缩微胶卷中再次摄影编排的图片约二十万张，另外还有画本、刺绣、壁画塑像等图片千余张。为保存原貌及资料的真实性，对损泐（"泐"读"le"，为石头裂开之意）不清处，也不旁注、不校改。

该书的编排顺序是英、中、法在前，其他各国在后。各国收藏品的编辑顺序是:英国部分仍旧用斯坦因编号，法国部

The Treasures of Dunhuang, considered to be the earliest and most comprehensive edition of facsimiles published on the subject of Dunhuang manuscripts, has played a major role in Dunhuang studies.

The serial began publication in 1980, with Huang Yongwu as the editor-in-chief. More than 100 volumes were published in succession from 1982 to 1986 by Taipei Xinwenfeng Publishing Company. About 200,000 re-photographed and re-edited photographs from Dunhuang's remaining manuscripts are featured in it, and in addition, almost 1,000 photos of paintings, embroideries, murals, and sculptures are included as well. To preserve the authenticity of the originals, there are no additional notes or corrections for the unclear or damaged sections.

The entries are arranged in order of collections from Great Britain, China, France, and then other countries respectively. The collections from Great Britain are numbered according to Aurel Stein's cataloguing method, and the ones in France are numbered according to Paul Pelliot's method. These two cataloguing styles have been widely accepted by international academia. The collections in the Beijing Library (present-day National Library of China), however, are numbered according to the format of *First Catalogue of Dunhuang Manuscripts*.

分也是用伯希和编号，因为这两个编号已经为国际学术界所通用；中国北京图书馆（今国家图书馆）所藏，则沿用《敦煌劫余录》的体例。

《敦煌宝藏》共 140 册，每 10 册为一辑。其中 1—55 册是斯坦因劫经录，即S.0001—S.7599 号；56—111 册是北京图书馆（今国家图书馆）藏卷，即北图 1—8738 号；112—135 册是伯希和劫经录，即 P.2001—P.6038 号；136—137 册是新文丰公司编辑部编撰的散录，即散 1—1608 号；138—140 册则是新文丰公司编辑部编辑的欣赏篇，即 P.2005 —P.5007 号，以及苏联列宁格勒（今俄罗斯圣彼得堡）东方学研究所藏 0096—2784 号。

为了配合《敦煌宝藏》的出版，黄永武教授还编印了《敦煌遗书最新目录》。本书以王重民等编《敦煌遗书总目索引》为基础，并补充了《总目索引》出版后的一些新发现，如 S.6980 号以后 600 号敦煌无名断片新标目和P.5579 号

There are 140 volumes in *The Treasures of Dunhuang*, with 14 albums containing 10 volumes each. The first 55 volumes (S.0001–S.7599) are from *Catalogue of Chinese Manuscripts in the Stein Collection*. Volumes 56–111(No.1–No.8738) are preserved in the Beijing Library (present-day National Library of China). Volumes 112–135 (P.2001–P.6038) are from *Catalogue of Chinese Manuscripts in the Pelliot Collection*. Volumes 136–137 (No.1–No.1608) are miscellaneous records that were edited by Taipei Xinwenfeng Publishing Company. Volumes 138–140 (P.2005–P.5007 & No.0096–No.2784) are mainly for aesthetic appreciation, which were also edited by Taipei Xinwenfeng Publishing Company, among which those manuscripts (No.0096–No.2784) are collected in the Institute of Oriental Studies of the USSR Academy of Sciences in Leningrad, Russia.

To assist in the publication of *The Treasures of Dunhuang*, Huang Yongwu compiled *New Catalogue of Dunhuang Manuscripts* as well. The book was created based on Wang Zhongmin's *General Index of Dunhuang Manuscripts*. Some new catalogues have been added to the book, including 600 unidentified fragments after S.6980 and P.5579. The translated version of *Catalogue of Dunhuang Manuscripts in the Soviet Union* by Lev N. Menshikov as well as the catalogue of Dunhuang manuscripts held in Japan have also been added.

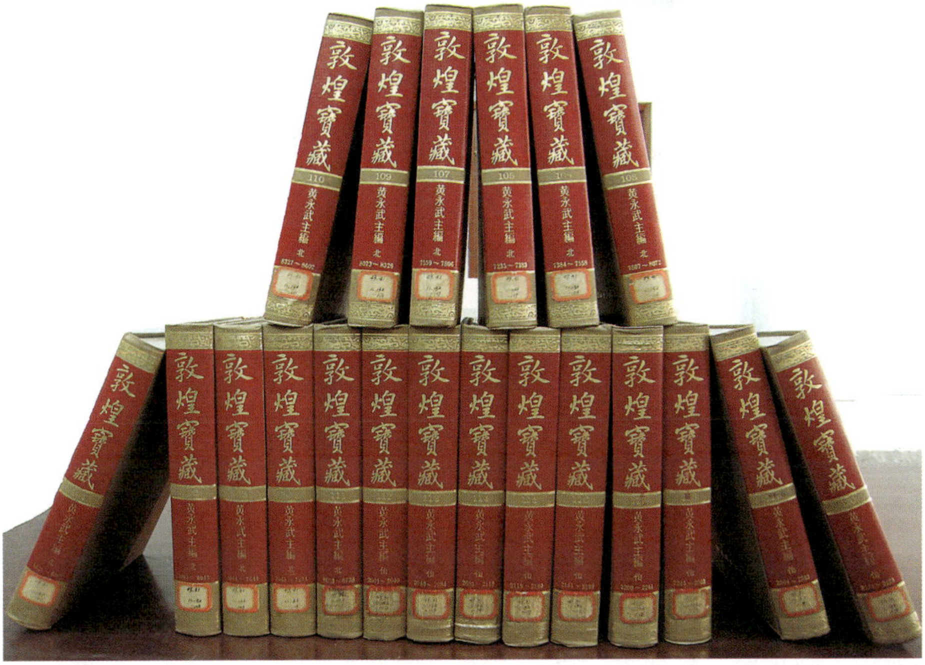

图 24 《敦煌宝藏》

Fig.24 The Treasures of Dunhuang

以后的新目录，同时，还将苏联孟列夫主编的《苏藏敦煌文献目录》翻译后补入，还补充了日本所藏敦煌文献的目录。

《敦煌宝藏》工程浩大，收录齐全，是敦煌文献发现后的第一次最全面整理，对推动敦煌学研究曾发挥过非常重要的作用。

当然，由于当时客观条件的限制，所有照片都是从缩微胶卷上拍摄的，从而使一些图片不大清楚。现在，随着

The unprecedented collections in *The Treasures of Dunhuang* were so comprehensive that they created new interest in promoting Dunhuang studies.

Because of the limited technology of that time, previous plates created using less advanced methods of photography were unclear and lacked resolution. However, with the successive publication of *Dunhuang Manuscripts in British Collections*, *Dunhuang Documents Held in Russia*, and *Dunhuang and Western Region Manuscripts Held in France*, *The Treasures of Dunhuang* has, to some extent, basically accomplished its mission of correcting this deficiency.

《英藏敦煌文献》《俄藏敦煌文献》《法藏敦煌西域文献》等大型图录的出版，《敦煌宝藏》可以说已基本完成了其使命。

在《敦煌宝藏》编辑结束、正在陆续出版之际，黄永武教授在新文丰出版公司的大力支持、赞助下，又编辑了一套大型敦煌学研究丛书——《敦煌丛刊初集》，于1985年6月由新文丰出版公司出版。

《敦煌丛刊初集》的编辑缘起和目的，正如该书的出版说明所说："敦煌资料之研究，乃当今国际汉学界之显学，随着本公司《敦煌宝藏》之辑印，更掀起广泛研究之热潮。非仅各方学术会议恒以敦煌学为重点，而各大学之纷纷开设'敦煌学'课程，尤为目下已蔚成之风尚。本公司为迎合潮流所趋，提供研究所需，促进文化复兴，特编辑民国以来中外重要之敦煌学工具书或经典之作，均为坊间绝版或难以购得之珍贵典籍，荟萃于一编，以利学术研讨之展开。"

《敦煌丛刊初集》共16册，即第一册：[英]翟理斯编《英伦

After that, Huang Yongwu, with great support and sponsorship from Taipei Xinwenfeng Publishing Company, edited a set of works on Dunhuang studies: *First Series of Dunhuang Documents*, which was published in June 1985 by Taipei Xinwenfeng Publishing Company.

The initial idea of editing these works was clearly stated in the foreword of its publication: "The study of Dunhuang is a distinguished school of international sinology, and there is a boom for further research with the publication of *The Treasures of Dunhuang*. Not only are the academic conferences focusing on it, but courses on 'Dunhuang studies' are becoming a trend. The study for it has now become quite standard in many universities. Our company, to follow this trend, to meet the demands of doing research, and to promote a cultural renaissance, has edited the most valuable reference books or classics on Dunhuang studies since the founding of the Republic of China (1912-1949)."

First Series of Dunhuang Documents consists of 16 volumes. The first volume includes *Catalogue of Chinese Dunhuang Manuscript Collections in the British Museum* edited by Herbert Allen Giles (English), supplemented by *New Discovery of Unidentified Dunhuang Manuscript Fragment Collections in the British Museum* and *New Catalogue of 600 Unidentified Dunhuang Manuscript Fragments* by Huang

博物馆汉文敦煌卷子收藏目录》，附黄永武撰《英伦所藏敦煌未知名残卷目录的新探索》和《敦煌六百无名断片的新标目》；第二册：王重民等编《敦煌遗书总目索引》，附黄永武撰《刘铭恕斯坦因劫经录之订补》；第三、四册：陈垣编《敦煌劫余录》；第五册：史岩《敦煌石室画像题识》、金祖同辑《流沙遗珍》、李证刚《敦煌石室经卷中未入藏经论著述目录》；第六、七、八册：罗振玉辑《敦煌石室遗书百廿种》；第九册：常钧《敦煌杂抄》和《敦煌随笔》、王重民《巴黎敦煌残卷叙录》、存古学会编《石室秘宝》；第十册：许国霖《敦煌石室写经题记》和《敦煌杂录》；第十一、十二册：[苏]孟列夫编《苏俄所劫敦煌卷子目录》；第十三册：[日]羽田亨辑《敦煌遗书》、[日]神田喜一郎《敦煌秘籍留真》和《敦煌秘籍留真新编》；第十四册：蒋礼鸿《敦煌变文字义通

Yongwu; the second volume includes *General Index of Dunhuang Manuscripts* by Wang Zhongmin, with the addition of *Addenda to the Catalogue of Chinese Manuscripts in the Stein Collection by Liu Mingshu* by Huang Yongwu; the third and fourth volumes include *First Catalogue of Dunhuang Manuscripts* by Chen Yuan; the fifth volume includes *Prefaces and Postscripts of Portraits in Dunhuang Caves* by Shi Yan, with two albums *Compilation of Turfan Manuscripts* and *Catalogue of Works Unlisted in Buddhist Scriptures in Dunhuang Caves* as supplemental materials by Jin Zutong and Li Zhenggang respectively; the sixth, seventh and eighth volumes include *One Hundred and Twenty Extant Manuscripts in Dunhuang Caves* by Luo Zhenyu; the ninth volume includes *Dunhuang Extracts* and *Dunhuang Essays* by Chang Jun, *Records of Dunhuang Manuscript Fragments in the Paris Collection* by Wang Zhongmin, *Facsimile Collections of Manuscripts in Dunhuang Caves* by Arihisa Gakkai; the tenth volume includes *Records of Buddhist Scriptures in Dunhuang Caves* and *Records of Dunhuang* by Xu Guoling; the eleventh and twelfth volumes include *Catalogue of Dunhuang Manuscripts in Russian Collections* by Russian editor Lev N. Menshikov; the thirteenth volume includes *Dunhuang Manuscripts* (Facsimile Edition) and *Original Manuscripts of Dunhuang Esoteric Buddhism* as well as its revised edition by Japanese editors Haneda Tōru and Kiichirou Kanda; the fourteenth volume includes *Explanation of Word Meanings in Dunhuang Bianwen* by Jiang Lihong; the fifteenth

释》；第十五册：刘复《敦煌掇琐》；第十六册：敦煌文物研究所编《敦煌莫高窟内容总录》。

重新编辑出版这些图书，主要是因为敦煌学已引起学术界的重视，但有关图书资料非常缺少，因而就选取民国以来世界各地已出版的敦煌学经典著作和工具书重印。

为了促进敦煌学的发展，20 世纪 90 年代初，新文丰出版公司又邀请东吴大学林聪明教授（现调入逢甲大学）主编《敦煌丛刊二集》。关于《二集》的主旨和内容，林聪明教授在序言中说："新文丰出版公司以弘扬敦煌学为己任，

volume includes *Dunhuang Folk Literature* by Liu Fu; and finally the sixteenth volume includes *General Catalogue of the Mogao Caves* by the Institute of Dunhuang Relics.

The major reason for re-editing these books was that Dunhuang studies had gained the attention of academic circles. However, due to the scarcity of relevant books and materials, it was imperative to select and reprint classics and reference books that had been published since 1912—the founding of the Republic of China.

In order to promote the development of Dunhuang studies, in the early 1990s, Professor Lin Tsong-ming of Soochow University in Taiwan was invited to edit *Second Series of Dunhuang Documents*. As for the content, Lin stated in the preface, "Shouldering the responsibility of disseminating Dunhuang studies, Taipei Xinwenfeng Publishing Company

图 25 《敦煌丛刊初集》
Fig.25 First Series of Dunhuang Documents

历年来不惜耗费巨资，大量编印相关资料。先后出版《敦煌宝藏》《敦煌丛刊初集》等丛书……为应敦煌学研究日新月异的趋势，因委托余筹编《敦煌丛刊二集》，收录当代中国学者的专著或论文集，从客观的角度呈现研究成果，供学界参考，希望此类丛刊的辑印，能有助于敦煌学的发展。"

《敦煌丛刊二集》从1993年开始出版，现已出版赵和平《敦煌写本书仪研究》、张鸿勋《敦煌讲唱文学概论》、张锡厚《敦煌本唐集研究》、项楚《敦煌歌辞总编匡补》、李正宇《敦煌史地新论》《敦煌乡土志八种笺证》、颜廷亮《敦煌文学概说》、邓文宽《敦煌吐鲁番学耕耘录》、饶宗颐《敦煌曲续论》、唐耕耦《敦煌寺院会计文书研究》、荣新江《鸣沙集》、刘进宝《敦煌文书与唐史研究》、左景权《敦煌文史学述》、林聪明《敦

has recently released a great amount of relevant materials, such as *The Treasures of Dunhuang*, and *First Series of Dunhuang Documents*, among others. Following this trend, *Second Series of Dunhuang Documents* has come into being, bringing together monographs and articles by contemporary Chinese scholars. These materials, objectively presenting these findings, can be used for academic reference and thus stimulate the development of Dunhuang studies."

Since 1993, *Second Series of Dunhuang Documents* has been published successively, including the following: *Research on Letter Formalities of Dunhuang Manuscripts* by Zhao Heping; *Introduction to Dunhuang Chanted Narrative Literature* by Zhang Hongxun; *Essay Collections on Tang Poetry from Dunhuang Manuscripts* by Zhang Xihou; *Addenda for Dunhuang Poems* by Xiang Chu; *New Perspectives on Dunhuang History and Geography* and *Eight Commentaries on Dunhuang Local Chronicles* by Li Zhengyu; *General Introduction to Dunhuang Literature* by Yan Tingliang; *Records of Dunhuang and Turfan Studies* by Deng Wenkuan; *A Sequel on Dunhuang Qu* by Jao Tsung-I; *Research on Accounting Documents of Dunhuang Temples* by Tang Geng'ou; *The Mingsha Collection—On the Academic History and Methodology of Dunhuang Studies* by Rong Xinjiang; *Research on Dunhuang Documents and the History of the Tang Dynasty* by Liu Jinbao; *On Dunhuang Literature and History* by Zuo Jingquan; and *Explanation of Dunhuang and Turfan Manuscripts* by Lin Tsong-ming.

煌吐鲁番文书解诂指例》等。

为了给初治敦煌学者提供一套全面系统的入门书，林聪明教授还主编了《敦煌学导论丛刊》。该《丛刊》的编辑目的和主要内容正如林聪明教授在序言中所说："新文丰出版公司董事长高本钊先生致力弘扬中国文化，近数年来尤全力支持敦煌学的研

To provide a series of comprehensive books for beginners, Professor Lin Tsong-ming also edited *Introduction to Dunhuang Studies* with the purpose and content mentioned in the preface, "Gao Benzhao, director of Taipei Xinwenfeng Publishing Company, has committed himself to spreading Chinese culture, and has especially given his full support to Dunhuang studies in the last few years. Nowadays, he is sparing no pains in publishing the research achievements of contemporary Dunhuang scholars on a large scale for reference and development in this area... Deeply appreciating his views and contributions, I edited the series entitled *Introduction to Dunhuang Studies*. Meanwhile, I would like to invite domestic and overseas scholars

图 26 作者与林聪明教授(左二)、新文丰出版公司总编高本钊先生(左三)、李正宇先生(右一)在一起(摄于 2000 年 8 月)

Fig.26 Lin Tsong-ming (Second from Left), Gao Benzhao (Second from Right), Li Zhengyu (Far Right) and the Author (Far Left), August, 2000

究。……今更不遗余力，欲大量出版当代敦煌学者的研究成果，供世人参考，俾有助于斯学的发展。余得知其用心，感佩其热诚，乃代为筹编《敦煌学导论丛刊》，邀请海内外中国学者，就其精研范围，以中文分类撰写导论……本丛刊的问世，期能使初治敦煌学者得窥其门径，专研有成者亦可助于会通，从而促进敦煌学的普及与发达，此诚为全体作者共同的愿望。”

《敦煌学导论丛刊》从 1991 年开始出版，共出版了 15 册，即林聪明《敦煌文书学》、周绍良《敦煌文学刍议及其他》、白化文《敦煌文物目录导论》、姜伯勤《敦煌社会文书导论》、高国藩《敦煌民俗资料导论》、季羡林《敦煌吐鲁番吐火罗语研究导论》、张鸿勋《敦煌话本、词文、俗赋导论》、项楚《敦煌诗歌导论》、陈祚龙《敦煌文物散论》、金荣华《敦煌文物外流关键人物探微》、王永兴《敦煌经济文书导论》、耿世民《敦煌突厥回鹘文书导论》、李正宇《敦煌历史地理导论》、谭蝉雪《敦煌岁时文化导论》、马德《敦煌石窟营建史导论》。

to write introductions to each issue in accordance with their research scope and interests... It is hoped that the publication of the series will benefit readers of different levels and thus promote the popularization and prosperity of Dunhuang studies.”

Since 1991, *Introduction to Dunhuang Studies* has been published 15 volumes successively: *Dunhuang Manuscript Studies* by Lin Tsong-ming; *On Dunhuang Literature and More* by Zhou Shaoliang; *Introduction to the Catalogue of Dunhuang Cultural Relics* by Bai Huawen; *Introduction to Dunhuang Social Documents* by Jiang Boqin; *Introduction to Dunhuang Folk Customs* by Gao Guofan; *Introduction to Research on Dunhuang and Turfan Tocharian Language* by Ji Xianlin; *Introduction to Storytelling, Ci, and Fu in Dunhuang Literature* by Zhang Hongxun; *Introduction to Dunhuang Poetry* by Xiang Chu; *Textual Criticisms and Explanations of Dunhuang Documents* by Chen Zuolong; *Key Figures in Dunhuang Relics Removal* by Jin Ronghua; *Introduction to Dunhuang Economic Documents* by Wang Yongxing; *Introduction to Dunhuang Turkic and Uyghur Documents* by Geng Shimin; *Introduction to Dunhuang History and Geography* by Li Zhengyu; *Introduction to Dunhuang Annual Calendar Customs* by Tan Chanxue and *Introduction to the Architectural History of the Dunhuang Caves* by Ma De.

《英藏敦煌文献》的刊布

Publication of *Dunhuang Manuscripts in British Collections*

1995年5月，大型图集《英藏敦煌文献·汉文佛经以外部分》14卷图版由四川人民出版社全部出版。

该书出版后，受到了海内外敦煌学者的广泛欢迎和高度评价，被认为是迄今为止，反映英藏敦煌文献最清晰、最完整、最准确的图版本，并荣获了1995年第二届国家图书奖。

《英藏敦煌文献》的编辑出版，是非常偶然的。当然，偶然中也包含着必然，这就是敦煌学研究发展到一定的程度后，研究者需要掌握全面的资料和清晰的图版。

当敦煌文献流散海外后，影印、抄写、整理、校录这些文献，就成了敦煌学者的夙愿。1954年，大英博物馆图书馆(后被分出成立为英国国家图书馆)在日

In May 1995, the large illustrated work *Dunhuang Manuscripts in British Collections* (*Chinese Texts Other than Buddhist Scriptures*), 14 volumes in total, was published by Sichuan People's Publishing House.

As the clearest, most complete, and most accurate facsimile version of the Dunhuang manuscripts in British collections up to now, the book has been widely accepted and praised by Dunhuang scholars both at home and abroad since its publication, which helped it garner the 2nd China's National Book Award in 1995.

The publication of *Dunhuang Manuscripts in British Collections* was done sporadically as the need arose. With the development of Dunhuang studies, comprehensive materials and clear facsimiles were greatly needed for doing further research.

As the Dunhuang manuscripts were scattered all over the world, the demand for handling, transcribing, reorganizing, and proofreading them began to develop among scholars. In 1954, with the assistance of Japanese Professor Kazuo Ue, the British Museum Library (present-day British Library) initially utilized the advanced technology of microfilm to reproduce more than 6,000 Dunhuang manuscripts in Britain on microfilm and had them issued worldwide. On September 13, 1954, Arthur Waley, along with

本学者榎一雄教授的协助下，首先采用先进的缩微技术，将英国所藏的6000多号敦煌文献制成缩微胶卷，向全世界发行。1954年9月13日，英国剑桥大学东方语言教研室以布莱伯兰克、穆尔、魏莱和李约瑟4人的名义，联名给中国科学院院长郭沫若写了一封信，提出能否有望得到我国北京图书馆等处收藏的我国出土的中世纪写本的缩微胶卷，尤其是敦煌文书的缩微胶卷，并提出可以用大英博物馆所藏敦煌文献的缩微胶卷交换。

中国科学院将此信的抄件转致北京图书馆后，经北图上报当时的文化部批准，开始了北京图书馆所藏敦煌文献的摄制工作，并于1957年完成了与英国的交换。很快中国科学院图书馆就得到了英国的缩微胶卷，中国科学院历史研究所也从图书馆获得了拷贝片，成为国内最早拥有这批缩微胶卷的科研单位。当时敦煌学家向达先生任历史所副所长，贺昌群先生也在历史所工作。正是因为有这样的机遇和条件，历史所就在向达、王重民、贺昌群等先生的策划、支持下，

Joseph Needham and others from the Faculty of Oriental Studies at the University of Cambridge, jointly wrote a letter to Guo Moruo, president of the Chinese Academy of Sciences, asking whether the National Library could provide them with microfilm copies of documents unearthed from the Medieval China (221–960). They especially wanted Dunhuang manuscripts, and in return, they could offer to them the microfilm of the Dunhuang manuscript collections in the British Library.

The Chinese Academy of Sciences made a copy of the letter and sent it to the National Library. After handing it over to the Ministry of Culture and getting approval, the National Library started taking photographs and exchanged these with Britain in 1957. Soon, the Library of Chinese Academy of Sciences received the microfilm from Great Britain and gave the copies of the microfilm to the History Research Institute. The latter therefore became the earliest Chinese scientific research institute with microfilm. Luckily, scholars including Xiang Da, vice dean of the institute, Wang Zhongmin, and He Changqun all worked there. Under their planning and support, the institute began to compile *Dunhuang Materials*, mainly consisting of these microfilm records, together with photographic plates taken in Paris and London by the National Library

决定利用这批胶卷和中华人民共和国成立前北京图书馆在巴黎、伦敦拍摄的部分照片以及向达、王重民先生早年在英、法所做的录文，编辑一套以敦煌社会文书为主的《敦煌资料》。

《敦煌资料》的具体编辑、录文是由阴法鲁、那向芹、虞明英等先生承担的。1961 年，中华书局出版了第一辑，同时完成了第二辑的初编工作。《敦煌资料》第一辑出版后，引起了中日学者的重视和关注。但由于当时国内搞各种"运动"，尤其是"文化大革命"的爆发而使这一非常有意义的工作被迫中断了。

1982 年，由国家文物局古文献研究室发起组织了《敦煌古文献》项目，同时，中国社会科学院历史所也组建了敦煌组，计划重新编辑、校勘《敦煌资料》。1983 年，中国敦煌吐鲁番学会成立后，《敦

of China before the founding of the People's Republic of China in 1949, and the transcriptions made by Xiang Da and Wang Zhongmin when they had studied in Britain and France that were also deposited in the National Library of China.

The editing and writing of *Dunhuang Materials* were done by Yin Falu, Na Xiangqin and Yu Mingying. In 1961, the first book was published by the Zhonghua Book Company, and the first edition of the second book was completed as well. The publication of the first book drew the attention and interest of both Chinese and Japanese scholars. However, this important work was suspended by various political campaigns in China, among which the Cultural Revolution was the major obstacle preventing its continuation.

In 1982, the project, *Ancient Dunhuang Manuscripts*, was inaugurated by the Research Laboratory of Ancient Documents in the State Administration of Cultural Heritage. Meanwhile, the Historical Research Institute also organized a team to re-edit and proofread *Dunhuang Materials*. In 1983, with the establishment of the Institute of Dunhuang and Turfan Studies of China, the Editorial Board of *Ancient Dunhuang Manuscripts* was assigned to the Institute of Dunhuang and Turfan Studies of China. The liaison work of the secretarial team was undertaken by the Dunhuang Team of the Historical Research Institute. Under such circumstances, the editing and proofreading of *Dunhuang Materials* and *Ancient Dunhuang Manuscripts* for the most part relied on the microfilm in China, Great Britain, and France, as

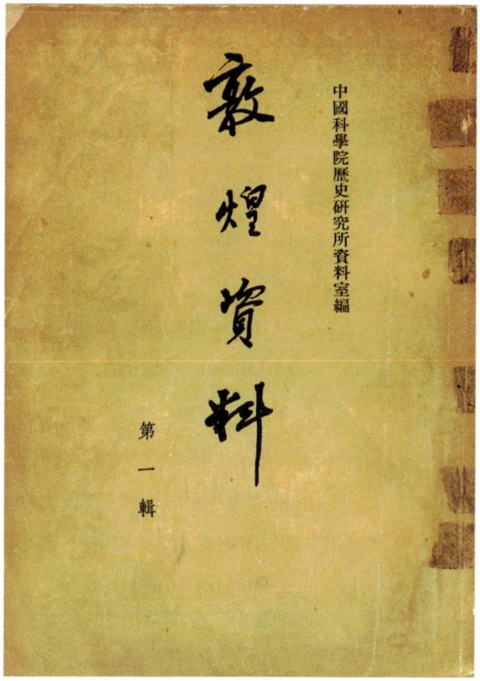

图 27 《敦煌资料》第一辑

Fig.27 Dunhuang Materials: Volume I

煌古文献》编委会改隶于敦煌吐鲁番学会，其秘书组的联络工作则由历史所敦煌组承担。在当时的条件下，不论是《敦煌资料》，还是《敦煌古文献》的编辑、校录，所依据的资料主要是中、英、法三国的缩微胶卷和海内外学者据原件所做的部分录文。而根据缩微胶卷放大的照片，有一些是不大清楚的，从而影响了学者的使用，其学术价值也就打了折扣。

20 世纪 70 年代末、80 年代初，日本学者池田温的《中国古代籍帐

well as transcriptions of the original scripts made by scholars both at home and abroad. As some plates enlarged from microfilm had poor resolution and were hard to read, their usefulness and academic value were diminished to some degree.

In the late 1970s and early 1980s, the first and second books *Research on Chinese Ancient Census Records* and *Tun-Huang and Turfan Documents: Concerning Social and Economic History* were published, written and edited by Japanese scholars Atsushi Ikeda and Tatsuro Yamamoto respectively. As the

研究》和山本达郎主编的《敦煌吐鲁番社会经济文书》第一、二辑先后出版。历史所重新校订的《敦煌资料》第一辑虽然吸收了国内外的研究成果，但毕竟没有利用英、法所藏原件，在总体上也就不能超越池田温和山本达郎的校录本。而当时正在进行的《敦煌古文献》，则计划是有图版有录文的分类全辑本，为了避免重复劳动，就决定将《敦煌资料》编成一部精选，只有录文，可供高等院校教学参考之用的普及本。

不论是编辑《敦煌资料》的普及本，还是编辑有图有文的《敦煌古文献》，都需要将已编成的录文用英、法所藏的原卷校订。为此，中国社会科学院就利用历史所与英国伦敦大学亚非学院的学术交流协议，于 1987 年 8 月派历史所副所长张弓和敦煌组负责人宋家钰两位先生前往伦敦，从事三个月的学术访问。

8 月 21 日下午，张弓和宋家钰先生到了英国国家图

first edition of *Dunhuang Materials* did not include images of original manuscripts preserved in Great Britain and France when it was re-edited by the Historical Research Institute, its academic value was lower than the two books written by the Japanese scholars, though it still absorbed research achievements both at home and abroad. The ongoing editing of *Ancient Dunhuang Manuscripts* was supposed to be thorough with both photos and transcriptions. As a result, the Historical Research Institute decided to refine *Dunhuang Materials* into transcriptions only to avoid redundancy, with the aim that *Dunhuang Materials* could be used as a popular edition for teaching reference in higher education.

The editing of both the popular edition of *Dunhuang Materials* and the illustrated *Ancient Dunhuang Manuscripts* needed to be proofread according to the original manuscripts in Great Britain and France. Thus, based on an academic exchange agreement between the Historical Research Institute and the School of Oriental and African Studies of the University of London, the Chinese Academy of Social Sciences sent assistant dean Zhang Gong and team leader of Dunhuang studies Song Jiayu to London as visiting scholars in August of 1987 for a three-month stay.

On the afternoon of August 21, Zhang Gong and Song Jiayu met Dr. Frances Wood and Beth Mckillop, the directors of the Department of Oriental Transcriptions and Books in the British Library. Both of them

书馆，见到了东方书籍与写本部(简称中文部) 主任吴芳思博士和马克乐女士。由于她们两人都毕业于剑桥大学，也都曾在北京大学历史系读书，因此能讲一口流利的汉语。张弓他们向吴芳思等说明了来意：以后三个月，将在这里借阅馆藏敦煌文书。二位女士对来自中国的朋友亲切热情。吴芳思放下手头工作，亲自领张弓、宋家钰到汉文阅览室参观，并介绍与出纳员相识；还帮他们照相、办理了临时借书证。

从第二天（8 月 22 日）开始，张弓和宋家钰先生就在英国国家图书馆阅读敦煌文书。第一天虽然只查对了两个卷号（S.0286、S.0329），但却有惊人发现，即国内所购缩微胶卷的扩印照片与敦煌写本原卷差别极大。如 S.0286 号是公元 10 世纪的《寺院诸色入历》。带来的扩印件模糊不能成行，原以为原卷如此，其实原卷基本完整而且清楚。尤

graduated from Cambridge University and could speak fluent Chinese due to their studies at the History Department of Peking University years earlier. Zhang and Song expressed their intention to read Dunhuang manuscripts there for the following three months. The two librarians showed great hospitality to them. Dr. Wood, putting aside what she was doing, guided them to the Chinese Reading Room and introduced them to the librarian there. In addition, she helped them register for reader passes.

On August 22, Zhang and Song started to read the Dunhuang manuscript collections in the library. Though they only proofread two volumes (S.0286 and S.0329), they discovered to their surprise that the enlarged photos once obtained by China differed greatly from the original transcriptions. Taking S.0286 (*Account Records of Buddhist Temples in Dunhuang*) written in the 10th century as an example, the enlarged photographic facsimiles they brought with them were too fuzzy to read, and people outside Great Britain supposedly thought the original looked exactly the same. Actually, the original was quite clear and almost complete, while the written words such as "wheat" and "jute," written in pale brown ink, could not be seen in the enlarged photos. Thus, the photographs lost much value because of difficulty in identification. As it was impossible to make corrections in the enlarged photographs, they had to spend an hour transcribing the original. They found these manuscripts were

其是土黄色墨迹所写入物名称“麦”“黄麻”等，照片上竟了无痕迹，完全隐没了。入历而不知所入物品名称，这件文书照片的价值也就减去大半。由于他们无法在扩印件上描补，只好用了一个小时的时间，对本件文书重新作了录文。从整个原卷情况看，英国保存得还好。但毕竟时历千余年，墨迹日见其淡。

他们两人就私下商量：可否与 SOAS(注：伦敦大学亚非学院简称）及英国国家图书馆合作，使用最新技术重拍照片。并写信向国内汇报，请示重拍。

在来伦敦时，张弓和宋家钰先生就随身携带了不清楚的照片复印件一千多张，现在看到原卷很清楚，就以此为契机，向英国方面介绍了《敦煌古文献》编委会在校录工作中，因部分缩微胶卷不清楚而遇到的一些困难，并希望重拍部分照片。当时吴芳思说：“我们的缩微胶卷是四十多年前制作的，我们知道其中少数质量不是很好。我们有责任为你们免费重拍。你们可以开列出需要重拍的斯坦因编号。”马克乐也说：“现在拍摄技术有很大进步，一

basically well-preserved in Great Britain, although the ink had faded after almost a thousand years.

In light of this situation, an idea occurred to them: Was it possible to cooperate with the School of Oriental and African Studies at the University of London (SOAS) and the British Library to re-shoot photos with the most current advanced technology? They reported the idea to the Historical Research Institute, asking for permission.

Zhang and Song brought more than 1,000 fuzzy, low-resolution images with them when they came to London. At the sight of the clear original manuscripts, they intended to seize this opportunity. They told the directors about the difficulties they had faced in transcribing *Ancient Dunhuang Manuscripts* due to the issues with their own facsimile copies and about their plan to re-shoot some photos. Dr. Wood replied, “The microfilm images we have were made over forty years ago and we know some pictures aren't clear enough. So we have the responsibility to re-photograph them free of charge. You can list the Stein numbers which need to be re-taken.” Beth Mckillop added, “Advancements in reproduction technology can accurately capture those words unseen by the naked eyes with infrared photography. We're thinking about re-imaging some

些肉眼完全不能辨识的字，采用红外线拍摄技术，就能清晰地显示出来。我们也在考虑重拍部分文书。”

正是由于吴芳思等人的理解与支持，英方同意了免费重拍部分文书。后双方又商量：既然缩微胶卷中的社会文书有三分之一要重拍，就不如全部重拍。所需经费，中国方面可以用将来在国内出版的相关图书抵偿。有此共识，双方遂草拟了《关于合作整理、出版英国所藏中国敦煌古文书的设想》的书面文件，以供讨论。该文件最后说：

> 英国图书馆过去拍摄的缩微胶卷……在四千五百多张非佛经的照片中，大约有近两千张照片完全不清楚，需要重拍；其余两千多张，也须按出版的要求，重新拍摄。为此，中国社会科学院历史研究所和中国敦煌吐鲁番学会《敦煌古文献》编委会希望能与英国图书馆东方部、伦敦大学亚非学院合作，共同编辑出版《英藏敦煌文献》一书。该书所需四千五百张斯坦因编号的敦煌文书照片，由英方负责重拍胶片，照片的放大和

manuscripts as well.”

Thanks to the understanding and support of Wood and Mckillop, the British side agreed to re-photograph part of the manuscripts free of charge. However, now that one third of the microfilm needed to be redone, it would be better to do all of them. As for the expense of the project, the British asked the Chinese side to use published books in the future as payment for the images. After reaching this consensus, both sides drafted the document “On Cooperative Collating and Publishing Ancient Dunhuang Manuscripts Held in Great Britain.” The last part of it was as follows:

> As for the microfilm taken by the British Library in the past... approximately 2,000 among 4,500 non-Buddhist photos needed re-photographing because of low resolution. The remaining 2,500 photos needed to be re-taken as well in accordance with the publishing requirements. Therefore, the Historical Research Institute of the Chinese Academy of Social Sciences and the Editorial Board of *Ancient Dunhuang Manuscripts* in the Institute of Dunhuang and Turfan Studies of China intend to cooperate with the Oriental Department of the British Library and School of Oriental and African Studies of the University of London (SOAS) to edit and publish *Dunhuang Manuscripts in British Collections* together. According to this agreement, the British side is responsible for re-photographing the 4,500 photos of Dunhuang manuscripts with Stein numbers,

编辑、出版，由中方负责。

while the Chinese side is responsible for the enlarging, editing, and publishing of the images.

这一建议，得到了中英双方的一致赞同，并很快达成协议：由中国社会科学院历史研究所、中国敦煌吐鲁番学会《敦煌古文献》编辑委员会、英国图书馆东方写本与书籍部、伦敦大学亚非学院两方四家，合作编辑出版《英藏敦煌文献·汉文佛经以外部分》。

This proposal won the agreement of both sides. *Dunhuang Manuscripts in British Collections* (*Chinese Texts Other than Buddhist Scriptures*) was to be published through the cooperation between the Chinese side—the Historical Research Institute of the Chinese Academy of Social Sciences and the Editorial Board of *Ancient Dunhuang Manuscripts* in the Institute of Dunhuang and Turfan Studies of China, and the British side—the Department of Oriental Transcriptions and Books in the British Library and the School of Oriental and African Studies of the University of London (SOAS).

1988年11月，中国敦煌吐鲁番学会副会长、著名敦煌学专家宁可教授飞赴伦敦，其任务是筛选全部英藏敦煌文献；1989年初，历史所高级工程师王杼携器材赴英，其任务是拍摄由宁可先生选定的文献（1990年，又派摄影师庄小明赴英补拍）。《英藏敦煌文献》的编辑工作正式启动。

In November 1988, Professor Ning Ke, vice president of the Institute of Dunhuang and Turfan Studies of China and expert in Dunhuang studies, flew to London to examine and select the Dunhuang manuscripts held in Britain. In the beginning of 1989, the senior engineer of the Historical Research Institute, Wang Zhu, went there with equipment to photograph those selected manuscripts by Ning. In 1990, photographer Zhuang Xiaoming was sent there to re-photograph some. The editing of *Dunhuang Manuscripts in British Collections* was officially launched.

文献的筛选是浩繁而又艰难的。千年古纸，脆薄易碎，长卷十多米，

The sorting and selection work was massive and arduous. Manuscripts covering a thousand years were thin and fragile, with the scrolls being more than 10 meters long and the fragments shorter than 3.33 centimeters, requiring great care in handling. To complicate things, other documents

残片不盈寸，翻阅时必须惜护留心；少量佛经以外的文献，同大量佛经掺杂交错，又大都字迹潦草随意，墨迹浓淡不一，再加上岁月的磨洗，实在是漫漶难辨。经过整整一年的工作，到 1989 年 11 月时，宁可先生过目了 15000 余件原卷，从中选出了 2000 余件。英国国家图书馆、英国印度事务部图书馆、英国国家博物馆所藏敦煌宝卷中的佛经以外文献，基本上被“一网打尽”了。中国学者阅过全部英藏敦煌文献者，宁可先生当是第一人。王杼则是拍摄英藏敦煌文献最多的人。他白天在英图铺放写卷、调机配光、精心拍摄，晚上则在公寓连夜调制药液，把胶卷冲洗出来，以便发现效果不佳者，次日能及时重拍。半年之内，拍黑白片 7000 张，彩照 400 多张。

由于敦煌文献涵盖人文社会科学的十多个学科，另外还有医药、天文、历法等方面的内容，编委会确定的工作原则是：按斯坦因编号流水分段，编委周绍良、沙知、宁可、宋家钰、张弓分任主编(首次发表的后面三

were mixed with the Buddhist sutras, and correct words were not easily identifiable due to illegible, scribbled writing and ink weathered over the years. For an entire year, Ning Ke had selected nearly 2,000 original manuscripts from all 15,000 in the British collection by November of 1989. All the manuscripts excluding Buddhist sutras were selected from the British Library, the India Office of the British Library and the British Museum. We can say that Ning Ke was the first one among the team of Chinese scholars who read all the Dunhuang manuscripts in Great Britain, and Wang Zhu was the one who photographed the most. Wang placed the manuscripts in sequential order and carefully took photos in the daytime, mixing the liquid and developing the film at night so as to pick out the blurred ones and re-photograph them the next day. Within half a year, he produced 7,000 black and white images and more than 400 color ones.

As Dunhuang manuscripts include more than 10 disciplines in the humanities and social sciences, as well as the materials such as medicine, astronomy, calendar and so on, the Editorial Board operated under the following principles: divide all manuscripts into several parts according to the order of Stein numbers, with Zhou Shaoliang, Sha Zhi, Ning Ke, Song Jiayu and Zhang Gong being editors-

卷，增加郝春文、荣新江为副主编）；充分吸收借鉴中外已有成果，给予系统整理，提出各卷文献定名初稿；每卷每条定名，都经编委会集体讨论研究确定；编委会难以认定的文献，请教专家。从1989年秋到1994春，历时四年半，定稿讨论会开了二十多次。除主编、副主编外，郭锋、王冀青、杨宝玉、李德龙、徐庆全等青年学者，也为《英藏敦煌文献》的编辑出版作出了很大的贡献。

《英藏敦煌文献》是从1990年开始出版的，其中1—11卷收录了英国国家图书馆已经公布的敦煌写本中的全部汉文非佛经文书。12—14卷则首次刊布了该馆所藏S.6981—S.13677之间的非佛教文书；英国博物馆东方古物部所藏敦煌写本、敦煌绢纸绘画上的供养人题名题记；英国印度事务部图书馆所藏敦煌汉文佛经以外的文书。正在编辑出版的第15卷是全书总目并编有多种索引。整套《英藏敦煌文献》的图版均据原件拍摄，清晰可辨，照片还附有比例尺，可以显示原文书的尺寸规格。

in-chief respectively (Hao Chunwen and Rong Xinjiang were assigned as associate editors for the last three volumes in the first publication); systematically reorganize domestic and overseas results by fully absorbing, learning and giving a temporary working name for each volume; determine the official name for each volume by group discussions of the Editorial Board; and consult experts when having difficulties. More than 20 meetings were held for discussing the final version, from autumn of 1989 to spring of 1994, almost four and a half years. Apart from editors-in-chief and associate editors, young scholars including Guo Feng, Wang Jiqing, Yang Baoyu, Li Delong, and Xu Qingquan also made great contributions to the editing and publishing of *Dunhuang Manuscripts in British Collections*.

Dunhuang Manuscripts in British Collections series was first published in 1990. The first 11 volumes consist of all the Chinese non-Buddhist Dunhuang manuscripts already published by the British Library. Volumes 12 to 14 consist of previously unpublished non-Buddhist manuscripts from the Stein collection from number S.6981 to S.13677 held in the British Library; Dunhuang manuscripts, dedicatory inscriptions on silk paper by Buddhist donors preserved in the British Museum;and non-Buddhist documents preserved in the India Office of the British

就在《英藏敦煌文献》陆续出版之时的1991年，北京大学历史系荣新江教授和北京图书馆善本部的方广锠博士，由王宽诚英国学术院奖学金资助，应英国国家图书馆邀请，前往伦敦编S.6981以下写本的目录。其中佛教部分由方广锠负责，非佛教部分由荣新江

Library. The 15th volume is a detailed table of contents, with various indexes. All plates in these books are original, clear, and true to scale.

In 1991, with the successive publication of *Dunhuang Manuscripts in British Collections*, Professor Rong Xinjiang of the History Department of Peking University and Dr. Fang Guangchang in the Department of Rare Books at the National Library, with funding by the Wang Kuancheng British

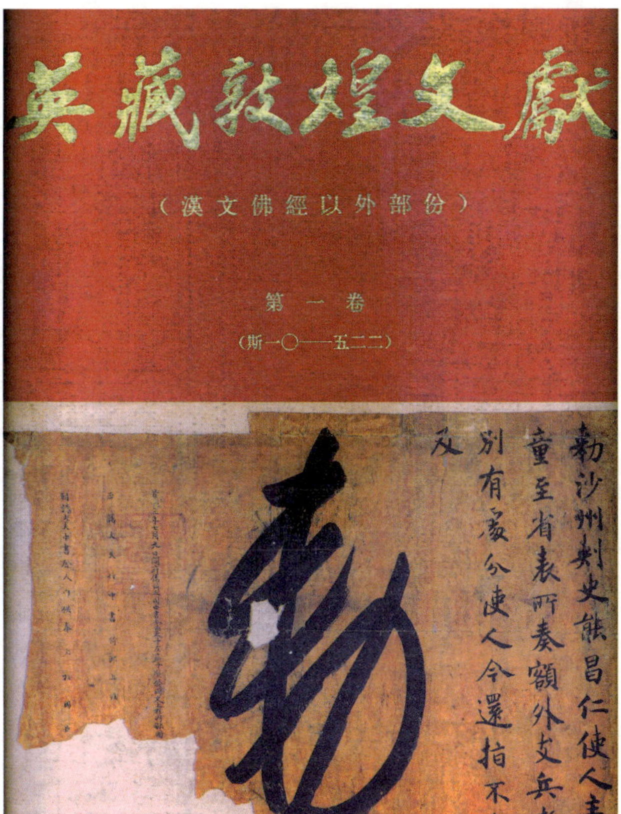

图28 《英藏敦煌文献》

Fig.28 Dunhuang Manuscripts in British Collections

编目。荣新江教授编著的《英国图书馆藏敦煌汉文非佛教文献残卷目录(S.6981—S.13624)》一书，由台北新文丰出版公司于1994年7月出版。由于荣新江先生学识渊博，尤精于敦煌文献，故该书是目前敦煌文献目录方面比较适用、权威的一部工具书。该目录除标题外，还包括

Academic Scholarship and by invitation from the British Library, went to London to compile the catalogues for manuscripts with numbers after S.6981. Fang took charge of the Buddhist manuscripts while Rong was responsible for non-Buddhist ones. *Catalogue of Non-Buddhist Fragments from Dunhuang in the British Library* (S.6981-S.13624), compiled and written by Rong, was published by Taipei Xinwenfeng Publishing Company in July 1994. His profound knowledge and

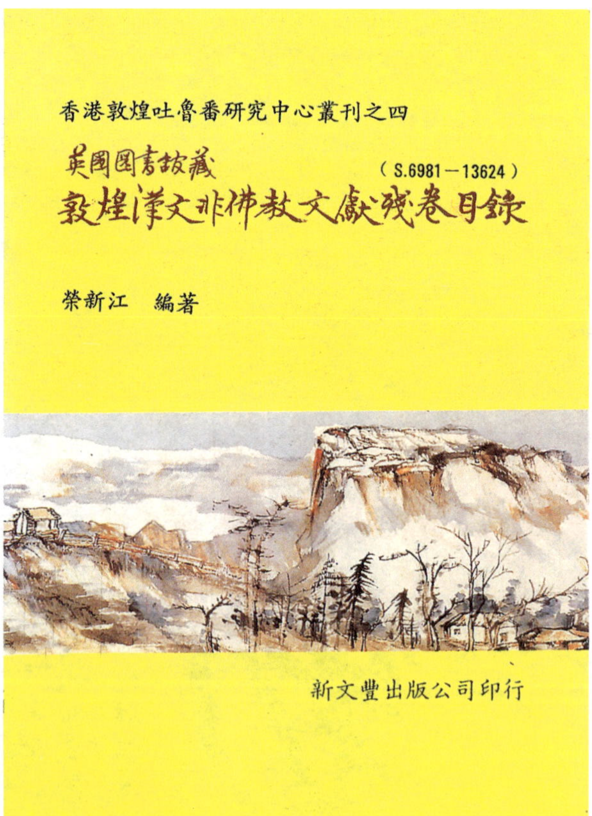

图29 《英国图书馆藏敦煌汉文非佛教文献残卷目录(S.6981—S.13624)》
Fig.29 Catalogue of Non-Buddhist Fragments from Dunhuang in the British Library (S.6981-13624)

诸如写本外观、内容、专有名词、题记、朱笔、印鉴、杂写、年代及其他与写本关联情况的提要，凡能找到的有关该号写本研究的文献和图版，亦作了著录说明。是我们阅读《英藏敦煌文献》12—14卷的重要参考书。方广锠博士编著的《英国图书馆藏敦煌遗书目录(S.6981 号—S.8400 号)》，于 2000 年由宗教文化出版社出版。按照原计划，荣新江编非佛教文献目录，方广锠编佛教文献目录，但方广锠博士在编写过程中又改为逐卷簿录，这样就出现了交叉著录的问题，正如该书"凡例"所说："本目录决定将《荣目》已经著录的五十四号也作为著录对象涵摄进来。"当然，对于使用者来说，未尝不是好事，这样使用起来就方便多了。

《英藏敦煌文献》的出版，是中英双方学术界友好合作的产物，也开启了海外所藏敦煌文献编辑照拍、整理出版的先河。

expertise in Dunhuang manuscripts enabled the book to become a useful and authoritative bibliographic tool. Besides titles, the book is also comprised of other descriptive information about the manuscripts, such as appearance, content, names and proper nouns, inscriptions, cinnabar markings, seals, miscellaneous notes, dates, abstracts and summary of contents, as well as illustrations of related research documents. Thus, it has become an important reference book for studying the manuscripts in volumes 12 to 14. *Catalogue of Chinese Manuscripts from Dunhuang in the British Library* (S.6981–S.8400) by Fang Guangchang was published by Religious Cultural Publishing House in 2000. As originally planned, Rong Xinjiang was in charge of the non-Buddhist references, while Fang was responsible for the Buddhist ones. But Fang changed his plan and ended up making a reference volume by volume. As a result, a cross-referenced directory took shape, just as mentioned in the preface, "The 54 lists made by Rong Xinjiang were also included in this book." Certainly, it is helpful to users.

Dunhuang Manuscripts in British Collections was the end product of a cooperative academic effort that brought together scholars from both China and Great Britain. It was a pioneering work that involved editing, imaging, collating, and publishing facsimiles of Dunhuang manuscripts housed overseas.

《俄藏敦煌文献》

Dunhuang Documents Held in Russia

如果说《英藏敦煌文献》从开始的设想、筹划、商谈到编辑出版，主要是敦煌学家努力的结果，那么《俄藏敦煌文献》的面世，则主要是出版家的功劳。

当《英藏敦煌文献》编辑完毕，即将由四川人民出版社全部出版之际，《俄藏敦煌文献》的编辑出版也被提上了议事日程。1989 年 8 月中旬，上海古籍出版社代表团访问了苏联，与苏联科学出版社东方文学部、苏联科学院东方学研究所列宁格勒分所就合作出版藏于列宁格勒的中国敦煌、吐鲁番与黑城文献进行了商谈，同时对艾尔米塔什(冬宫)博物馆所藏中国新疆、敦煌与黑城艺术品进行了比较详细的考察。

作为《敦煌吐鲁番文献集

If the successful publication of *Dunhuang Manuscripts in British Collections* was mainly due to efforts by Dunhuang scholars, then the birth of *Dunhuang Documents Held in Russia* can be attributed to its publishers.

When *Dunhuang Manuscripts in British Collections* had been edited and was ready for publication by Sichuan People's Publishing House, the issue of editing and publishing *Dunhuang Documents Held in Russia* was next on the agenda. In mid-August 1989, a delegation from Shanghai Classics Publishing House visited the Soviet Union and held negotiations with the publishers from the Oriental Literature Department of the Soviet Sciences Publishing House and the Institute of Oriental Studies of the USSR Academy of Sciences[1] on co-publishing documents from Dunhuang, Turfan and Khara-Khoto preserved in Leningrad. Meanwhile, a detailed investigation was conducted on the artworks of Xinjiang, Dunhuang, and Khara-Khoto preserved in the Elmi Tash Museum at the State Hermitage Museum in Russia.

Boris L. Riftin, a scholar at the Academy of Sciences of the Soviet Union, advised Wei

---

① The Institute of Oriental Studies of the USSR Academy of Sciences is presently known as the Institute of Oriental Manuscripts of the Russian Academy of Sciences, located in St. Petersburg.

图 30　俄罗斯科学院东方学研究所藏敦煌卷子

Fig.30　Dunhuang Scrolls in the Institute of Oriental Manuscripts of the Russian Academy of Sciences

成》主体项目的《俄藏敦煌文献》，是苏联科学院通讯院士李福清向上海古籍出版社魏同贤社长推荐的。

20 世纪 80 年代初，中苏关系尚未解冻，李福清以私人身份来到中国。在上海时，他曾与魏同贤谈到了列宁格勒的东方学研究所藏有一抄本《石头记》，并说台湾的潘重规先生曾经看过。这一信息引起了魏同贤的极大兴趣，李福清也表示愿意促成。后来，苏藏《石头记》在中华书局出版。1987 年，当李福清院士与魏同贤社长再次见面时，既谈到了《石头记》在中华的出版，又谈到东方学研究所收藏敦煌文书之事，而在此前不久，《读书》月刊（1986 年第 10 期）刚公布了郑振铎 1957 年在列宁格勒阅读敦煌文献的信件。当魏同贤提出有兴趣出版俄藏敦煌文献时，李福清当即表示愿意从中牵线。

后来，经李福清的介绍，上海古籍出版社的领导认识了苏联科学出版社东方

Tongxian, president of Shanghai Classics Publishing House, to edit *Dunhuang Documents Held in Russia*, the major part of *Dunhuang and Turfan Manuscript Collections*.

In the early 1980s, the Sino-Soviet relationship was still strained, requiring Riftin to make a personal visit to China. In Shanghai, he had a talk with Wei Tongxian about the copy of *A Dream of the Red Mansions* (also translated *The Story of the Stone*) held by the Institute of Oriental Studies in Leningrad, and told him that Pan Chonggui had read it, arousing Wei's interest. Later, with the assistance of Riftin, *A Dream of the Red Mansions* was published by Zhonghua Book Company. In 1987, when Riftin and Wei met again, they talked about the publication of the book as well as the preservation of the Dunhuang manuscripts in the Institute of Oriental Studies. Not long before that, in 1986, some letters had been published in the 10th issue of *Reading*, indicating that Zheng Zhenduo had read the Dunhuang manuscripts in 1957 while he was in Leningrad. When Wei expressed his interest in publishing *Dunhuang Documents Held in Russia*, Riftin immediately showed his willingness to offer help.

Thanks to the help of Riftin, the editor-in-chief of Shanghai Classics Publishing House became acquainted with O. K. Dreyer, the editor-in-chief in the Oriental Literature Department of the Soviet Sciences Publishing House and Lev N. Menshikov, an expert on Dunhuang studies in the Institute of Oriental

文学部总编辑德列尔和东方学研究所的敦煌学专家孟列夫。

经过中苏双方的多次电函往返后，就有了1989年8月上海古籍出版社代表团的苏联之行。

随后，苏联有关方面又到上海进行了访问商谈。1990年10月，上海古籍出版社派遣李伟国、府宪展等前往苏联进行现场工作。1991年2月，以苏联科学出版社东方文学部主任德列尔、列宁格勒东方学研究所所长彼得罗相、敦煌学专家孟列夫组成的苏方代表团来到上海，与中国方面签订了出版协议。

当中苏双方达成协议，合作影印出版藏于列宁格勒的全部敦煌、吐鲁番与黑城文献后，上海古籍出版社为此还专门组建了敦煌吐鲁番文献编辑室(现改为敦煌文博编辑室)。后来，苏联解体，虽然其政治制度发生了重大变化，但《俄藏敦煌文献》的编辑出版却仍在继续进行。

合作编辑出版《俄藏敦煌

Studies.

After several rounds of correspondence between both sides, in August 1989, a delegation from the Shanghai Classics Publishing House paid an academic visit to the Soviet Union.

Later, the Soviet delegation visited Shanghai. In October 1990, Li Weiguo and Fu Xianzhan were sent by the Shanghai Classics Publishing House to the Soviet Union for preliminary work. In February 1991, the delegation consisting of O. K. Dreyer, the editor-in-chief of the Oriental Literature Department of the Soviet Sciences Publishing House, Y. A. Petrosyan, the director of the Institute of Oriental Studies in Leningrad, and Lev N. Menshikov, an expert on Dunhuang studies, went to Shanghai and signed a publishing agreement with the Chinese side.

According to the agreement, all manuscripts from Dunhuang, Turfan and Khara-Khoto housed in Leningrad were co-published with photographed facsimiles. Shanghai Classics Publishing House set up a special editing room for the Dunhuang and Turfan manuscripts, presently known as the Dunhuang Wenbo Editing Room. Later, with the collapse of the Soviet Union, although its political system changed significantly, the editing and publishing of *Dunhuang Documents Held in Russia* continued on as before.

Despite the success of the agreement, an unexpected situation arose when text editors

文献》的协议已经签订，但当上海古籍出版社的文字编辑府宪展、蒋维崧和摄影师严克勤于 1992 年初乘车赶往俄罗斯准备拍摄胶卷时，却出现了意外——俄罗斯东方学研究所所长提出：在他们的学者还没有研究清楚俄藏写卷并写出论著之前，不允许中国方面拍摄文献原卷，而只能阅读。当然，协议中的书将来还是可以出版，但必须分类分册出版，每一册书的前面是俄罗斯专家的论著，后面是相关的若干原卷。

当时俄罗斯方面研究敦煌文献的学者主要是孟列夫和丘古耶夫斯基教授，他们是真正的学者，都将其一生献给了敦煌文献研究。因此，李伟国先生首先说服他们二位:第一，按照目前的整理程度，要分类出版是不可能的;第二，你们要写专著，作专题研究，都可以继续进行，我们也愿意帮助出版；第三，你们两位本身就是国际敦煌学界的著名学者，现在又是《俄藏敦煌文献》的主编，《俄藏敦煌文献》的编辑出版将是你们对敦煌学的重大贡献，

Fu Xianzhan, Jiang Weisong, and photographer Yan Keqin from Shanghai Classics Publishing House arrived in Russia to photograph the manuscripts in early 1992. The director of the Institute of Oriental Studies claimed that the Chinese scholars were only allowed to read the manuscripts instead of photographing them, unless Russian scholars had previously studied and published relevant academic works on the Russian collections. In addition, he said that the manuscripts in the agreement could be published at some future point, but they first needed to be classified and published volume by volume, with works by Russian academics at the earlier part of each volume, followed by the manuscript facsimiles.

At the time, professors including Lev N. Menshikov and Leonid Chuguevsky were prominent scholars who had devoted their careers to the study of the Dunhuang manuscripts. Li Weiguo, associate editor of Shanghai Classics Publishing House, managed to convince them to allow the Chinese scholars to participate in the research by giving the following arguments: firstly, in terms of current progress, it was impossible to classify and publish facsimiles in complete volumes. Secondly, Russian scholars could continue their research in writing books or making monographic studies, and the Chinese side would try their best to help. Finally, as prestigious scholars in the international academic circles

图 31　作者与孟列夫先生在玉门关(摄于 2000 年 8 月)

Fig.31　Lev N. Menshikov and the Author at the Yumen Pass, August, 2000

全世界的学者都会感谢你们。

这几条非常真诚的理由，说服了孟列夫和丘古耶夫斯基教授。当由他们二位再去做所长的说服工作时就顺利多了。结果仍然按原来的计划，按号数一件件地阅读、编辑、拍摄，一卷一卷地出版。

这样，上海古籍出版社的正式工作小组在 1992 年取得了实质性进展，拍摄了第一册到第五册的全部“Дx”编号的照片，完成了著录卡片，

and editors-in-chief of *Dunhuang Documents Held in Russia*, the publication of the series would be in large part due to them, and scholars all over the world would greatly appreciate their efforts.

The two experts were finally persuaded. Naturally, it seemed much easier for them to persuade the director to agree to the publication. As a result, the work went on following the original plan—reading, editing, photographing images according to accession numbers, and publishing facsimiles volume by volume.

Not surprisingly, Shanghai Classics Publishing House made substantial progress

并在当年出版了具有决定意义的《俄藏敦煌文献》第一册。

《俄藏敦煌文献》的全称是《俄罗斯科学院东方研究所圣彼得堡分所藏敦煌文献》，它作为上海古籍出版社策划出版的大型项目《敦煌吐鲁番文献集成》之一，由俄罗斯科学院东方研究所圣彼得堡分所、俄罗斯科学出版社东方文学部和上海古籍出版社合编（主

in 1992. All the photos with Russian "Дх" numbers in the first five books had been photographed and catalogued; and the first volume was published in the same year.

The full name of *Dunhuang Documents Held in Russia* is *Dunhuang Documents Held in the Institute of Oriental Studies at the USSR Academy of Sciences*. It was one of the major projects of *Dunhuang and Turfan Manuscript Collections*, jointly edited by the Leningrad Branch of the Institute of Oriental Studies of the USSR Academy of Sciences, the Department of Oriental Literature of the Russian Sciences Publishing House and Shanghai Classics Publishing House. The

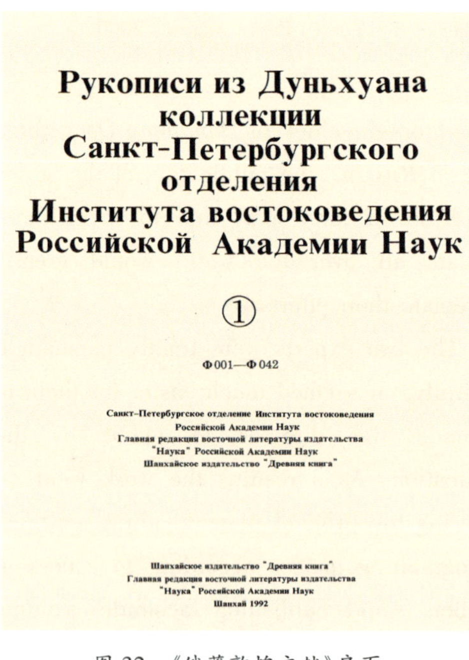
Рукописи из Дуньхуана
коллекции
Санкт-Петербургского
отделения
Института востоковедения
Российской Академии Наук

①

Ф001—Ф042

Санкт-Петербургское отделение Института востоковедения
Российской Академии Наук
Главная редакция восточной литературы издательства
"Наука" Российской Академии Наук
Шанхайское издательство "Древняя книга"

Шанхайское издательство "Древняя книга"
Главная редакция восточной литературы издательства
"Наука" Российской Академии Наук
Шанхай 1992

图 32 《俄藏敦煌文献》扉页

Fig.32 Preface to *Dunhuang Documents Held in Russia*

图 33 《俄藏敦煌艺术品》

Fig.33 Dunhuang Artworks Collected in Russia

编:[俄]孟列夫、[中]钱伯城;副主编:[俄] 丘古耶夫斯基、[中]李伟国),上海古籍出版社和俄罗斯科学出版社东方文学部于1992年12月开始联合出版。

该书是俄罗斯科学院东方研究所圣彼得堡分所藏敦煌写本的大型完整图录集。书前有孟列夫撰《前言》,对俄藏敦煌文献有概括介绍。每册前还有彩色图版若干,展示最有价值和朱笔较多的文献。

通过上海古籍出版社与俄罗斯科学院东方研究所圣彼得堡分所、俄罗斯科学出版社东方文学部的多年筹划合作,《俄藏敦煌文献》共17册、18000余号(后面碎片特多),目前已全部出版。

除此之外,1993年8月,在时任上海古籍出版社副总编、《俄藏敦煌文献》中方副主编李伟国先生与其诸多同仁的共同努力下,上海古籍出版社与俄罗斯冬宫博物馆签订出版合同,并于其后出版了6册《俄藏敦煌艺术品》和11册《俄藏黑水城文献》。

editors-in-chief were: Lev N. Menshikov, Qian Bocheng, and the associate editors were: Leonid Chuguevsky and Li Weiguo. In December 1992, it was co-published by Shanghai Classics Publishing House and the Department of Oriental Literature of the Russian Sciences Publishing House.

The book is a complete collection of images of manuscripts preserved in the Leningrad Branch of the Institute of Oriental Studies of the USSR Academy of Sciences. The preface of the book includes a brief introduction to the Dunhuang manuscripts in Russia, written by Professor Menshikov. In addition, many pictures in full color were included at the beginning of each volume to illustrate the importance of particular manuscripts.

Through the endeavors made by the three parties, *Dunhuang Documents Held in Russia* was successfully published, with a total of 17 volumes comprising over 18,000 numbered manuscripts, including many fragments.

At the same time, Li Weiguo, associate editor of *Dunhuang Documents Held in Russia*, together with his colleagues, faithfully upheld the publishing agreement between Shanghai Classics Publishing House and the State Hermitage Museum in August 1993. Thus, six volumes of *Dunhuang Artworks Collected in Russia* and 11 volumes of *Documents from Khara-Khoto Collected in Russia* were later published.

《敦煌吐鲁番文献集成》及其他

Dunhuang and Turfan Manuscript Collections and Other Documents

在《俄藏敦煌文献》的编辑过程中，上海古籍出版社的领导认识到，如果能将散藏在世界各地的敦煌文献都像《俄藏敦煌文献》一样影印出版，就能为学界提供敦煌吐鲁番文献的全貌，这样会省去学者们到世界各地奔波旅行、四方求阅之烦。因此，他们又积极与法国国家图书馆以及国内的上海博物馆、上海图书馆、北京大学图书馆、天津艺术博物馆等单位联系，并得到了这些单位及有关人士的热情支持。这就有了《敦煌吐鲁番文献集成》的编辑出版。

《法藏敦煌西域文献》是《集成》的又一主体项目。当出版《敦煌吐鲁番文献集成》的主体《俄藏敦煌文献》时，上海古籍出版社就聘请季羡林、潘重规、饶宗颐先生为《集成》的顾问。通过饶宗颐、潘重规和吴其昱先生的撮合，1992年，魏同贤、李伟国访问了巴黎，

During the editing of *Dunhuang Documents Held in Russia*, leaders at Shanghai Classics Publishing House realized that if Dunhuang manuscripts scattered all over the world could be reproduced and published, it would save a great amount of work on behalf of researchers. Therefore, they soon made contact with and successfully received support from la Bibliothèque nationale de France, the Shanghai Museum, the Shanghai Library, the Peking University Library, and the Tianjin Museum of Art, all of which assisted in the editing and publishing of *Dunhuang and Turfan Manuscript Collections*.

Dunhuang and Western Region Manuscripts Held in France was one of the main projects of *Dunhuang and Turfan Manuscript Collections*. Shanghai Classics Publishing House invited Ji Xianlin, Pan Chonggui, and Jao Tsung-I as consultants when *Dunhuang Documents Held in Russia* was in the planning stages. Later, through the recommendation of Jao Tsung-I, Pan Chonggui, and Wu Qiyu, in 1992, Wei Tongxian and Li Weiguo visited Paris to discuss the issue of publishing *Dunhuang and Western Region Manuscripts Held in*

图 34　巴黎法国国家图书馆阅览室

Fig.34　Reading Room in la Bibliothèque nationale de France

与法国方面商谈法藏敦煌西域文献在中国的出版问题，并签订了协定草案。此后通过多次的书信往来，签订了正式的协议。1993 年 7 月至 10 月，李伟国与府宪展在法国国家图书馆进行了

France, and they signed a preliminary agreement. In the following days, the two sides had correspondence with each other. Thanks to their efforts, a formal agreement was signed eventually. From July to October of 1993, Li Weiguo and Fu Xianzhan researched and compiled the first ten volumes in la Bibliothèque nationale de France. In the meantime, they did considerable investigation into Dunhuang manuscript collections in France,

现场编辑工作，主要是查阅和著录了预定前10册所收的文献，调查了法藏敦煌西域文献的编号和收藏情况，制作了反映法藏概貌的七十多件文献的彩色图版，同时还商定并开始重新制作部分不合格的底片。

《法藏敦煌西域文献》是上海古籍出版社与法国国家图书馆合作编辑的，全书包括法国国家图书馆所藏全部汉文和非汉文敦煌西域文献的图版，补拍以前出版物中的缺号卷子和模糊不清的照片，并给予新的定名，共34册，由上海古籍出版社于1994年开始出版，目前已全部出版。

《敦煌吐鲁番文献集成》总策划：魏同贤；顾问：季羡林、潘重规、饶宗颐。该《集成》除《俄藏敦煌文献》全17册、《法藏敦煌西域文献》34册外，还有《俄藏黑水城文献》全11册；《俄藏敦煌艺术品》全6册；《天津市艺术博物馆藏敦煌文献》全7册；《上海博物馆藏敦煌吐鲁番文献》全2册；《上海图书馆藏敦煌文献》全4册；《北京大学藏敦煌文献》全2册。

creating a colored facsimile version of over seventy prominent manuscripts to show the average preservation condition. Furthermore, a number of poor quality plates were planned for re-photographing.

Shanghai Classics Publishing House collaborated with la Bibliothèque nationale de France to edit *Dunhuang and Western Region Manuscripts Held in France*. It contained all pictures of the Western Region manuscripts preserved in la Bibliothèque nationale de France both in Chinese and in other languages. Meanwhile, incomplete fragments and fuzzy images were re-photographed and renamed. With 34 volumes in total, it commenced publication in 1994 by Shanghai Classics Publishing House, and its publication has been completed.

The executive director of the *Dunhuang and Turfan Manuscript Collections* was Wei Tongxian, with consultants Ji Xianlin, Pan Chonggui, and Jao Tsung-I. It comprises seventeen volumes of *Dunhuang Documents Held in Russia*; thirty-four volumes of *Dunhuang and Western Region Manuscripts Held in France*; eleven volumes of *Documents from Khara-Khoto Collected in Russia*; six volumes of *Dunhuang Artworks Collected in Russia*; seven volumes of *Dunhuang Manuscripts in the Tianjin Museum of Art*; two volumes of *Dunhuang and Turfan Manuscripts in the Shanghai*

从已出各辑《敦煌吐鲁番文献集成》可知，其有如下特点：

第一，相对完备。尽力搜求、辑集，将敦煌地区出现的各种文字资料和艺术资料，尽可能完整地反映出来，使其成为一部总汇式的集成文献。

第二，力求存真。敦煌吐鲁番文书具有文献和文物两重价值，这就要求对文献的印制必须逼真，其大小、长短、形状、色彩、字迹、残损自不必说，即使是纸质、卷轴、包封等也不宜忽略。

第三，定名准确。当然，由于各种原因，已出《敦煌吐鲁番文献集成》，在个别文献的定名、分类等方面可能还有一些不当之处，这也是可以理解的。

第四，编排合理。由于本《集成》是一套大型的资料用书，中心目的是给学术界提供一份全面可信的原始资料，因而，文字部分如前言、凡例、目录、题解、索引等等，均需说明性质，意在方便使用；图版部分则按序排列，重在实用，兼

Museum; four volumes of *Dunhuang Manuscripts in the Shanghai Library*; and two volumes of *Dunhuang Manuscripts in the Peking University*.

The characteristics of *Dunhuang and Turfan Manuscript Collections* are as follows:

I. Comprehensiveness: it contains for the most part all materials from multiple languages and scripts, and is an integration of documents.

II. Authenticity: it contains documents and cultural relics that require accurate and authentic reproduction, including the size, shape, color and handwriting; in addition, the quality of paper, scroll, and covers have not been overlooked.

III. Accuracy of document names: most of the manuscripts are named accurately.

IV. Easy-to-use layout: as a reference book, *Dunhuang and Turfan Manuscript Collections* intends to provide complete and authoritative primary sources for academic research. The preface, user's guide, contents, notes, and indexes explain the essence of the sources and are easy to use. Meanwhile, the plates are arranged in order for easy reference, with accompanying text providing optimal results.

In consideration of the excellence of *Dunhuang and Turfan Manuscript Collections*, with more than 80 volumes, we cannot help appreciating the scholars and publishers of the project for their hard work and enduring contributions.

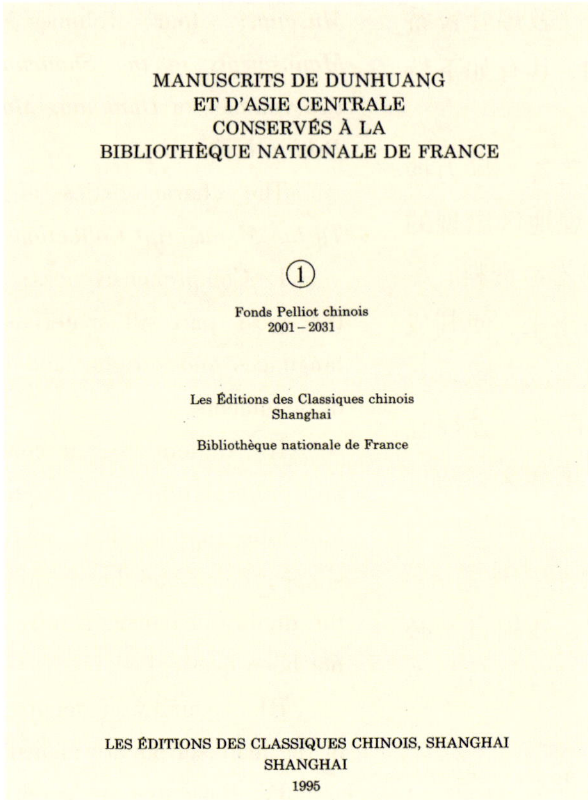
MANUSCRITS DE DUNHUANG
ET D'ASIE CENTRALE
CONSERVÉS À LA
BIBLIOTHÈQUE NATIONALE DE FRANCE

①

Fonds Pelliot chinois
2001 – 2031

Les Éditions des Classiques chinois
Shanghai

Bibliothèque nationale de France

LES ÉDITIONS DES CLASSIQUES CHINOIS, SHANGHAI
SHANGHAI
1995

图 35 《法藏敦煌西域文献》扉页

Fig.35 Preface to *Dunhuang and Western Region Manuscripts Held in France*

及欣赏。做到图文结合，以发挥资料用书的最佳效果。

现在，当我们看到装帧精美、印制优良的八十多册《敦煌吐鲁番文献集成》时，我们不得不从内心感谢那些为此艰辛奔波、作出了巨大贡献的学者和出版家。没有他们的艰辛劳动，就不可能有今天的硕果。

我们不应该也不能忘记魏同贤、钱伯城、李国章、赵昌平、王兴康等先生，

We can never forget Wei Tongxian, Qian Bocheng, Li Guozhang, Zhao Changping, and Wang Xingkang, who took great effort to publish these Dunhuang documents. Li Weiguo wrote in *Dunhuang Discourses*, "Scholars such as Wei Tongxian and Qian Bocheng didn't study Dunhuang, but had the ambition to go abroad to research Dunhuang manuscripts and edited many books on

图 36 《敦煌吐鲁番文献集成》顾问季羡林先生

Fig.36 Ji Xianlin, Consultant of *Dunhuang and Turfan Manuscript Collections*

他们虽然不是敦煌学家，但他们是真正的出版家，为出版敦煌文献付出了自己的心血。正如李伟国先生在《敦煌话语》中所说："当年主事的魏同贤、钱伯城先生，都很有学者风度和眼光，虽然他们并不研究敦煌，即使由他们主编出版了那么多的有关敦煌的书，他们个人的研究仍不涉猎敦煌，但他们却有走出国门，找回'敦煌'的决心和魄力。……在钱、魏两先生相继退

Dunhuang as well. After their retirement and my transfer, my colleagues Fu Xianzhan and Jiang Weisong were under great financial pressure since they didn't realize any immediate compensation from these projects. Fortunately, they didn't give up, and were helped by Li Guozhang, Zhao Changping, and Wang Xingkang." All of their names should be recorded in the history of Dunhuang studies.

休，我又被调离以后，以我的同事府宪展、蒋维崧为主任的编辑室，因为短期内不见经济效益，曾经承受了巨大的压力，不理解的社内同事对他们侧目而视，幸好有李国章、赵昌平、王兴康等先生的苦苦撑持，方得继续，没有半途而废。”真的，当将来编写敦煌学史时，人们不应该遗忘他们。

当然，还有李伟国、府宪展、蒋维崧、郭子健、刘景云等等，他们干一行，爱一行，因编辑出版敦煌文献而成了敦煌学研究者。由编辑而学者，编辑兼学者，在老一代的中华人中能找出很多，如李侃先生的中国近代史研究、赵守俨先生的唐史研究、程毅中先生的唐代小说研究等。而在上海古籍出版社从事敦煌文献出版的这些编辑中，我们看到的是薪火相传。他们默默无闻、不计功名利禄，其敬业奉献精神、责任心和事业心，都是值得我们学习的。

其实，应该记住的人还有很多很多，正如李伟国先生在《敦煌话语》中所说：“当我走进书店，默默地翻看着这部来之不易的大书的时候，我想起了慈眉善目的丘古耶夫斯基教授，他已经永远离开我们了；我想起了与丘教授同岁的孟列夫教授，这位聪明绝顶，精力充沛的学者，也已白发苍苍，

Among the editors who worked in the editing and publishing of Dunhuang documents in Shanghai Classics Publishing House, some became experts in Dunhuang studies, such as Li Weiguo, Fu Xianzhan, Jiang Weisong, Guo Zijian, and Liu Jingyun. Some were both editors and scholars. For example, Li Kan was engaged in studying the modern history of China, Zhao Shouyan the history of the Tang Dynasty, and Cheng Yizhong the novels of the Tang Dynasty. They exemplified a strong sense of responsibility and dedication to their careers.

There were many more people we should remember, just as Li Weiguo commented in *Dunhuang Discourses*, “When I went to the bookstore, silently reading this book, I thought of Professor Chuguyevsky who had left us forever; Professor Menshikov, a brilliant and energetic scholar, now elderly with gray hair; Dr. Zhang Huiming who had married in France and was out of contact; and my own ex-wife who had already been gone for so many years. I wanted to buy the set of books and write their names on it as a souvenir, but the expense made me hesitate.”

渐现老态；我想起了张惠明博士，她早已远嫁法国，杳无音信；我想起了我的前妻，她也早已长眠地下。我想买一部书，把他们的名字都写上，留作纪念，但是昂贵的价格又叫我下不了决心。”

2005 年 10 月 29 日，孟列夫教授因病去世。在墓地的葬礼上，东方所的负责人宣读了来自敦煌研究院、中国敦煌吐鲁番学会、上海古籍出版社的唁函，有关刊物发表了柴剑虹、府宪展等中国学者的纪念文章，表达了对这位俄罗斯敦煌学家的深切怀念与高度赞扬。

不论是四川人民出版社出版的《英藏敦煌文献》，还是上海古籍出版社已经出版的《敦煌吐鲁番文献集成》各卷，都是汉文文献。而在敦煌发现的文书中，除汉文文献外，还有大量的民族文字文献，其中就有许多藏文文献的卷子，而且主要收藏在英国国家图书馆和法国国家图书馆中。

这些藏文卷子具有涉及多种学科的重要史料价值，国际上的研究还只是停留在编目阶

On October 29, 2005, Professor Menshikov died from natural causes. At his funeral, a representative from the Institute of Oriental Studies read a letter of condolence from the Dunhuang Academy, the Institute of Dunhuang and Turfan Studies of China, and Shanghai Classics Publishing House. Commemorative articles from Chai Jianhong, Fu Xianzhan, and other Chinese scholars were published to express great respect for this Russian expert in Dunhuang studies.

The Dunhuang manuscripts comprise both Chinese and numerous minority language documents. The former is represented by *Dunhuang Manuscripts in British Collections* published by Sichuan People's Publishing House and *Dunhuang and Turfan Manuscript Collections* by Shanghai Classics Publishing House. Minority language documents include many Tibetan scrolls mostly preserved in the British Library and la Bibliothèque nationale de France.

The Tibetan manuscripts, covering a wide range of disciplines, bear tremendous historical value. The international research on them at this point, however, has still been in the cataloguing stage, and it has been difficult for Chinese scholars to access them, thus limiting academic research and development.

Recently, Northwest Minzu University, la Bibliothèque nationale de France, the

段，并未全面刊布，中国学者更是难以亲睹其面，从而限制了学术的繁荣和发展。

最近，经过多方商讨，西北民族大学、法国国家图书馆、英国国家图书馆和上海古籍出版社达成协议，联合编纂出版敦煌西域藏文文献。经过前期准备工作，现在已开始了《法藏敦煌藏文文献》《法藏敦煌胡语文献》，以及《英藏敦煌藏文文献》的编辑出版工作。由于懂得古藏文的学者和编辑人数不多，从而使编辑出版工作困难重重。可以说，无论在规模上还是在学术难度上，藏文文献的编辑出版都将会超过汉文文献，全部工程预计在2年至3年中完成。

British Library, and Shanghai Classics Publishing House reached an agreement to jointly compile and publish Dunhuang and Western Region manuscripts in Tibetan language. They have begun editing and publishing *Tibetan Language Manuscripts from Dunhuang in French Collections*, *Hu Minority Language Manuscripts from Dunhuang in French Collections*, and *Tibetan Language Manuscripts from Dunhuang in British Collections*. Because only a few scholars and editors are proficient in ancient Tibetan, the editing and publishing of the book has been more difficult than those of the Chinese documents, and as a result the entire project is expected to continue for two to three more years.

图 37 《法国国家图书馆藏敦煌藏文文献》
Fig.37 Tibetan Language Dunhuang Manuscript Collections in la Bibliothèque nationale de France

《国家图书馆藏敦煌遗书》及其他

Dunhuang Manuscripts Reserved by the National Library of China and Other Documents

伴随着《敦煌吐鲁番文献集成》的出版，由国家图书馆（前北京图书馆）馆长任继愈先生主编的《中国国家图书馆藏敦煌遗书》也开始由江苏古籍出版社出版。

中国国家图书馆现收藏敦煌遗书约16000余号，包括四个部分：(1)劫余录部分。即陈垣先生《敦煌劫余录》所著录的部分，计8738号。(2)详目续编部分。1927年前后，从解京的敦煌遗书中又整理出1192号比较完整的遗书，定名为《敦煌石窟写经详目续编》。(3)残卷部分。解京的敦煌遗书经过上述两

After the publication of *Dunhuang and Turfan Manuscript Collections*, another work, *Dunhuang Manuscripts Reserved by the National Library of China* edited by Ren Jiyu, former director of the National Library of China (the former Beijing Library), is soon to be published by Jiangsu Classics Publishing House①.

There are 16,000 Dunhuang manuscripts in the National Library of China, generally in four categories: 1) The remaining manuscripts left after the removal of the bulk of the documents by Westerners, 8,738 volumes in total, which were compiled into *First Catalogue of Dunhuang Manuscripts* by Chen Yuan; 2) The catalogued 1,192 intact documents included in *A Sequel to Catalogue of Scriptures from the Dunhuang Caves*, which were sorted and catalogued in 1927; 3) Damaged parts, totalling approximately 4,000 manuscript fragments, which had been sorted and cataloged twice; 4) New materials—manuscripts which were gradually collected over decades by

① *Dunhuang Manuscripts Reserved by the National Library of China* (1–7) had been published by the end of 2001 by Jiangsu Classics Publishing House, and after then, it was suspended for some reasons.

次整理编目的残存部分，总计近4000号。(4)新字号部分。指除甘肃解京的敦煌遗书外，图书馆于其后数十年间陆续收藏的敦煌遗书。

《中国国家图书馆藏敦煌遗书》包括以上四个部分，并全部重新拍摄。拍摄所据的原件，已经过专家进一步修复整理，未经修复时所制缩微胶卷中存在的遗书背面漏拍，以及首尾残破、皱折叠压或墨迹深浅不一、难以辨认等问题，得以避免，从而使本书的图版更加完整、清晰。

江苏古籍出版社出版的《中国国家图书馆藏敦煌遗书》为8开本，每册约460页，在正文图版之后，编有叙录、新旧编码对照表等，原计划全套出版约100册，但在出版了7册以后，不知什么原因，再未能继续出版。从2005年开始，国家图书馆又重新编辑，仍由任继愈先生主编，定名为《国家图书馆藏敦煌遗书》，由北

the National Library with the exception of those delivered to Beijing by Gansu Province.

All the collections have already been re-photographed. The originals were repaired by conservation experts to solve problems such as the reverse side of documents not being transcribed or photographed, as well as broken, folded, or smudged parts of the manuscripts, so as to make them complete and legible to read.

Published by Jiangsu Classics Publishing House, the paper size of *Dunhuang Manuscripts Reserved by the National Library of China* is 260 × 370mm, with each volume containing 460 pages. There are descriptions of the manuscripts and comparison tables of old and new codes after the main text. Unfortunately, only seven volumes out of the originally planned 100 were finished for various reasons. The National Library of China began to recompile a new edition in 2005 with Ren Jiyu at the helm, renaming it *Dunhuang Manuscripts Reserved by the National Library*. Currently, 79 volumes have been issued, and the entire set of the book, 150 volumes altogether, will be published by the end of 2008[1].

① Up till February of 2008, *Dunhuang Manuscripts Reserved by the National Library* (Volumns 1-146) have been re-edited and published by Beijing Library Press.

京图书馆出版社出版，目前已出版了 79 册，全套共计 150 册，计划于 2008 年全部出版。

由于敦煌文书的大部分被劫往国外，因此早期中国学者主要是赴海外阅读、抄写、摄制有关资料，在此基础上，出版了一些专科的整理文献，如王重民的《敦煌曲子词集》(1950 年)、周绍良的《敦煌变文汇录》(1954 年)、任二北的《敦煌曲校录》(1955 年)、王重民等的《敦煌变文集》(1957 年)、中国科学院历史研究所资料室的《敦煌资料》第一辑(1961 年)等。

这些专科资料虽然有限，但为我国的敦煌文献研究曾起过巨大的作用。如《敦煌变文集》就是 1954 年由王重民、王庆菽发起，向达主持，周一良、启功、曾毅公参加，在广泛摄录、抄写国内外公私收藏的变文资料的基础上，过录了 187 个写本，经过认真的整理后选编了 78 种而编成的。

Earlier Chinese scholars studied Dunhuang manuscripts mainly by reading, copying, and photographing those which had been removed overseas. In this way, they published special collections of documents such as *A Collection of Dunhuang Quzi Ci* (1950) by Wang Zhongmin; *A Collection of Dunhuang Bianwen* (1954) by Zhou Shaoliang; *A Collation and Collection of Songs from Dunhuang* (1955) by Ren Erbei; *An Anthology of Dunhuang Bianwen* (1957) primarily by Wang Zhongmin; *Dunhuang Materials: Volume I* (1961) by the History Research Institute of the Chinese Academy of Sciences.

The above-mentioned achievements have played a large role in the study of Dunhuang manuscripts. Take *An Anthology of Dunhuang Bianwen* as an example. In 1954, Wang Zhongmin and Wang Qingshu initiated the compilation of this work, which won the support of Xiang Da, Zhou Yiliang, Qi Gong, and Zeng Yigong, who then went to locate the manuscripts both at home and abroad. In total, they identified 187 manuscripts, from which they selected and compiled 78. *An Anthology of Dunhuang Bianwen* was the most successful work at the time in China for the study of narrative literature. Its publication in 1957 by People's Literature Publishing House exerted great influence on promoting the study of Chinese folk literature. In addition, *Dunhuang Materials: Volume I*,

《敦煌变文集》是当时我国学者对变文写卷进行的规模最大的一次整理成果，也是收集资料最丰富的一部变文总集，1957年由人民文学出版社出版后，对推动我国变文及民间文学的研究起了很大的作用。另如《敦煌资料》第一辑，就是一部综合性的敦煌文献集，它由中国科学院历史研究所编

edited by the History Research Institute of the Chinese Academy of Sciences, was quite comprehensive. Published by Zhonghua Book Company in 1961, it became an essential reference for scholars studying the economy of Dunhuang and the history of the Tang Dynasty. The book was of great value in promoting the study of the economic history of Medieval China.

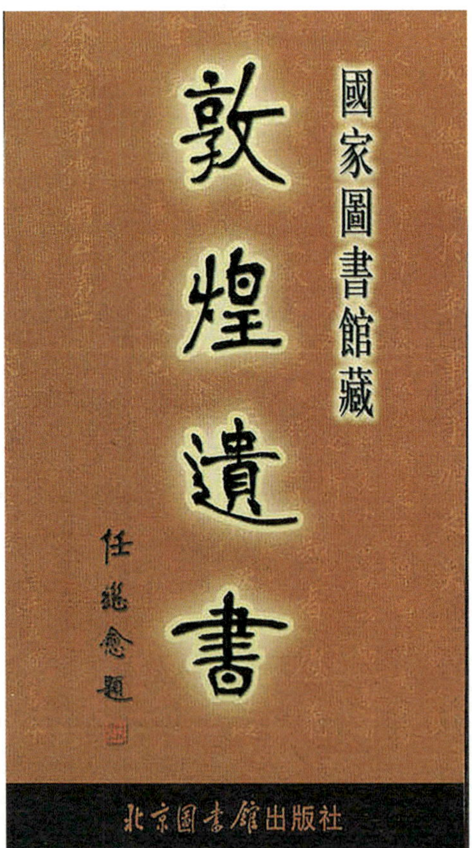

图 38 《国家图书馆藏敦煌遗书》

Fig.38 Dunhuang Manuscripts Reserved by the National Library (Chinese Edition)

辑，主要是辑录社会经济方面的资料，1961 年由中华书局出版后即成了敦煌经济文书和唐史研究者的案头必备书，对推动我国中古经济史及唐史研究发挥了重要作用。

20 世纪 80 年代以来，我国学者更重视资料的整理与刊布。除前述《英藏敦煌文献》《俄藏敦煌文献》《法藏敦煌西域文献》和《国家图书馆藏敦煌遗书》外，还有一些零星的、专科的和分类的整理出版，也是很有价值的。如张锡厚《王梵志诗校辑》就整理出王梵志诗 366 首，是敦煌资料搜集整理方面的可喜收获。在此基础上，项楚又搜集了一些新发现和公布的资料，并作了精细校注，完成了《王梵志诗校注》一书，使王梵志诗的整理、研究更趋完善。任半塘(任二北)在《敦煌曲校录》的基础上，又不断搜集整理，编著了 100 多万字的《敦煌歌辞总编》，于 1987 年由上海古籍出版社出版。该书收辞 1300 余首，是目前所见收辞最多、品种最全、范围最广的歌辞总编，体现了半

Since the 1980s, Chinese scholars have paid more attention to the arrangement and publication of the documents. In addition to *Dunhuang Manuscripts in British Collections*, *Dunhuang Documents Held in Russia*, *Dunhuang and Western Region Manuscripts Held in France* and *Dunhuang Manuscripts Reserved by the National Library*, there were still scattered, specialized, and classified collections of great value. For example, there were 366 poems of Wang Fanzhi in *A Collation and Compilation of the Poetry of Wang Fanzhi* compiled by Zhang Xihou. On this basis, Xiang Chu then located additional related materials and completed his study of the poems, writing *An Annotation of the Poetry of Wang Fanzhi*. With *A Collation and Collection of Songs from Dunhuang* as its foundation, Ren Bantang (Ren Erbei) compiled *A General Collection of Lyrics from Dunhuang*, with 1,300 lyrics and more than one million Chinese characters in total, being the most comprehensive research on song lyrics. It was published by Shanghai Classics Publishing House in 1987. *A Supplement to the Anthology of Dunhuang Bianwen*, coedited by Zhou Shaoliang, Bai Huawen, and Li Dingxia, contains 15 newly discovered Dunhuang *bianwen*—or "transformation texts"—a popular form of vernacular narrative literature which flourished during the Tang Dynasty, with

个多世纪敦煌歌辞的研究成果。周绍良、白化文、李鼎霞合编的《敦煌变文集补编》，收录了《敦煌变文集》出版后新发现的变文 15 篇，既有录文，又有原件照片，后面还附有俗字表。黄征、张涌泉的《敦煌变文校注》则是敦煌变文校注方面的集大成著作。

1986 年，书目文献出版社出版了唐耕耦、陆宏基所编《敦煌社会经济文献真迹释录》(以下简称《释录》) 第一辑，1990 年，全国图书馆文献缩微复制中心又出版了该书的第二至五辑。由于编者唐耕耦先生是历史学出身，又以研究唐代社会经济而著名，因此《释录》是敦煌社会经济文献整理、刊布的集大成著作。编者从英、法、俄、日等国及我国收藏的敦煌文献中，将有关社会经济方面的资料辑出，按类编排，分成五辑，用原件的照片与录文对照，兼附前人研究原件的论著出处，图文并茂，极便于敦煌学者之利用。

《释录》是迄今为止敦煌文献整理方面有关社会经济文

alternate prose and rhymed parts for chanting and singing, often on Buddhist themes. It contains transcribed *bianwen* with facsimiles of the original documents, and a table of the written characters in vernacular form. *Annotated Dunhuang Bianwen*, edited by Huang Zheng and Zhang Yongquan, was an unprecedented masterpiece in regard to the research, verification, and annotation of Dunhuang *bianwen*.

In 1986, Bibliography Press published *A Compilation of Dunhuang Secular Manuscripts: Volume I*, edited by Tang Geng'ou and Lu Hongji. In 1990, the China National Microfilm Center for Library Resources carried out work on Volume II–V. It is a comprehensive work on Dunhuang socioeconomic documents, as Tang Geng'ou was renowned for his academic work on the economy of the Tang Dynasty. This book, through worldwide selection and meticulous classification of documents, as well as excellent plates and text on the society and economics of Dunhuang, is an essential reference book for scholars in Dunhuang studies.

A Compilation of Dunhuang Secular Manuscripts includes 34 categories of secular and socioeconomic documents, such as local chronicles, clan and family gazettes, records of residency and taxation, group clubs and organizations, written complaints, eulogies, and private writings on rituals. It

书收录最丰富的一部文献集，它包括地志、氏族志、籍账、社邑、牒、状、邈真赞、书仪等 34 类，释录文书 1664 件。既收录了籍账、契据、土地、赋税、财政、寺院经济等经济资料，也收录了一些虽不属经济但又与经济相关的文书，如告身、表、书、律、

also includes 1,664 economic, legal, and administrative documents such as records of residence, contracts, land deeds, taxation, finance, temple economies, as well as other materials such as appointment letters, statements, letters, laws, orders, and other official documents. This monumental work constitutes the largest and most important collection of Dunhuang secular manuscript facsimiles. Every document is titled, classified,

图 39 唐耕耦、陆宏基编《敦煌社会经济文献真迹释录》
Fig.39 *A Compilation of Dunhuang Secular Manuscripts*, Edited by Tang Geng'ou and Lu Hongji

令、格、式等，这些社会历史文献都是敦煌世俗文献中最重要的。同时，《释录》对每件文书都作了定名或拟题，按性质分类，每类中再分为若干细目，按年代先后排列。尤其是作者对每件文书都作了详细的辨识录文，并采用上图下文的方式，尽可能提供文书原件的图版与录文的对比阅读。这在《英藏敦煌文献》《俄藏敦煌文献》《法藏敦煌西域文献》和《中国国家图书馆藏敦煌文献》都还没有提上议事日程的80年代，就显得更加珍贵、更加难得了。《释录》的出版改变了国内绝大多数学者看不到原卷图片的困惑，对推动敦煌社会经济文书的整理研究和魏晋隋唐史研究发挥了重要作用。

此外，由甘肃藏敦煌文献编委会、甘肃省文物局等单位编纂的《甘肃藏敦煌文献》，也已由甘肃人民出版社出版。

《甘肃藏敦煌文献》全面系统地刊布了甘肃全省各单位收藏的敦煌遗书700余

and arranged in chronological order. Each plate is supplemented with descriptive text for easy identification, which was a great innovation during the 1980s when the editing and publication of *Dunhuang Manuscripts in British Collections*, *Dunhuang Documents Held in Russia*, *Dunhuang and Western Region Manuscripts Held in France*, and *Dunhuang Manuscripts Reserved by the National Library of China* were not yet on the horizon. Fortunately, the publication of *A Compilation of Dunhuang Secular Manuscripts* not only solved the problem of most scholars lacking access to the original sources, but promoted the study of Dunhuang secular documents and that of the history of the Wei, Jin, Sui, and Tang dynasties.

In addition to the documents mentioned above, *Dunhuang Manuscript Collections in Gansu Province*, compiled by the Gansu Provincial Bureau of Cultural Relics, has also been published by Gansu People's Publishing House.

In total it contains 700 Dunhuang manuscripts preserved in Gansu, in six volumes. The first volume is *Dunhuang Manuscript Collections in the Dunhuang Academy: Volume I*; the second volume includes *Dunhuang Manuscript Collections in the Dunhuang Academy: Volume II*, and *Dunhuang Manuscript Collections in Jiuquan Museum*; the third volume includes

图 40 《甘肃藏敦煌文献》

Fig.40 Dunhuang Manuscript Collections in Gansu Province

号，真实完整地展示了甘藏敦煌文献的全貌。

《甘肃藏敦煌文献》共 6 卷，第一卷为《敦煌研究院藏敦煌文献（上）》；第二卷为《敦煌研究院藏敦煌文献（下）》和《酒泉市博物馆藏敦煌文献》；第三卷包括《甘肃省图书馆藏

Dunhuang Manuscript Collections in Gansu Provincial Library, *Dunhuang Manuscript Collections in Northwest Normal University*, *Dunhuang Manuscript Collections in Yongdeng County Museum*, *Dunhuang Manuscript Collections in Gansu College of Traditional Chinese Medicine*, and *Dunhuang Manuscript Collections in Zhangye Museum*; the fourth volume is

敦煌文献》《西北师范大学藏敦煌文献》《永登县博物馆藏敦煌文献》《甘肃中医学院藏敦煌文献》和《张掖市博物馆藏敦煌文献》；第四卷为《甘肃省博物馆藏敦煌文献（上）》；第五卷为《甘肃省博物馆藏敦煌文献（下）》；第六卷包括《敦煌市博物馆藏敦煌文献》《定西县博物馆藏敦煌文献》和《高台县博物馆藏敦煌文献》。

《浙藏敦煌遗书》一册也已于 2000 年由浙江教育出版社出版。

在各地刊布敦煌原卷图版的良好基础上，敦煌文献的整理更趋于专精，即分类校注。这一方面的典范当推《敦煌文献分类录校丛刊》。该《丛刊》由周绍良主编，由江苏古籍出版社于 1995 年—1998 年出版，共 10 卷、12 册，即邓文宽《敦煌天文历法辑校》，张锡厚《敦煌赋汇》，宁可、郝春文《敦煌社邑文书辑校》，沙知《敦煌契约文书辑校》，马继兴《敦煌医药文献辑校》，方广锠《敦

Dunhuang Manuscript Collections in Gansu Museum: Volume I; the fifth volume is *Dunhuang Manuscript Collections in Gansu Museum: Volume II*; the sixth volume includes *Dunhuang Manuscript Collections in Dunhuang Museum*, *Dunhuang Manuscript Collections in Dingxi County Museum*, and *Dunhuang Manuscript Collections in Gaotai County Museum*.

In addition, *Dunhuang Manuscript Collections in Zhejiang Province* was published by Zhejiang Educational Press in 2000.

With achievements made in publishing facsimiles of original Dunhuang manuscripts, the arrangement of them has become more and more specialized as far as classification and annotation are concerned. The prototype in this regard has been *Dunhuang Document Classification and Recording Series*, a total of 10 volumes in 12 books, edited by Zhou Shaoliang and published by Jiangsu Classics Publishing House from 1995 to 1998. It consists of *A Compilation of Dunhuang Astronomy and Calendar Manuscripts* by Deng Wenkuan; *A Collection of Dunhuang Fu Poetry* by Zhang Xihou; *A Compilation of Dunhuang Documents from Clubs and Organizations* by Ning Ke and Hao Chunwen; *A Compilation of Dunhuang Contract Documents* by Sha Zhi; *A Compilation of Dunhuang Documents on Medicine* by Ma Jixing; *A Compilation of*

煌佛教经录辑校》(上、下)，周绍良、张涌泉、黄征《敦煌变文讲经文因缘辑校》(上、下)，赵和平《敦煌表状笺启书仪辑校》，王素、李方《敦煌〈论语集解〉校证》，邓文宽、荣新江《敦博本禅籍录校》。

《丛刊》所收每篇文献基本包括四项内容，即定性、定名、定年；原件录文；题解或说明；校勘记。每辑之后附有“主要论著参考书目”和该辑所用敦煌文献“卷号索引”，便于读者查阅。

Dunhuang Buddhist Scriptures: Volumes I and II by Fang Guangchang; *Selected Dunhuang Bianwen on the Subject of Avadana Tales* by Zhou Shaoliang, Zhang Yongquan, and Huang Zheng; *A Compilation of Dunhuang Correspondence and Ritual Manuscripts* by Zhao Heping; *A Compilation of Explications of Confucian Analects Found in Dunhuang* by Wang Su and Li Fang; and *A Compilation of Zen Texts Found in Dunhuang* by Deng Wenkuan and Rong Xinjiang.

Each work in *Dunhuang Document Classification and Recording Series* includes four parts: labeling and dating; transcribing the original text; explanation and notes on collation; and proofreading records. References and indexes of scroll numbers are available for ease of use.

图 41 《敦煌文献分类录校丛刊》

Fig.41 Dunhuang Document Classification and Recording Series

《丛刊》每辑的校录者，都是敦煌文献整理、研究方面的专家(起码也是他校辑的这一方面的专家)，是国内从事这一工作的最佳人选，从而也就保证了辑校工作的质量。

正在进行的《英藏敦煌社会历史文献释录》是郝春文教授主编的大型文献释录。在已经有了英、法、俄藏图录集和《敦煌文献分类录校丛刊》的情况下，为什么还要出版没有图版、只有文字释录的《英藏敦煌社会历史文献释录》? 这主要是由于:第一，由于敦煌文献的内容复杂，不少文书目前还难以进行分类和归类，因此，分类校录本不能反映敦煌文献的全貌；第二，由于大多数分类校录本的作者都是依据目录调查某一类文献，而现有的各种目录又不完备，因而分类校录本对所需的文献很难搜集齐全；第三，分类校录容易忽略各类文书之间、各个专题之间的联系，不利于对敦煌文献进行综合、宏观的研究。正是考虑到这些因素，郝春文教授就按英国图书馆藏流水号，依次对每件敦煌汉文社会历史文献进行释录。每件文

The editors were experts in the classification or study of Dunhuang manuscripts, ensuring the quality of *Dunhuang Document Classification and Recording Series*.

Professor Hao Chunwen edited the documents selected for *An Interpretation of Dunhuang Secular Manuscript Collections in Great Britain*. There was an abundance of available Dunhuang materials by then, such as facsimile collections from Great Britain, France, and Russia as well as *Dunhuang Document Classification and Recording Series*. Why, however, did Hao publish a purely textual version of the manuscripts without any accompanying images? The reasons were complex. First, the intricacy of the Dunhuang manuscripts complicated the classification of certain documents and accordingly caused problems with accuracy. Second, previous incomplete cataloguing could not meet the need to select proper materials through catalogues alone. Third, previous classification likely overlooked the connections among different categories of documents, which was not suitable for a large-scale study of Dunhuang manuscripts. Taking these factors into account, Professor Hao summarized and recorded every piece of social and historical literature in the Chinese language according to the

图 42　已出版的国内外收藏的敦煌文献

Fig.42　Dunhuang Documents Published Within China and Overseas

书一般都包括标题、释文、说明、校记和参考文献几个部分。全书计划 30 卷，现已出版 5 卷（其中第一卷由科学出版社出版，从第二卷开始，改由社会科学文献出版社出版）。

此外，由浙江大学古籍所张涌泉教授领衔主编的《敦煌文献合集》的编撰

catalogue numbers in the British Library collections. In this way, each volume involved the title, summary of contents, description and explanation, notes on collation, and references. Presently, five out of the originally planned 30 volumes have been published, among which Volume I was published by Science Press, and Volume II–V were published by Social Sciences Academic Press.

In addition to the books mentioned above, *Dunhuang Manuscripts of Traditional Chinese*

工作也正在紧张地进行之中，其中《敦煌经部文献》可望于2007年正式出版发行。

Texts, with Zhang Yongquan from the Institute of Ancient Books of Zhejiang University, as the editor-in-chief, is in progress, and its subset, *Dunhuang Manuscripts of the Classics* (*Jing*) *Category*[1], is expected to be published in 2007.

① *Dunhuang Manuscripts of the Classics* (*Jing*) *Category* was officially published in August, 2008 by Zhonghua Book Company.

敦煌艺术探索

Art Explorations in Dunhuang

1937年日军发动侵华战争后，随着日本侵略者的一步步紧逼，国民政府也在一步步后退，先是从南京退居武汉，后又从武汉进一步退居重庆。相应的，沦陷区的大学和研究机构也纷纷转入西部，以前不大为人所关注的西南，则成了各种文化人和知识分子汇聚的宝地。随着政府重心的西移，以兰州为中心的西北就成了抗战的大后方，自然就引起了各方面的关注。了解西北、开发西北、建设西北就成了时人关心的新课题。正是在这样的大背景下，从40年代初开始，由政府有关部门或学术机构组成的各种考察团便开赴西北。

在此之前，学术界对敦煌的关注及对敦煌学的研究，主要是藏经洞文书。而这一阶段，不论是由官方组织的考察团，如“西北艺术文物考察团”“西北史地考察团”，还是官员、个人的考察、视察或朝圣，如于右任、张大千等，乃至奉命筹备敦煌艺术研究所的常书鸿及其追随者，基本上都是以艺术见长，他们关注的也主要是石窟保护和壁画艺术。

正是由于他们的关注及考察，尤其是他们所临摹的敦煌壁画在全国各地的展出，向世人宣传了敦煌，也使世人了解了敦煌艺术的博大精深。而他们在那种艰难困苦的条件下，对敦煌艺术的探索、临摹、展览、宣传，对敦煌石窟的保护，则更是我们应该永远铭记在心的。

In 1937, Japan invaded China, launching the War of Aggression Against China, which caused the Kuomintang government of China to retreat from Nanjing to Wuhan, then from Wuhan to Chongqing. As a result, universities and research institutes in the occupied areas moved west as well, following the westward migration of intellectuals and the government. Northwestern China—with its center in Lanzhou—became a significant area of conflict in the War of Resistance Against Japanese Aggression and naturally aroused concern in different circles. Many people shifted their attention towards the development and construction of the northwest at the time. Under these conditions, beginning in the early 1940s, numerous delegations were sent there by various governmental departments and academic institutions.

Prior to this, the study of Dunhuang had focused on the manuscripts found in the Library Cave at Mogao. During the war years, however, archaeological teams sent to Dunhuang by official organizations such as the Northwestern Art and Cultural Relics Expedition, the Northwestern Historical and Geographical Expedition, as well as private citizens embarking on their own explorations including Yu Youren, Zhang Daqian, and Chang Shuhong, began to turn to the study of Dunhuang art, and became increasingly concerned about the protection of historically significant cave temples and murals.

Their explorations, and especially the exhibitions of their reproductions of murals, made Dunhuang known to the world and aroused interest in Dunhuang art. Their devotion to the study and protection of Dunhuang art under challenging circumstances will not be forgotten.

王子云的敦煌考察

Wang Ziyun's Expedition to Dunhuang

王子云(1897—1990)，安徽萧县人，生前系西安美术学院教授、陕西美协名誉主席。早年毕业于江苏省立第七师范学校，后肄业于上海美术学校和北京美术专科学校。1930年底至1937年初在法国留学并游历欧洲。1937年

Wang Ziyun (1897-1990), born in Xiaoxian County, Anhui Province, was a professor at the Xi'an Academy of Fine Arts, and the honorary chairman of the Shaanxi Art Association. He graduated from Jiangsu No.7 High School, later studying at the Shanghai Fine Arts School and the School of Fine Arts in Beijing. From late 1930 until early 1937, he studied in France and traveled all over Europe. Upon his return, he became a professor at the China Academy of

图43　西北艺术文物考察团团长王子云

Fig.43　Wang Ziyun, Head of the Northwestern Art and Cultural Relics Expedition

回国后，被聘为国立杭州艺术专科学校教授。抗战爆发后随杭州艺专流亡西南各地，1939 年到达重庆。因他曾经帮助欧洲著名雕塑家朗多维斯基完成南京中山陵国父坐像，又是著名雕塑家刘开渠小学时期的老师，在国内雕塑界为一时之选，遂被委以设计重庆抗日无名英雄纪念碑的重任。由于日机狂轰滥炸，工程无法继续。其时，地处日寇沦陷区的山西大同石窟、河北涿县白带山石窟、辽宁义县万佛堂石窟等正惨遭破坏。而其他尚未沦陷的地区，其古迹文物又面临着灭顶之灾。因此，王子云毅然于 1940 年 5 月向国民政府教育部上呈报告，建议迅速组建艺术文物考察团奔赴西北，以摄影、临摹、拓印、复制、测绘、记录等方式，抢救收集尚未被日军占领地区的古代艺术文物。

1940 年 8 月，国民政府正式组建“艺术文物考察

Art in Hangzhou, but after the outbreak of the War of Resistance Against Japanese Aggression, he and his colleagues were forced to seek refuge in Chongqing in southwestern China in 1939. There he was assigned a great task: to design a monument known as the “Unknown Heroes of the War of Resistance Against Japanese” in Chongqing. He was chosen partly because he had helped Paul Landowski, a prominent monument sculptor from Europe, with creating the marble statue of Sun Yat-sen at the Sun Yat-sen Mausoleum in Nanjing, and partly because he had once taught the famous sculptor Liu Kaiqu while Liu was still in primary school. Unfortunately, the project was suspended because of the bombing by the Japanese forces. At that time, many historical icons in the occupied areas were damaged or destroyed by invaders: the Yungang Grottoes in Datong, Shanxi Province; the Baidaishan Grottoes in Zhuoxian County, Hebei Province; and the Wanfotang Grottoes in Yixian County, Liaoning Province. As the Japanese invasion threatened relics in a number of other places, Wang Ziyun asked the Ministry of Education of the National Government of the Republic of China to set up an expedition team whose job was to survey ancient cultural relics in the unoccupied areas. They were to do this by taking photographs, drawing sketches and copies, making ink rubbings, and mapping and surveying the relics.

The Northwestern Art and Cultural Relics Expedition was officially established in August of 1940. The expedition team was under the

团”，直属教育部领导（考察团因此也被称为“教育部艺术文物考察团”），聘任王子云为团长，成员主要由沦陷区撤退来重庆的美术教员和重庆国立艺专即将毕业的优秀生组成。考察团的任务是考察陕西西汉帝陵、唐帝陵及宗教寺院，甘肃敦煌石窟、安西万佛峡石窟，青海佛教寺院等西北古代历史文化遗迹、古代艺术品和社会民俗。由于该考察团的主要工作基本上都在西北地区的陕、甘、青三省，因此又被称为“西北艺术文物考察团”。

考察团开始组建时，其考察对象虽然有敦煌石窟，但显然不是重点和首选。后来还是因为于右任的建议，才将敦煌列为主要的考察对象。正如王子云在《从长安到雅典——中外美术考古游记》中所回忆的：“1941 年，于右任从西北视察回来后，对我们说敦煌莫高窟是我国最大的艺术宝窟，藏有许多古代的壁

direction of the Ministry of Education, and thus it was also known as the Northwestern Art and Cultural Relics Expedition under the Ministry of Education. Members of the team were primarily art teachers who had been evacuated to Chongqing from the occupied areas, as well as outstanding students who were about to graduate from Chongqing National Arts Training College. With Wang Ziyun as the leader, the team was assigned the task of researching ancient works of art, ancient social customs, and ancient historical and cultural relics in the northwest of China. Such places included the mausoleums of emperors from the Western Han Dynasty (202 BC–AD 8) in Shaanxi Province, mausoleums and Buddhist temples from the Tang Dynasty, the Dunhuang Caves in Gansu Province, the Ten Thousand Buddha Gorge (the Yulin Caves) in Anxi County, Gansu Province, and Buddhist temples in Qinghai Province. The team was also known as the Northwestern Art and Cultural Relics Expedition, as their work mainly covered three northwest provinces: Shaanxi, Gansu, and Qinghai.

When the team was first established, the Mogao Caves in Dunhuang were not the focus of their research, until this was later strongly recommended by Yu Youren, a senior statesman of the Kuomintang government. As Wang Ziyun remarked in the book *From Chang'an to Athens—Travel Notes on Art and Archaeology at Home and Abroad*, "In 1941, when Yu Youren returned from his expedition in the northwest, he told us that the Mogao Caves in

画和彩塑珍品，要我们去看看，调查调查。于是由当时政府的有关单位主持，组织了一个共有十多个人参加的考察团，其中包括历史、考古、美术等各方面的专家，由我担任团长。我们于1941年冬从西安出发，到敦煌时，张大千先生早已在敦煌莫高窟工作半年了。"(王子云的回忆，虽然有时间上的误记，不十分准确，但大体上是当时实际情况的反映)

考察团从1940年12月开始到1945年初结束，历时近五年，辗转奔波于川、陕、豫、甘、青的大部分地区，在非常艰苦的环境下，进行了一系列科学考察和研究，并做了一些力所能及的保护工作，取得了丰硕的成果。

原计划的考察范围，本来不包括河南洛阳，但由于洛阳龙门石窟也属于佛教石窟雕刻，再加上离西安不远，为了多了解其与敦煌千佛洞的不同，并作比较研究，考察团就在去敦煌之前先到洛阳龙门进行了调查。

Dunhuang were the biggest art treasure, with many ancient murals and rare painted sculptures. So he suggested that we explore them ourselves. Sponsored by the local government, we organized an expedition team led by me, with a total of more than 10 experts, specializing in history, archaeology, art, and other fields. We set off from Xi'an in the winter of 1941. By the time we arrived in Dunhuang, Zhang Daqian had already been working there for half a year." Although Wang's remark was not completely accurate in time, it offers a general picture of the situation at the time.

The team began their expedition in December 1940 and finished in early 1945. By the end of their expedition, they had traversed through most of Sichuan, Shaanxi, Henan, Gansu, and Qinghai, making great achievements and contributing significantly to research of these regions.

Originally they had not planned to do a research in Luoyang, Henan Province. However, since the Longmen Grottoes also contained Buddhist rock-cut architecture and sculptures, and it was not far from Xi'an, the team went to Luoyang before heading towards Dunhuang in order to learn more about the differences between the Longmen Grottoes and the Mogao Caves, known as the Thousand Buddha Caves at the time.

In the 1940s, traveling from Lanzhou to Dunhuang was difficult. The team had to first traverse the Hexi Corridor by bus across

图 44　西北艺术文物考察团全体合影(左一为何正璜，左二为王子云)
Fig.44　Members of the Northwestern Art and Cultural Relics Expedition: He Zhenghuang (Far Left), Wang Ziyun (Second from Left)

20 世纪 40 年代，由内地到敦煌，路途是非常艰苦的。从兰州去敦煌，先坐汽车经河西走廊，即经武威、张掖、酒泉；酒泉到安西约 280 公里，需专雇畜力车走三天；安西到敦煌 180 公里，连畜力车也难通行，只能坐农家的木轮牛车，在这样一段行程里，有三个休息站，都是在沙窝里搭的小草棚。

王子云率领的“西北艺

Wuwei, Zhangye, and Jiuquan, and then spent three days traveling from Jiuquan to Anxi (about 280 kilometers) by hired, animal-drawn wagons. The road from Anxi to Dunhuang (about 180 kilometers) was impossible even for the wagons to pass; they then had to ride in ox carts into local villages, as this was the only means of transportation available. In the last part of the journey to Dunhuang, they rested at three different stops, in small huts on the desert.

There were twelve members in the team led by Wang Ziyun. Due to a lack of funding, only three people finally reached the Mogao Caves in October of 1941. Some team members had to stay in Xi'an to deal with unfinished work, and

术文物考察团”共有 12 人，1941 年 10 月到达敦煌莫高窟的只有 3 人，这主要是由于经费的限制，“其他的团员有的留在西安继续未完成的工作，有的留在兰州听候调遣”。考察团从 1941 年 10 月到 1943 年春，在莫高窟断断续续工作了两年半，有时是 4 人，有时则只有 2 人。

虽然考察团在敦煌的时间不长，人数又少，但仍然取得了巨大的成绩：

第一，王子云绘制了莫高窟全景写生图。该图长 5. 5 米，宽 0. 233 米，是采用艺术和写实相结合的手

others stayed in Lanzhou waiting for further instructions. The team worked in Dunhuang from October 1941 until the spring of 1943, sometimes with a team of four people, and sometimes with a team of only two.

The team made enormous achievements despite a brief stay with a minimum number of people.

First, Wang Ziyun created a panoramic painting of the Mogao Caves by using a realistic painting style mixed with creative elements. As it was 5.5 meters long and 0.233 meter wide, it was not only a graceful landscape painting of the Mogao

图 45 西北艺术文物考察团从安西赴敦煌途中

Fig.45 The Northwestern Art and Cultural Relics Expedition on the Road from Anxi to Dunhuang

法绘制的。它既是一幅优美的莫高窟外貌风景画，极具观赏价值，又是一幅莫高窟实位勘测图，具有很高的学术史价值。1998 年，在陕西省举行的王子云教授诞辰百年纪念会上，向与会者展示了这件作品。王子云先生去世之后，其夫人何正璜遵其遗嘱将此图捐献给了敦煌研究院。

第二，拍摄了一些珍贵照片。在考察过程中，考察团一路拍摄了许多照片，其中在莫高窟拍摄的照片就有 120 多张。由于时光的流逝，这些照片已成了莫高窟历史形象的珍贵记录。20 世纪 90 年代，根据王子云先生生前提供的线索，在西北大学文博资料室发现了《教育部艺术文物考察团西北摄影集选》10 辑，每辑 1 册，每册约 50 页，每页的上半部是粘贴的照片，下半部是文字说明。其中第七辑是《敦煌千佛洞壁画》，第八辑是《敦煌及其它壁画集》，收集敦煌照片 83 张。在第一辑的《史

Caves, but also a realistic map of their on-site exploration, with substantial academic value. In 1998 the painting was shown to those who attended the 100th anniversary of Wang Ziyun's birth, which was held in Shaanxi Province. After Wang's death, his wife He Zhenghuang donated the painting to the Dunhuang Academy, according to his will.

The second achievement of the expedition was producing a set of valuable photographs, among which 120 were taken in the Mogao Caves. Eventually, these photos became an invaluable historical record. In the 1990s, by following clues offered by Wang Ziyun, the team located a rare collection of the photographs in the Wenbo Reference Room of Northwest University in Xi'an. The collection they found was known as the *Photographic Anthology of the Northwestern Art and Cultural Relics Expedition Appointed by the Ministry of Education*. It consisted of 10 albums or volumes in total, with each album containing approximately 50 pages. On each page, there was a photograph on the upper part, and below was a written description of the photograph. The seventh album was *An Anthology of Murals from the Mogao Caves in Dunhuang*, and the eighth was *An Anthology of Murals from Dunhuang and Other Caves*. A total of 83 photos were collected in these two albums. The first album, the *Anthology of Places of Historic Interest and Scenic Beauty*, included a panoramic photograph of the Crescent Moon Spring, which lies at the foot

图 46 王子云等人测绘的敦煌千佛洞全景图卷(局部)
Fig.46 Section of *Panorama of the Mogao Caves* by Wang Ziyun

迹名胜集》中，还有鸣沙山下的月牙泉全景，由此使我们看到了月牙泉自然变迁的直观资料。

第三，撰写了莫高窟现状调查报告。考察团成员、王子云先生的夫人何正璜女士1942年撰写的《敦煌莫高窟现存佛窟概况之调查》(发表于1943年出版的《说文月刊》3卷10期"西北专号")，是实地考察莫高窟，利用第一手资料撰写的我国第一份莫高窟内容总录。它比较系统地对莫高窟的沿革历史及洞窟形式等问题进行了梳理与整合，并根据文献和实物资料，粗分了洞窟的类型，探讨了石窟形制的特点和艺术风格。由于是第一个莫高窟内容总录，虽然还

of the Mingsha Mountain, enabling researchers to detect natural changes to the site over the years.

The third achievement produced by the expedition was field reports on the Mogao Caves. He Zhenghuang, a member of the team and Wang Ziyun's wife, finished writing the "Overview and Survey of Extant Mogao Caves in Dunhuang" in 1942, which was published in *Shuowen Monthly* in 1943. It was the first general report and catalogue of Dunhuang relics in China that was based on first-hand materials from field research. The report systematically analyzed the history of the Mogao Caves and their architectural forms. Using relevant literature and physical data, the report roughly categorized the caves into different types, examining their type characteristics and artistic styles. Although it was, to some degree, incomplete or even inaccurate in some parts, the report was still of value for reference. For example, in the chapter on "Serial Numbers of Caves," the

有不完备,甚至在今天看来不准确之处,但仍有重要的参考价值。如在“洞窟之编号”一节中说:“就莫高窟悬崖现存之佛窟，可分为南北二段，总计不下五六百窟，惟北段各窟除一二魏窟及元代欢喜佛洞以外，余多空无所有，因此历来调查者多仅就南段佛窟编号。”的确，伯希和、张大千都是如此。北区的编号是20 世纪 90 年代考古的新收获。

另外，考察团还临摹了一部分壁画。但与当时同在莫高窟的张大千的创造性临摹不同，考察团成员临摹壁画是从文物工作者的角度出发，“描旧如旧”，即壁画当时是什么样子就画成什么样子。

考察团的成果很快就以展览的形式向社会公布。在考察过程中，曾于 1941 年—1944 年分别在西安、兰州、重庆等地举办过展览。考察团成员王子云、何正璜、雷震、卢善群、邹道龙

author wrote, “There are more than five or six hundred Buddhist caves in the Mogao Caves, which can be divided into the north and south sections. On the north end, except for one or two caves which were built during the Wei Dynasty (220–265) and the Mandkesvara Cave (also known as Yab–Yum Cave or the Happy Buddha Cave) which was built during the Yuan Dynasty (1271–1368), the other caves were deserted, with nothing in them. Thus, from a historical perspective, investigators mainly studied the south end.” Actually, that was true for both Paul Pelliot and Zhang Daqian as well. Cave numbers for the north section were not assigned until the 1990s.

In addition, the team also copied some murals from Dunhuang, but their reproductions were different from the creative imitation of Zhang Daqian, who was also exploring the Mogao Caves at that time. Acting in their roles as researchers of historical relics, the team members reproduced the murals according to the principle of “letting the old be the old,” that is, to copy them exactly as they were in a realistic, objective style.

The achievements of the team were soon exhibited to the public. They had already held exhibitions in several cities, including Xi'an, Lanzhou, and Chongqing between 1941 and 1944 during their expedition. Some team members including Wang Ziyun, He Zhenghuang, Lei Zhen, Lu Shanqun, and Zou Daolong had also already held some personal exhibitions. Once they had finished the expedition in Dunhuang,

图 47 王子云与夫人何正璜 1941 年在考察途中
Fig.47 Wang Ziyun and his Wife He Zhenghuang on an Archeological Expedition, 1941

等还举办过不同形式的个人展览。如完成敦煌的工作后，就先在兰州举办了成果展，又于 1943 年元月在重庆举办了第一次敦煌艺术展览。由于参观者太多，拥挤得无法继续进行，教育部又决定在中央图书馆单独展览一周，有 3 万人参观。

敦煌的考察结束后，考察团又对甘肃河西走廊诸石窟、甘南

they held an exhibition on Dunhuang arts in Lanzhou, and then in Chongqing in January of 1943. Due to the large number of visitors who were attracted to the exhibitions, the Ministry of Education of the National Government decided to hold a special exhibition for an entire week in the National Library, attracting more than 30,000 visitors.

Following their on-site expedition of Dunhuang, the team conducted another field study of caves along the Hexi

图 48　王子云绘制的鸣沙山、三危山长卷外景图(局部)。这幅作品长 330 厘米、高 39 厘米,真实、完整地再现了 20 世纪 40 年代的敦煌莫高窟

Fig.48　Section of *Panorama of the Mingsha and Sanwei Moutains* by Wang Ziyun. 330 Centimeters Long by 39 Centimeters High, Presenting an Accurate Representation of the Mogao Caves in the 1940s

拉卜楞寺、兰州、西安等地进行了考察。1944 年,由于货币贬值,考察团经费实在困难,无法继续维持,便报请政府要求解散。1945 年初,"西北艺术文物考察团"被撤销。经协商,教育部指令由西北大学处理善后工作。这主要是因为此时徐朗秋(与王子云是师范学校同学)任西北大学教务长,而刘季洪(王子云老乡)又是西北大学校长,萧一山为西北大学文学院长。这样,西北大学就成立了西北文物研究室,由王子云先生任主任并兼历史系教授,继续从事西北历史文物和敦煌石窟的研究工作。考察团收集的文物和资料也交给了西北大学。

在考察团考察期间,敦

Corridor, in the Labrang Monastery in Gannan Tibetan Autonomous Prefecture, in Lanzhou, and in Xi'an. In 1944, the team was running out of funds due to currency devaluation and had to ask to be dissolved by the government, for which they received approval in early 1945. Following that, the Ministry of Education demanded that Northwest University take over the expedition. Xu Langqiu, Wang Ziyun's schoolmate, was then a dean at the university; Liu Jihong, who was from the same town as Wang Ziyun, was president of the university. Xiao Yishan was dean of the Faculty of Arts. Because of this, Northwest University established the Research Center of Northwestern Cultural Relics, appointing Wang Ziyun as director of the center and professor of the Department of History to continue his research on historical relics in northwestern China, including the research on the Dunhuang Caves. The cultural relics and materials that had been collected by the team up until that point were handed over to the Northwest University.

The founding of the National Research Institute on Dunhuang Art was an important event in the history of Dunhuang studies. Yu

煌艺术研究所的成立是不能不说的，这是敦煌学史上的重大事件。对于成立敦煌艺术研究所的建议，是谁最先提出来的，目前所能见到的原始文字只有于右任 1942 年 12 月 15 日的“提议”。但无论是谁先提出的，作为国民政府大员的于右任，对于在敦煌设立研究机关显然起过重大作用。敦煌艺术研究所筹备委员会成立于 1943 年 1 月 18 日，距于右任发表“提议”仅一月，可以说，最后决策此事和于右任有直接关系。当时的筹备委员会主任也不是常书鸿，而是国民政府监察院甘青监察使高一涵（于右任当时任国民政府监察院长），这也可以说明于右任对此事的影响。当时发表的名单中，张大千、王子云、常书鸿都是委员。1943 年 3 月，敦煌艺术研究所筹备委员会举行第一次会议，张大千和王子云都没有出席，也没有参加研究所以后的活动。王子云对常书鸿任筹备委员会副主任一职只有一句评价，即“常一直是画西洋油画的专业者”，言下之意，对雕塑艺术还是外行，由

Youren, the first person who came up with the idea and put it on written record on December 15, 1942, was a high-ranking official in the Kuomintang government, which meant that, obviously, he played a vital role in the institute's founding. The committee to make preparations for the National Research Institute on Dunhuang Art was established on January 18,1943, only a month after Yu Youren's proposal. The director of the preparatory committee was not Chang Shuhong, but Gao Yihan, who was supervisory commissioner of Gansu and Qinghai, while Yu was director of Ministry of Supervision during this period. As a result, Yu could exert great influence over the establishment of the institute. At the time Zhang Daqian, Wang Ziyun, and Chang Shuhong were the committee members. However, when the preparatory committee of the National Research Institute on Dunhuang Art held the first meeting in March 1943, neither Zhang Daqian nor Wang Ziyun attended the meeting or participated in the subsequent activities of the institute. Regarding Chang Shuhong, who was appointed vice-director of the institute, Wang Ziyun commented with one sentence, "Chang has always been an expert in Western oil paintings." This might have implied that he thought Chang was no expert in sculpture and so it made no sense for Chang to be assigned such a task.

他“来筹备这样的工作似乎没有道理”。

或曰，在于右任“提议”之前，教育部对敦煌的考察和机构设置已经在筹划进行之中。因“西北艺术文物考察团”早在1940年8月就成立。当时决定此事的是教育部长陈立夫和社会教育司长陈礼江，而为王子云递呈报告的是王子云当年的师范学校同学徐朗秋，其时正在社会教育司做科员，官不大，但是很能办事，以后做了西北大学教务长。他在1955年的“交代”里说：王子云和当时教育部上层无一人相识，被任命为考察团团长，就是因为陈立夫和陈礼江“口袋里没有这样的专业人才”。考察团成立之初，敦煌就是最重要的目标，而进行了一年多时间的内地考察，也等于是为敦煌考察练兵，提出成立研究机构的建议，正在考察团分内。虽然现在找不到王子云“建议”的文字，但他从事此项工作之初，便招收的是艺术专科学校的毕业生，其

Some experts believed that the Ministry of Education had already planned to launch an exploration of Dunhuang before Yu made his proposal, because the Northwestern Art and Cultural Relics Expedition was established early in August 1940 by order of Chen Lifu, minister of education, and Chen Lijiang, director of the Social Education Department. However, the person who submitted the proposal on behalf of Wang Ziyun was his schoolmate Xu Langqiu, who was a clerk in the Sociology Education Department, a minor but capable official. In 1955, he recalled the situation at the time, “Wang Ziyun had no contacts in the Ministry of Education at that time. The only reason why he was appointed as the head of the team was that Chen Lifu and Chen Lijiang couldn't find any other experts.” Since the establishment of the expedition team, Dunhuang had been the major destination for exploration, but they had worked in other provinces for more than a year to prepare for their expedition to Dunhuang. It seemed very likely that setting up a research institute was one of the aims of the team. Although there was no written record of Wang Ziyun's proposal to create such an institute, Wang had been engaged in related work for years and had recruited graduates from art colleges to work in a way that was similar to the suggestions made in the proposal by Yu Youren. It can be concluded that establishing an art institute had been one of the primary

工作方式，与于右任“建议”所云“招收大学艺术学生，就地研习，寓保管于研究之中”本趋一致。显然，对敦煌艺术研究所的考虑，考察团成立之初，便为题中之义。

关于研究所的成立，王子云在《从长安到雅典——中外美术考古游记》中回忆：考察团“到敦煌后不久，即致函重庆教育部，建议设立敦煌艺术研究所，并列出具体计划。建议书寄到重庆，恰在此时，重庆国民党教育部为了安置一些因抗战流亡的艺术界人士，特设立一个闲散机构艺术教育委员会，油画家常书鸿在这个委员会当秘书。我们的建议当然先送艺术教育委员会，于是不仅批准，而且常自告奋勇，愿意远去边塞，筹备研究所的成立”。筹备委员会由常书鸿任副主任，王子云任秘书。王子云认为常书鸿是个专业油画家，让他来主持敦煌研究不甚合理，于是不肯居常之下，没有参加敦煌研究所的工作。

objectives of the expedition since its inception.

Wang Ziyun wrote in *From Chang'an to Athens—Travel Notes on Art and Archaeology at Home and Abroad* about the establishment of the institute, "Shortly after the team arrived in Chongqing, I wrote to the Ministry of Education in Chongqing and suggested establishing the National Research Institute on Dunhuang Art, with a detailed plan. After my proposal was sent to Chongqing, the officials just happened to set up a committee of Art Education and appointed Chang Shuhong, an oil painter, as the secretary. As soon as the proposal was sent to the committee, Chang Shuhong not only approved it but also volunteered to go to Dunhuang to prepare for the establishment of the institute." Chang Shuhong held the post of deputy director and Wang Ziyun served as secretary. However, Wang thought that it was inappropriate for Chang to be in charge of the committee, because Chang was a professional oil painter and did not specialize in sculpture. Thus, Wang was unwilling to be secretary and as a result did not serve the institute once it was established.

敦煌考察中的向达

Xiang Da's Expedition to Dunhuang

向达（1900—1966），字觉明，笔名方回，1919年考入南京高等师范学校。1930年，任北平图书馆编纂委员会委员，利用馆藏丰富文献，着重于敦煌俗文学和中西文化交流等领域的研究。1935年秋赴欧洲，在伦敦、巴黎、柏林等地阅读敦煌吐鲁番文

Xiang Da (1900-1966), courtesy name Jueming, and pseudonym Fang Hui, was admitted to Nanjing Higher Teachers' College (present-day Nanjing University) in 1919. In 1930, as a member of the editorial committee of the Beiping Library (present-day Beijing Library), he made full use of the library to focus on the research of popular literature from Dunhuang and Chinese-Western cultural exchanges. In the autumn of 1935, he traveled

图 49　向达

Fig.49　Xiang Da

献。1938年回国后，先后任浙江大学、西南联合大学教授。抗战胜利后，任北京大学历史系教授兼掌北大图书馆。中华人民共和国成立后，任北京大学历史系教授、图书馆馆长，中国科学院哲学社会科学部委员、历史研究所第二所副所长等。《唐代长安与西域文明》是其学术代表作，奠定了其在学术界的地位。另外还有《大唐西域记古本三种》《中西交通史》《敦煌变文集》(合编)等，译有《斯坦因西域考古记》等。

作为著名敦煌学家的向达，在敦煌学上的贡献是多方面的，下面仅对20世纪40年代向达先生从事敦煌考察的成就作一简述。

第一次敦煌考察

据向达先生《西征小记》记述："三十一年(1942年)春，"国立中央研究院"有西北史地考察团之

to several cities in Europe, including London, Paris, and Berlin, to study Dunhuang and Turfan documents. After he returned in 1938, he served as a professor at Zhejiang University and then at the National Southwest Associated University. Later he became a professor in the History Department and director of the Library of Peking University after China's victory in the War of Resistance Against Japanese Aggression. Afterward, he held several other posts, including serving as a committee member in the Department of Philosophy and Social Sciences in the Chinese Academy of Sciences, and as the deputy director of the History Research Institute. His masterpiece, *Chang'an and the Civilizations of the Western Regions in the Tang Dynasty*, established his position in academia. His other works include *Three Ancient Versions of Buddhist Records of the Western Regions*, *The History of Communication Between China and the West*, *An Anthology of Dunhuang Bianwen*; and his translated work of Aurel Stein's *Ruins of Desert Cathay: Personal Narrative of Explorations in Central Asia and Westernmost China.*

As a great scholar, Xiang Da made contributions to Dunhuang studies in different areas. The following is only a brief overview of his achievements in the expedition of Dunhuang during the 1940s.

The First Expedition to Dunhuang

In the article "Notes on a Westward Expedition," Xiang Da wrote, "In the spring of 1942, the Academia Sinica set up a team to explore northwestern history and geography in Gansu,

组织。考察范围为甘肃、宁夏、青海三省，其用意于纯粹的学术研究外，盖亦思以其所得供当时从事西北建设者之参考。”由此可见，当时的学术考察，也有一定的现实目的，即在抗战的艰难时期，想开发大后方，为现实服务。

1942年4月中旬，中央研究院“西北史地考察团”即在重庆组建。西北农学院院长辛树炽任团长，中国地理研究所所长李承三任总干事兼地理组主任，北京大学教授向达任历史组主任，同济大学教授吴静禅任植物组主任，中央研究院历史语言研究所劳干为历史组组员兼文书，史语所的石璋如为历史组组员兼会计，地理所的周廷儒为地理组组员兼事务。5月4日，全团成员到达兰州后，各组分别进行工作。而向达先生由于当时正在昆明的西南联大任教，并要赴重庆安排家属等，故迟至10月9日

Ningxia, and Qinghai. Apart from doing pure academic research, another purpose of this expedition was to provide guidance for the development of the northwest at the time." It can thus be seen that the academic research had a certain practical purpose: to explore the northwestern areas of China during the harsh period of the War of Resistance Against Japanese Aggression.

In the mid-April 1942, the Northwestern Historical and Geographical Expedition was established in Chongqing. The following personnel were appointed: Xin Shuchi, president of Northwest Agricultural College, served as the head of the expedition; Li Chengsan, director of the Geography Research Institute of China, served as secretary-general and the head of the geography team; Xiang Da, a professor at Peking University, served as the head of the history team; Wu Jingchan, a professor at Tongji University, served as the head of the botany team; Lao Gan from the History and Language Institute of the Academia Sinica served as a member and the secretary of the history team; Shi Zhangru from the History and Language Institute served as a member and the accountant of the history team; and Zhou Tingru from the Geography Institute served as a member and the service staff of the geography team. On May 4, upon arriving in Lanzhou, all the teams started their work except Xiang Da, who postponed his journey to Dunhuang until October 9, because he had to finish his teaching work at the National Southwest Associated University, and also because he had to make arrangements for his

才到敦煌。正如《西征小记》所述："余应研究院之约，奉校命参加考察。以滇西变起仓卒，交通艰阻，迟至八月方克入川。九月下旬自渝抵兰，十月初西行，经武威、张掖、酒泉，出嘉峪关以抵敦煌。"

9日中午到达敦煌后，向达先生即于下午4时启程赴莫高窟，晚8时到达后住于中寺。从此在敦煌一带考察、生活达九个多月。《西征小记》记其事曰："余于三十一年十月九日午抵敦煌，下午即去千佛洞，住其间者凡九阅月。中于同年十月中旬至南湖一访阳关遗址，三十二年三月旬往游大方盘、小方盘，探玉关之胜迹，访河仓之旧城。其年四月复自敦煌至南湖，由南湖北行越中戈壁以至西湖，再访玉关，然后东行以归敦煌。五月至安西，礼万

family in Chongqing. He recorded in "Notes on a Westward Expedition": "On invitation by the Research Institute, I participated in the exploratory commission, but traffic was blocked in western Yunnan Province, delaying my arrival in Sichuan until August; I then reached Lanzhou in late September. At the beginning of October, I continued traveling westward through Wuwei, Zhangye, Jiuquan, and the Jiayu Pass, and then on to Dunhuang at last."

After he arrived in Dunhuang at midday on October 9, Xiang Da set out at 4 o'clock in the afternoon and reached the Mogao Caves at 8 o'clock, spending the night in the middle temple. He stayed there to conduct his field research for more than nine months. He recorded his experience in "Notes on a Westward Expedition": "After I arrived in Dunhuang at noon on October 9, 1942, I headed for the Thousand Buddha Caves (the Mogao Caves) in the afternoon. I lived there for the next nine months, except for short periods when I traveled to explore other places. For example, in mid-October, I went to Nanhu Lake to look at the ruins of the Yangguan Pass, and in March of the next year I traveled to the Big Fangpan Warehouse and the Small Fangpan Warehouse to explore the amazing site of the Yumen Pass and the old city of Hecang. In April, I headed towards Nanhu Lake from Dunhuang, and traveled northward through the middle of the Gobi desert to Xihu Lake. Then I revisited the Yumen Pass, and continued eastward, to return to Dunhuang. In May, I went to Anxi and stayed there to explore the cave shrines of the Ten Thousand Buddha Gorge (the Yulin Caves) for one week and then came back to the Thousand Buddha Caves (the Mogao Caves). In July, I returned to Chongqing. I

图 50　西北史地考察团由兰州赴敦煌途中

Fig.50　Northwestern Historical and Geographical Expedition on the Road from Lanzhou to Dunhuang

佛峡诸窟，历时一周，复返千佛洞。七月遂东归返川。以在敦煌历时稍久，见闻较多。”

向达先生到达千佛洞的第二天（10 日），就与西北史地考察团地理组成员、教育部艺术文物考察团(即王子云率领的考察团)成员以及张大千会面，并由艺术文物考察团的卢善群导游，游览了莫高窟。

随后，向达就赴南湖一带考察，他考察了西千佛

stayed in Dunhuang for a long time and learned a tremendous amount.”

On the day after his arrival at the Mogao Caves, Xiang Da met with members of the geography team of Northwestern Historical and Geographical Expedition and the members of the Northwestern Art and Cultural Relics Expedition (led by Wang Ziyun), as well as Zhang Daqian. Meanwhile, Xiang visited the caves, guided by Lu Shanqun.

Later Xiang Da went to the Nanhu Lake area, where he explored the Western Thousand Buddha Caves, the ruins of Shouchang City, Gudongtan, and the Yangguan Pass. After he returned to the Mogao Caves on the 23rd of that month, he focused on the caves there, making

洞、寿昌城遗址、古董滩、阳关等地。23日回到莫高窟后，即潜心于洞窟考察，同时还作详细的记录。到了11月初，向达已对莫高窟的三分之一洞窟作了详细考察。有感于张大千一行任意勾勒、剥离壁画，他用三天的时间，写成了在敦煌学和莫高窟历史上有重大影响的《论敦煌千佛洞的管理研究以及其他连带的几个问题》，建议将千佛洞收归国有，由学术机构管理。他将此文寄给傅斯年，请其推荐发表。该文经傅斯年推荐，以“方回”为笔名，在《大公报》1942年12月27日至30日连载刊登。

在撰写和寄送《论敦煌千佛洞的管理研究以及其他连带的几个问题》一文的同时，向达还给中央研究院史语所的傅斯年、李济和中央博物馆的曾昭燏写信，既汇报西行考察情况，又谈及张大千破坏壁画及千佛洞保护问题。在致曾昭燏的信中，向达写道：“最近骝先先生（教育部长朱家骅）来电，嘱

detailed field notes. By early November, Xiang Da had carefully studied about one third of the Mogao Caves. Shocked and frustrated by Zhang Daqian's team, who had carelessly drawn on the wall paintings and even peeled off layers from some of them, Xiang Da wrote an influential article on the history of Dunhuang studies over the next three days with the title "On the Administration and Research of the Thousand Buddha Caves (the Mogao Caves) in Dunhuang and Related Issues." In the article, he suggested that the Mogao Caves should be made a national heritage site and put under the supervision of an academic institution. Later, he sent this article to Fu Sinian and asked him for a recommendation for publication. With the help of Fu, the article, under the pseudonym of "Fang Hui," was published in a series in the newspaper *Ta Kung Pao* from December 27 to 30, 1942.

Besides writing and publishing the article, Xiang Da also wrote letters to Fu Sinian and Li Ji at the History and Language Institute of the Academia Sinica, and Zeng Zhaoyu in the Central Museum, to give an account of his expedition, the mural destruction by Zhang Daqian, and the condition of the Mogao Caves. In his letter to Zeng, he wrote, "Zhu Jiahua, the minister of education, telegraphed me recently, advising me to stay here for some time and not to send written reports back, because the work here is to be continued and the plan for the next year is being drafted. So I intend to stay here for

論敦煌千佛洞的管理研究以及其他連帶的幾個問題（中）

方回

图 51　1942 年，向达发表在《大公报》的文章

Fig.51　Article of Xiang Da Published in *Ta Kung Pao*, 1942

暂留此，不必亟返，西北工作，尚待继续，正拟明年计划云云。达拟在此再留三月，将千佛洞逐窟作一详细记录，于每一窟之壁画塑像名目、保存情形、前人题记等一一备录，整理蒇事，往安西万佛峡一游，再访布隆吉遗存洞窟，然后东归酒泉，以待后命。”在给李济、傅斯年的信中也

another three months to record each cave temple in detail, including the names of statues in each cave, their current condition, and any inscriptions by predecessors. In addition, I plan to visit the Ten Thousand Buddha Gorge (the Yulin Caves) in Anxi, and then the remaining caves in Bulongji. Afterward, I will return to Jiuquan in the east to await further orders.” In his letters to Li Ji and Fu Sinian, Xiang Da also wrote, “My current plan is to survey all the caves three times and to note down various details at length, such as the degree of preservation of the murals and statues, and the inscriptions of

说:“目前计划，拟普看三遍，将各窟壁画、塑像保存情形，供养人题记诸项，逐窟详予纪录。”

随后，向达对莫高窟诸窟进行了比较详细的考察，又对敦煌周围各地如西北长城沿线的大方盘城（河仓城)、小方盘城(玉门关)等进行了考察，抄写了一些当时能在敦煌见到的文书。

7 月初从敦煌东归，20 日到兰州，26 日赴重庆，结束了第一次敦煌考察。

向达的第一次敦煌考察，固然有巨大的成绩，但也有许多的无奈。在向达看来，他参加考察团，乃是代表北京大学，而考察的组织者是中央研究院和中央博物馆，只有历史组是与北大合作，而北大也只有向达一人参加，再加上当时可能没有形成文字的协议，而向达又由于诸事迟到约四个月，在考察团及历史组诸位心中，就有意或无意地未将向达看成考察团的成员，甚至没有给向达留下必需的经费。向达在

donors.”

Later, Xiang Da did in fact make detailed records of each cave as well as surrounding sites, such as the Big Fangpan Warehouse (Hecang City) and the Small Fangpan Warehouse (the Yumen Pass), and he also transcribed some Dunhuang manuscripts available to him then.

In early July, he finished his first expedition and started his journey back. He reached Lanzhou on July 20 and then arrived in Chongqing on July 26.

In spite of the achievements of his first expedition, Xiang Da became disappointed and disillusioned during the journey. From his point of view, he had participated in the expedition on behalf of Peking University, but in fact it was the Academia Sinica and the Central Museum that had organized the expedition, rather than Peking University. Only the history team had collaborated with Peking University, and Xiang Da was the only participant from Peking University. Moreover, because he had no written agreement and due to his four-month delay in joining the team, Xiang Da felt that he was excluded from the team and even deprived of funds that were indispensable for his follow-up work. He wrote to Zeng Zhaoyu on March 5, 1943, “Regrettably, the Northwestern Historical and Geographical Expedition was launched by the Academia Sinica and the Central Museum, and the history team was actually a cooperative organization between the two and Peking University. I participated in this expedition on behalf of my university, not personally, so I

1943年3月5日致曾昭燏的信中就提到了这一点："所不幸者，西北史地考察团之组织，虽出自研究院与博物院，而历史组则为两者与北大合作之事业。而达之来，亦为代表学校，并非以个人资格参加，此种情形，最少北大方面，有此谅解。惜呼考察团自组织以至出发，于此点未尝正式声明；历史、考古两组中人，于此中经过，尤其未能明了。"

expected Peking University at least to understand my position. It was a shame that the expedition team did not make any official claim about this from the beginning. Even the members of the history and archeology teams knew nothing about this."

图52　1942年，石璋如和劳干在莫高窟

Fig.52　Shi Zhangru and Lao Gan at the Mogao Caves, 1942

另外，当向达于 1942 年到达敦煌时，张大千一行和王子云率领的教育部“西北艺术文物考察团”也在千佛洞。张大千等人居住在莫高窟上寺，向达住在上寺隔壁的中寺，王子云一行则住在稍微远一些的下寺。

从现有资料看来，向达与王子云率领的“西北艺术文物考察团”的关系比较融洽，而与张大千一行的关系则比较紧张，其原因可能与前述向达对敦煌艺术的看法，尤其是在《大公报》发表的文章有关。

当傅斯年将向达的《论敦煌千佛洞的管理研究以及其他连带的几个问题》交《大公报》发表时，虽然用了“方回”的笔名，但从文章的内容，尤其是傅斯年在按语中所说“此君乃今日史学界之权威，其研究中外交通，遍观各国所藏敦煌遗物，尤称独步”的话中，人们不难知道作者是谁。当张大千得知此事后，双方的关系就开始紧张起来，有的朋友甚至为向达的安全考虑。向达的文章发表不久，甘肃省政府主

Furthermore, when Xiang Da arrived in Dunhuang in 1942, Zhang Daqian's team and the Northwestern Art and Cultural Relics Expedition led by Wang Ziyun were also in the Mogao Caves. Zhang's team stayed in the upper temple, Xiang Da was in the middle temple—next door—and Wang's team were in the lower temple, slightly further away.

According to available documents, Xiang Da got along well with Wang's team, but his relationship with Zhang's team was tense, probably because they had differing views on Dunhuang art, and especially because of the complaints Xiang Da had raised in his article published in the newspaper *Ta Kung Pao*.

Although Fu Sinian had submitted the article to *Ta Kung Pao* under the pseudonym of "Fang Hui," it was easy to deduce the writer from the content of the article, especially from the remarks by Fu in the annotations, "The writer, who is an authority in historiography circles, has studied Dunhuang relics collected both at home and abroad, and is justifiably regarded as an unmatched scholar." The publication of this article created a tense relationship between Xiang Da and Zhang's team, causing some friends even to worry about Xiang Da's safety. Soon after the publication of the article, Gu Zhenglun, chairman of Gansu Provincial Government, sent a telegraph to the governor of Dunhuang county in late March which read, "There have been a number of complaints from all sides about Zhang Daqian's long stay in Dunhuang.

席谷正伦就在 3 月中下旬致电敦煌县长:"张君大千，久留敦煌，中央各方，颇有烦言。敕转告张君大千，对于壁画，勿稍污损，免滋误会。"

Please tell him not to deface the murals, for fear of causing any misunderstanding."

第二次敦煌考察

The Second Expedition to Dunhuang

1943 年，中央研究院史语所、中央博物馆筹备处、中国地理研究所与北京大学文科研究所又组织了"西北科学考察

In 1943, the Northwestern Scientific Research Expedition was organized by the History and Language Institute of the Academia Sinica, the Preparatory Office of the Central Museum, the Geography Research Institute of China, and the Art Research Institute of Peking University. Xia Nai, from the History and Language Institute, Li Chengsan and Zhou Tingru,

图 53 考古学家夏鼐(1910—1985)

Fig.53 Archaeologist Xia Nai (1910–1985)

团”。史语所派夏鼐参加，中国地理研究所派李承三、周廷儒参加，北大文科研究所派向达、阎文儒参加。这次组建“西北科学考察团”的目的和上次一样，除了纯粹的学术研究外，主要是为当时的西北建设服务，以考察“所得供从事西北建设者之参考”，因此，除了历史考古组外，还有地理组、地质组、矿产组、动物组、植物组等。

早在第一次考察时，向达就曾极力推荐夏鼐为第二次敦煌考察的负责人，但“西北科学考察团”任命向达为考古组组长，夏鼐、阎文儒为成员。夏鼐虽然是考古学科班出身，但他对向达的道德文章非常敬佩，而阎文儒又是向达在北大文科研究所的研究生，正是因为有这样的关系，所以他们三人的合作是很愉快的。

考察组原计划 1943 年 9 月出发，临行前由于夏鼐先生生病而不得不推迟

from the Geography Research Institute of China, as well as Xiang Da and Yan Wenru, from the Art Research Institute of Peking University, were all members. The purpose of the second expedition was the same as the first: to do academic research and to aid the development of northwestern China. In addition to the archeology team, a geography team, a geology team, a mineralogy team, a zoology team, and a botany team were also components of the expedition.

As early as the beginning of the first expedition, Xiang Da had strongly recommended Xia Nai's appointment as the team leader, but instead Xiang was appointed as the leader of the archeology team, with Xia Nai and Yan Wenru as team members. Xia greatly admired the morality Xiang displayed in his articles—although Xia himself was a professional archeologist—and Yan was taught by Xiang in his postgraduate studies at the Research Institute of Arts of Peking University. This past acquaintance laid a solid foundation for a friendly cooperation among the three.

The team had originally planned to depart in September 1943, but they were delayed for about six months because Xia unexpectedly became ill. On March 21, 1944, Xiang flew to Lanzhou from Chongqing, while Xia was forced to take the next flight to Lanzhou on April 4, due to limited seats. After they had both arrived, the archeological expedition was officially launched. On April 17, they rushed to the Hexi area for an expedition, and on May 12, Yan Wenru joined them in Jiuquan. On May 14, they headed back westward from Jiuquan, via Yumen and Anxi, and arrived

了半年。1944 年 3 月 21 日，向达由重庆飞抵兰州，夏鼐乘下一航班于 4 月 4 日抵兰（由于飞机座位有限的缘故），开始了考古组的工作。17 日，向达、夏鼐即赴河西考察。5 月 12 日，考察团另一成员阎文儒赶到，于酒泉汇合后，14 日，又从酒泉启程西行，经玉门到安西，19 日早晨抵敦煌，22 日参观千佛洞，30 日移住佛爷庙工作站，31 日开始发掘魏晋墓葬。

第二次敦煌考察，向达的时间更少，只有 4 个多月。当佛爷庙西区墓地的发掘工作结束后，向达即于 10 月 19 日启程东归。31 日，夏鼐、阎文儒由敦煌前往西北汉长城遗址考察，发掘了小方盘城北的汉代遗址和大方盘城东南土台，获得汉代简牍若干及晋泰始十一年乐生题记石。12 月 6 日，夏鼐、阎文儒赴安西、酒泉考察。1945 年 2 月 17 日回到兰州，随后又曾到武威、民勤、张掖等地发掘考察。

第二次敦煌考察，除了对阳关、玉门关、河仓城等著

at Dunhuang on the morning of May 19. On May 22, they visited the Mogao Caves and moved in to live at their temporary base at Foyemiao on May 30. The next day they started excavating tombs from the Wei and Jin dynasties.

Xiang Da's second expedition only lasted about four months. After completing the excavation of the western cemetery at Foyemiao, Xiang headed back home on October 19. On October 31, Xia Nai and Yan Wenru left Dunhuang and traveled to the remains of the Han Dynasty Great Wall, where they excavated Han relics located north of the Small Fangpan Warehouse as well as the earthen banks to the southeast of the Big Fangpan Warehouse. They discovered dozens of bamboo and wooden slips from the Han Dynasty and stones with inscriptions written by musicians during the 11th year (275) of Taishi Era of the Jin Dynasty (265–420). They went to Anxi and Jiuquan on December 6, and returned to Lanzhou on February 17, 1945. After that, they occasionally went to Wuwei, Minqin, and Zhangye to do further research.

Apart from the expedition of the ruins of the Yangguan Pass, the Yumen Pass, and Hecang, the team also made discoveries in their excavations of cemeteries. Xiang Da, in his "Notes on a Westward Expedition" wrote, "I first arrived in Dunhuang in the winter of 1942, and heard about mounds of gravel on the way from Foyemiao to the Mogao Caves, which were thought to indicate the existence of an

图 54　考古学家阎文儒(1912—1994)
Fig.54　Archaeologist Yan Wenru (1912–1994)

名遗址进行考察外，还在墓葬的发掘方面做出了成绩。向达在《西征小记》中曾说:“三十一年冬始至敦煌，即闻人言佛爷庙至千佛洞中途戈壁上有砾石堆甚多，疑是古代墓葬遗址。”“就其形式观之，与斯坦因、黄仲良(文弼)诸人在高昌所发掘之六朝以及隋、唐古墓绝相类似，则其为古代之墓葬群，盖无可疑也。”在 1943 年 1 月 13 日致曾昭燏信中，向达先生

ancient cemetery. With regards to their external form, they were quite similar to the ancient cemeteries of the Six Dynasties[①] (222–589), the Sui (581–618), and the Tang (618–907) that were discovered by Stein and Huang Zhongliang in Gaochang. Thus, it was undoubtedly an ancient burial ground.” In his letter to Zeng Zhaoyu on January 13, 1943, Xiang said, “We found more than one hundred cemeteries along the Gobi desert between the Mogao Caves and Dunhuang, most of which are rectangular in form... In my opinion, they are the graves of Shazhou (an ancient name for Dunhuang)

① Six Dynasties refers to the Wu, Eastern Jin, Song, Qi, Liang, and Chen dynasties.

说:"近在千佛洞至敦煌中途戈壁上，见到古代墓葬群百余，大都作长方形……达以为此是唐代沙州人墓地，毫无可疑。盖唐代沙州，距千佛洞二十五里，在其西北，适当今敦煌人称为佛爷庙之地，至今其地废基颓垣，弥望皆是，迤逦长达数里。按诸距千佛洞里数、方位，俱甚相合，而墓葬群即在古沙州东南约五里左右，南为鸣沙山，不能营葬地，则此必是墓地也。"

向达的这种推论，1944 年就被考古组的发掘所证实。

1944 年 6 月 30 日至 7 月 11 日，向达、夏鼐、阎文儒在敦煌城东约 9 公里的佛爷庙发掘了一墓葬，其墓门内两侧站立着一对高 1. 2 米的武士像，在武士像稍后的右首，站立着一对骆驼，高达 0. 85 米，各有一个驼夫牵引。再向后就是放置木棺的平台，台前排立着大批的小陶俑，共 41 件。这些马夫和驼夫，都身穿大翻领的狭袖短大衣，足穿长筒的黑靴子。其中的两个不仅穿胡服，而且高鼻圆目，发辫盘在头

people from the Tang Dynasty. Shazhou, which is the area now known as Foyemiao, was about 25 *li* (8 miles) to the northwest of the Mogao Caves during the Tang Dynasty. There the deserted, barren land stretches as far as the eye can see. Its location and distance from Mogao tallies with the written records. Furthermore, it must be a cemetery because the burial ground was recorded to be about 5 *li* (2 miles) to the southeast of ancient Shazhou, with the Mingsha Mountain to its south. Nowhere else could be found that held so many tombs."

This conclusion was confirmed by subsequent excavations by the archeological team in 1944.

From June 30 until July 11, 1944, Xiang Da, together with Xia Nai and Yan Wenru, excavated a tomb at Foyemiao, almost nine kilometers to the east of Dunhuang City. A pair of warrior statues stood on each side of the tomb door respectively. Each statue was 1.2 meters in height, and behind each warrior on their right was a pair of camel statues, 0.85 meter tall, each drawn by a camel driver. Further back, there was a flat platform on which a coffin would have been placed, with 41 small clay figurines standing in front. The camel drivers were dressed in narrow-sleeved jackets with wide lapels and long black boots. Two of them were wearing Hu ethnic clothing, and they had high-bridged noses, round eyes, and braided hair; these were probably statues of Hu

图 55　西北科学考察团历史考古组在佛爷庙进行考古测量
Fig.55　Archeology Team of the Northwestern Scientific Research Expedition at the Foyemiao Site

上，可能血统也是胡人。此外，还有带金箔的铜片、开元通宝钱、玻璃细条和玻璃珠等。从其内容判断，它是盛唐时代的墓葬。

科学考察结束后，考察团成员利用历史考古所得，撰写了丰富的研究成果，如向达先生的《西征小记》《两关杂考》《莫高、榆林二窟杂考》《罗叔言〈补唐书张义潮传〉补正》《记敦煌石室出晋天福十年写本寿昌县地境》，夏鼐先生的《新获之敦煌汉简》

people. Also in the tomb were gilded copper coins, Kaiyuan Tongbao coins from the Tang Dynasty (618–907), as well as thin strips and beads made from glass. On inspecting all the objects found in the tomb, the archaeologists could deduce that the tomb was built during the High Tang period (713–766).

After finishing their field work, the expedition members made full use of the materials they had found to publish a series of works. Xiang Da's published research includes "Notes on a Westward Expedition," "A Miscellaneous Study of the Yumen Pass and the Yangguan Pass," "A Miscellaneous Study of the Mogao and Yulin Caves," "Addenda to 'Supplementary Information on the Biography of Zhang Yichao during the Tang Dynasty' by Luo Shuyan," and "Record of Jin Dynasty 'Geography of Shouchang County' Unearthed in the Dunhuang Caves." Xia Nai published the following: "Newly Discovered Dunhuang Han Bamboo and Wooden Slips," "Newly Discovered Han Bamboo and

《玉门关发掘新获的汉简》《武威唐代吐谷浑慕容氏墓志》《敦煌考古漫记》，阎文儒先生的《河西考古杂记》等。

而向达先生发表的《论敦煌千佛洞的管理研究及其连带的几个问题》，在敦煌学史上占有非常重要的地位。他关于保护千佛洞的建议，对促进“敦煌艺术研究所”的设立起了重要作用。

Wooden Slips Unearthed at the Yumen Pass," "Epitaph of the Murong Family of Tuyuhun in the Tang Dynasty from Wuwei," and "Records on the Expedition to Dunhuang." Yan Wenru published "Miscellaneous Records on the Expedition to Hexi."

Of all their research publications, Xiang Da's article"On the Administration and Research of the Thousand Buddha Caves (the Mogao Caves) in Dunhuang and Several Other Incidental Problems" played an especially important role in the study of the history of Dunhuang. His suggestions for preserving the Mogao Caves encouraged the establishment of the National Research Institute on Dunhuang Art.

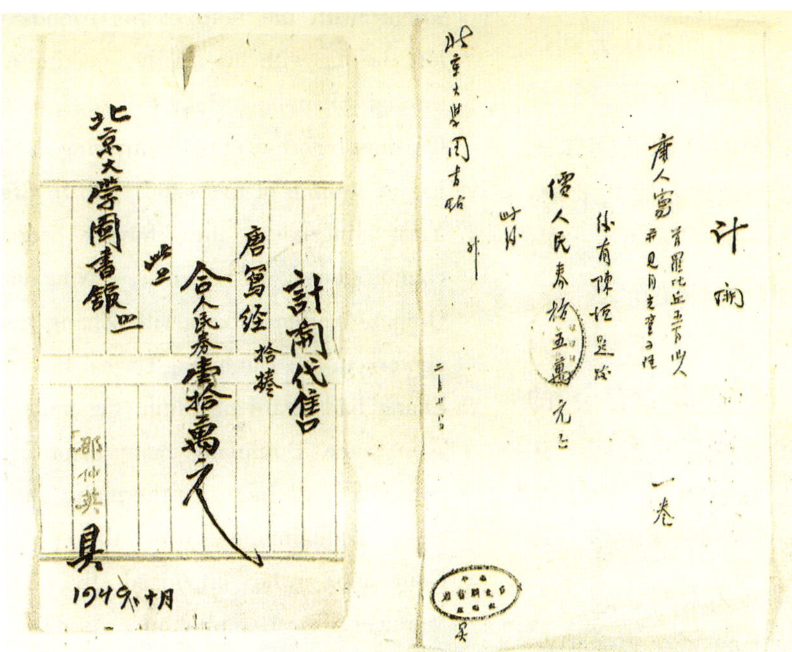

图 56　20 世纪 50 年代购买敦煌文献的收据及向达先生的信函

Fig.56　Xiang Da's Receipt for Purchase of Dunhuang Documents and Personal Correspondence, circa 1950s

面壁敦煌的张大千

Zhang Daqian in Dunhuang

西北有深厚的文化底蕴，敦煌的艺术世界闻名。因此，在抗日战争时期各方关注西北的浪潮中，敦煌也就为世人所瞩目。张大千也正是在这种背景下赴敦煌的。

抗战开始时，张大千住在北平。1938 年初夏，在朋友们的帮助下，张大千携家属离开北平，绕道上海、香港、广西、贵州，于同年秋天到达成都。在成都时，曾担任过甘宁青监察使的严敬斋向张大千多次谈到敦煌石窟艺术。在此之前，张大千已经听说过敦煌，还亲眼见过零散的敦煌写经和绢画。在北平时，他与发起组织“敦煌经籍辑存会”的书画家叶恭绰交往密切。在抗日炮火中的成都，张大千无事可做，当听到严敬斋多次谈到敦煌艺术时，他的心动了。他查阅了有关敦煌的资料后，于 1940 年秋决定：西出嘉峪关，前往敦煌。

Dunhuang art is known throughout the world for its record of the vast history of northwestern China. During the War of Resistance Against Japanese Aggression, because much attention was being given to the northwest, Dunhuang also caught the attention of the wider world. Zhang Daqian went to Dunhuang under these conditions.

Zhang had lived in Beijing before the War of Resistance Against Japanese Aggression, until the early summer of 1938, when—with the help of his friends—Zhang left Beijing with his family, making a detour through Shanghai, Hong Kong, Guangxi, and Guizhou before eventually arriving in Chengdu in the autumn of the same year. In Chengdu, Yan Jingzhai, the former supervisory commissioner of Gansu, Ningxia, and Qinghai, often talked with Zhang about the artwork in the Dunhuang Caves. Prior to this, Zhang had heard of Dunhuang and also had seen some Dunhuang manuscript fragments and silk paintings. Furthermore, he had a close acquaintance with the painter Ye Gongchuo, who organized the Dunhuang Manuscripts Compilation Association in Beijing. But the flames of war were raging around Chengdu, and Zhang had no choice but to remain at home, though Yan Jingzhai's

当张大千行至广元，正欲动身前往甘肃麦积山时，传来了噩耗——为抗日赈灾回国才半个月的二哥张善子，因劳累过度，旧病复发，于 10 月 20 日在重庆去世。张大千仓促回重庆奔丧。同年底，张大千的长子张心亮因病在西安去世，年仅 18 岁。张大千“方哭兄逝，又哭子亡，此等刺激真非寻常人所能受者”。第一次敦煌之行就这样流产了。

1941 年 5 月，张大千带着夫人杨宛君、次子张心智再赴敦煌。

在当时那种艰难困苦的条件下，张大千义无反顾地去敦煌，是有多种原因的，除了敦煌作为艺术宝库的吸引外，张大千个人也想通过敦煌探求中国艺术的源流。另外还有一个原因，就是张大千听从叶恭绰的建议，为改变画风去敦煌学习技法。叶恭绰素赏张大千的画，曾力劝张大千弃山水花竹专攻

repeated conversations with Zhang about Dunhuang art had sparked his interest. After doing some preliminary research, Zhang Daqian decided to set out for Dunhuang via the Jiayu Pass in the autumn of 1940.

After Zhang arrived in Guangyuan and was about to depart for the Maiji Mountain in Gansu, however, he received some tragic news: his elder brother, Zhang Shanzi, who had returned home on sick leave for half a month, had died on October 20 in Chongqing from over-work and exhaustion. Zhang rushed back for his brother's funeral. To make things worse, Zhang's eldest son, Zhang Xinliang, who was only 18 years old, died of an illness in Xi'an before the end of the year. Grieving from the death of his family members, Zhang abandoned his first trip to Dunhuang halfway.

In May 1941, Zhang—this time together with his wife Yang Wanjun, and his younger son Zhang Xinzhi—headed to Dunhuang once again.

Despite the difficult conditions at the time, Zhang had several reasons for his determination to reach Dunhuang: first, Dunhuang was a treasury of art, which naturally attracted Zhang, who wanted to explore the origins of Chinese art; second, following Ye Gongchuo's advice, Zhang went to Dunhuang to learn new techniques for improving his style of painting. Because Ye appreciated Zhang's talent in painting, he persuaded Zhang to abandon landscape painting and to focus on figure painting instead, so as to return figure painting to greater prominence in China.

人物，以刷新我国人物画的颓风。

当时的西北、当时的河西、当时的敦煌，其自然、气候、交通、物产等各方面都是比较差的，曾有"一出嘉峪关，两眼泪不干。前看戈壁滩，后望鬼门关"之说。当1941年张大千一行到达嘉峪关时，曾对随行的人说：在成都出发以前，就有人介绍了西北的艰苦情况，还特别说到河西走廊和关外（嘉峪关以西），说路上吃的是凉水拌炒面，有时没有水喝，实在不行，还要啃西瓜皮，甚至喝马尿。我们现在的条件应该说是比较好的，起码还不至于喝马尿，但要准备吃苦。《西游记》里的唐僧带着他的三个徒弟，历尽千辛万苦才到西方取经，我们到敦煌来，也是为了取"经"，不过这是取艺术上的"经"。我们的条件比唐僧好多了，吃的苦也比唐僧差远了。

到达莫高窟的前三天，张大千一直陪同范振绪参

At the time of their journey, they were faced with a harsh climate, poor transportation, and inadequate food supplies in the northwest. A line from a classic poem depicts the Hexi Corridor area and Dunhuang, "Out of the Jiayu Pass / Tears well up in the eyes / In front of you is the Gobi desert / Behind you is the gate to hell." When Zhang and his team arrived at the Jiayu Pass, he recalled, "Before we left Chengdu, I had been warned about the brutal conditions in the northwest, especially in the Hexi Corridor and west of the Jiayu Pass. Travelers in the past only had dried flour mixed with water and sometimes were even forced to eat watermelon rinds and drink horse urine if water ran out during their journey. Compared to that of the past, our conditions are relatively better, but hardships are unavoidable. The journey is a little like the one described in the book *Journey to the West*, where Xuanzang and his three disciples, after experiencing all kinds of hardships, finally obtain Buddhist sutras in the Western Paradise. Our visit to Dunhuang is to seek the essence of art—the genuine techniques of painting. Luckily, we have much better conditions than Xuanzang, who suffered a lot."

During the first three days after their arrival at the Mogao Caves, Zhang, escorting Fan Zhenxu, visited the cave temples there. After Fan left, Zhang began to explore and document what he saw. In order to record the murals, Zhang had to produce exact copies of them by painting. A ladder was necessary for the

图 57 张大千在莫高窟住地上寺门前逗玩喂养的黄鸭(1941 年春)
Fig.57 Zhang Daqian Feeding Ducks in Front of the Upper Temple, Spring, 1941

观石窟。范振绪离开后，他就开始了考察和记录。由于许多壁画需要拷贝、用画稿记录下来，因此，很多地方就要先搭上梯子，高处要用绳子把两架梯子连接在一起，有时还需要两副梯子并排而立，一架梯子由张大千记录，一架由别人提着马灯照明。这样工作起来，既慢又危险，张大千就请来了两位油工师傅——窦占彪和李复(中华人民共和国成立后，他们二人都在

artist to stand on, and if the murals were too high, two ladders were connected together with a rope. Sometimes two ladders were placed side by side, one supporting Zhang who was copying the wall paintings, and the other supporting an assistant who was holding a lantern. This way of working was not only inefficient, but also dangerous. Zhang asked two oil painters to help him: Dou Zhanbiao and Li Fu, both of whom later worked in the Research Institute on Cultural Relics of Dunhuang (present-day Dunhuang Academy) after the founding of the People's Republic of China. The Commander Ma of the military troops stationed in the city also sent several soldiers to help and as a result the progress of the project was greatly accelerated.

敦煌文物研究所工作），城里驻军的马团长也派来了几名士兵帮忙，这样就加快了速度。

记录工作进行了四五个月后，张大千对敦煌石窟已有了大致的了解，这时，他改变了原计划，不想马上回成都了，而且还请画家谢稚柳和学生刘力上、肖建初也来敦煌从事壁画的临摹。

在临摹前，张大千为了记录的方便，还给洞窟重新编号。

在临摹壁画前，张大千还到青海请了藏族画师，并买了藏蓝（石青）、藏绿（石绿）、朱砂等矿质颜料。

在石窟里临摹壁画是比较困难的，当临摹大幅壁画的上面部分时，要一手提着煤油灯，一手拿着画笔爬在梯子上，上下仔细观察，看清楚一点就在画布上画一点。而临摹洞窟底部的画面时，就要铺着羊毛毡或油布趴在地上勾线、着色，这样不到一个小时，脖子和手臂就酸得抬不起来。

After the team had been copying the murals for four or five months, Zhang gained a rough understanding of the Mogao Caves, so he changed his original plan. Instead of going back to Chengdu, he invited another painter, Xie Zhiliu, and his students Liu Lishang and Xiao Jianchu, to help make facsimiles of the murals.

Before this, Zhang had been assigning numbers to the caves to make the recording of them more convenient.

Zhang also went to Qinghai to recruit some Tibetan artists for his project and to buy mineral pigments such as azurite, malachite, and cinnabar.

Making copies of the murals was an extremely difficult process, particularly in the caves. To copy the figures on the upper part of one large mural, Zhang had to stand on a ladder and observe the mural from one end to another, with a kerosene lamp in one hand and a brush in the other. Then he would paint it bit by bit on the canvas. While making a copy of the bottom part of a cave, the artist had to kneel down on the ground covered with wool or cloth while drawing lines and adding colors. Consequently, his neck and arms were too sore to lift up after about an hour working this way.

The winter in Dunhuang was intensely cold, and there were no doors in most of the cave temples at Mogao; at the coldest times, dripping water froze almost immediately. To copy a mural, Zhang had to remain in the same position for several hours. Although they were

敦煌的冬天是特别寒冷的，莫高窟的绝大多数洞窟都没有窟门，而一些小窟离洞外又很近，最冷的时候，会滴水成冰，而要临摹一幅壁画，就要在一堵墙壁的某一位置连续工作较长时间，尽管他们身穿老羊皮大衣，但仍然冻得非常难受。有时刚把颜色着在画布上，就被冻住了。张大千也常常是一头砂土，满身颜色，他曾打趣地说："我们简直就跟犯人一样，跑到这里来受徒刑，而且还是心甘情愿！"

从 1941 年 6 月到敦煌，1943 年 10 月离开，在两年多的时间里，张大千除给莫高窟、榆林窟、西千佛洞等编号、记录，写了二十多万字的学术著作《敦煌石室记》外，主要是临摹了敦煌壁画 276 幅，他为调查、临摹、保护、研究、宣传敦煌艺术付出了极大的努力和无数的心血。正如叶浅予在《张大千临摹敦煌壁画画册序》中所说："作为一个在艺术上已有很大成就的画家，为了追寻六朝隋唐遗迹，不避艰辛，投荒面壁将近三载，去完成只有国家

dressed in sheepskin overcoats, it was still difficult to endure the freezing temperatures. Sometimes the paint froze as soon as it touched the canvas, and most of the time Zhang had sand, dust, and paint in his hair and on his clothes. He jokingly said, "It's almost like we're prisoners being tortured here, but we're willing!"

After more than two years, from June 1941 until October 1943 in Dunhuang, apart from numbering and recording the Mogao Caves, the Yulin Caves, and the Western Thousand Buddha Caves, Zhang also finished an academic work of more than 200,000 Chinese characters: *Records of the Dunhuang Caves*. His main contribution was in copying 276 murals, in the process of which he made great progress in investigating, reproducing, protecting, and promoting Dunhuang art. Ye Qianyu remarked in the preface to *Dunhuang Mural Facsimile Paintings by Zhang Daqian*, "As an accomplished painter, Zhang suffered great hardships in Dunhuang, making facsimiles of the murals for nearly three years for the sake of exploring and recording the remains of the Six Dynasties (222–589), the Sui (581–618), and the Tang (618–907) dynasties. He dared to undertake a huge project that ought only to have been possible to accomplish with the support of the government, and his adventures exceeded the demands of academic research. Although the National Research Institute on Dunhuang Art, later founded by the government, did

图 58　张大千在莫高窟临摹壁画
Fig.58　Zhang Daqian's Reproduction of Murals in the Mogao Caves

财力才能做到的事，他的大胆行动已超出个人做学问的范围。尽管后来国家组织了敦煌艺术研究所，为保护石窟和艺术研究做了大量工作，但不能不承认张大千在这个事业上富于想象力的贡献及其先行者的地位。"

张大千在敦煌取得巨大的成绩，其原因是多方面

much for the protection of the caves and artistic research, Zhang's contributions to the study of Dunhuang, as a pioneer in art history, should not be ignored."

Zhang's great success in Dunhuang can be attributed to several causes. In addition to his own artistic skill, three other advantages are worth mentioning: first, he was accompanied by dedicated experts, painters, and volunteers; second, he was assisted by Tibetan artists invited from Qinghai; and third, he was supported by people from all walks of life in the

的。除了他本人的艺术素养外，还有三个有利的条件，即人多，力量集中；有从青海请来的藏族画师协助；得到了西北各方面，尤其是敦煌各界的支持。

由于张大千是有名的画家，其画在市场上很抢手，他在莫高窟时，经常是白天记录、临摹，晚上在所住的上寺作画，然后寄回成都出卖，以维持在敦煌的庞大开支；各地官绅都相继求画，而大千一般也都是有求必应，再加上他和国民党元老、监察院长于右任有深交，和西北地方军政方面如甘肃省参议会副议长范振绪、青海省财政厅厅长魏兰芳等也有交往，同时还得到了青海的土皇帝马步芳，河西走廊驻军骑兵第五军军长、马步芳的哥哥马步青，马步青的女婿、骑兵第五军第五师师长马呈祥等人的帮助，正是有这样许多的因素，他和敦煌的地方长官及达官贵人均能处理好关系，因此能得到各方面的关照，经济上也是很好的。当时同在敦煌的王子云、向达曾对此有记载，如王子云说：我们这个由官方组织的考察团，经费

northwest, particularly in Dunhuang.

Since Zhang was a famous painter, his works were in high demand on the art market. When he was at Mogao, he usually recorded or copied the murals during the day, and painted his own works in the upper temple where he slept at night. He sent his works to Chengdu to be sold in order to meet his substantial expenses in Dunhuang. Zhang had a deep friendship with Yu Youren, a senior statesman of the Kuomintang and head of the Ministry of Supervision. He also kept contact with military and political officials in the northwest such as Fan Zhenxu, vice-president of the Gansu Council, and Wei Lanfang, director of the Qinghai Finance Department. Furthermore, he received assistance from the Ma clan including Ma Bufang, a local autocrat in Qinghai, his brother Ma Buqing, commander of the Fifth Cavalry in the Hexi Corridor, and Ma Buqing's son-in-law Ma Chengxiang, division commander of the Fifth Cavalry. It was for such reasons that he had a good relationship with local officials, and it was due to their support that he had relatively good living conditions there. Wang Ziyun and Xiang Da were also in Dunhuang at the time, as Wang recorded, "Though our expedition team is organized and supported by the government, now and then we're short of money. Zhang, however, arrived

图 59 张大千临摹榆林窟第 17 窟壁画

Fig.59 Zhang Daqian's Reproduction of a Mural in Yulin Cave 17

却微乎其微。张大千虽是私人自费出来临摹，随行的人也不少，但比起我们，则要阔气得多了。

张大千选择了敦煌，敦煌也成就了张大千。由于张大千临摹的敦煌壁画在许多城市展出，使国人知道了敦煌，了解了敦煌艺术。而张大千本人，也通过对敦煌艺术的“触摸”、弘扬，迎来了自己的又一个艺术高峰，成了中国画坛的领袖人物。

张大千对敦煌石窟艺术的贡献是多方面的，首先是他临摹了大批壁画，并在全国各地展出，宣传了敦煌艺术。张大千在敦煌前后居住了近三年，临摹了二百多幅壁画，在重庆、成都、兰州、上海等地都举办过展览，使敦煌艺术为大多数人所了解，甚至可以说，就是张大千开创了敦煌艺术的研究。因为在此之前，敦煌学研究重视的是藏经洞发现的文书，此后，敦煌艺术成了敦煌学研究的另一个重要方面。陈寅恪先生在看过张大

here with many companions and works at his own expense, yet he lives a better life than us."

Zhang contributed to the study of Dunhuang, and Dunhuang offered a platform for him to achieve more. Since his mural reproductions were displayed in many cities, gradually more and more Chinese people learned about Dunhuang and Dunhuang art. By being in direct contact with Dunhuang art and promoting Dunhuang art to the wider world, Zhang reached the zenith of his career: being deemed the greatest living painter in China.

Zhang's contributions to Dunhuang art are numerous: first and foremost, he made a large number of facsimiles of cave murals, up to 200 during his stay in Dunhuang for nearly three years. Meanwhile, he held exhibitions throughout the country, such as in Chongqing, Chengdu, Lanzhou, and Shanghai, through which Dunhuang art was exhibited to the public and as a result, known by ordinary people. It could even be said that it was Zhang who founded the field of Dunhuang art research. Before him, Dunhuang studies mainly focused on manuscripts discovered in the Library Cave, but Zhang's exploration shed light on the cave temple artwork. Chen Yinque, after attending Zhang's exhibition of Dunhuang mural reproductions, wrote about his feelings of delight, "Since the discovery of treasures in Dunhuang, domestic research has been

图 60　张大千临摹敦煌莫高窟《反弹琵琶图》
Fig.60　Zhang Daqian's Reproduction of *Playing the Pipa in Reverse*

千临摹的敦煌壁画展览后，专门写了其观感以推崇："自敦煌宝藏发见以来，吾国人研究此历劫仅存之国宝者，止局于文籍之考证，至艺术方面，则犹有待。大千先生临摹北朝唐五代之壁画，介绍于世人，使得窥见此国宝之一斑，其成绩固已超出以前研究之范围，何况其天才特具，虽是临摹之本，兼有创造之功，实能于吾民族艺术上别辟一新境界，其为敦煌学领域中不朽之盛事，更无论矣。故欢喜赞叹，略缀数语，以告观者。"

其次，张大千还注意学习敦煌艺术遗产，他不仅继承，而且还能推陈出新，发扬光大。他除了临摹敦煌壁画外，还在临摹的同时，创造了新的绘画手法，如他用古代的绘画传统来表现现代题材，使人耳目一新，很受群众喜爱。正是通过敦煌壁画的临摹，使他的线描更加成熟了，在人物画方面也有了长足的进步和很大的发展，可以说，敦煌成就了张大千，敦煌壁画的临摹，使张大千成了一位世界级画家。

再次，张大千对敦煌壁画的临摹，尤其是在各地的展出，不

limited to the historical study of manuscripts, and artistic research has been accorded little significance. Fortunately, by copying the murals of the Northern Dynasty (386–581), the Tang Dynasty (618–907), and the Five Dynasties (907–979), Zhang introduced these treasures to the wider world as well. His achievements in some ways are beyond the previous scope of research. Moreover, as Zhang himself is an extremely talented painter, his skill is apparent in his replicas as well. Indeed, he has opened up a new realm of national art studies, which marks a milestone in the field of Dunhuang studies."

In addition, Zhang Daqian not only learned from Dunhuang art, but also made his own innovations, which helped promote an artistic style as found in Dunhuang murals. In the process of copying the murals, he had created a new painting technique; he adapted a traditional painting approach with more modern themes, which was refreshing and very popular with the masses. His line drawing techniques developed to maturity by making facsimiles, allowing him to make great progress in figure painting. It can be said that Dunhuang provided a channel for Zhang to achieve success in his art; in other words, Zhang became a world-class artist because of his work—creating reproductions of the wall art in Dunhuang.

Furthermore, by copying Dunhuang

图 61　张大千临摹《初唐大势至菩萨》
Fig.61　Zhang Daqian's Reproduction of *Mahasthamaprapta Bodhisattva During the Early Tang Period*

仅宣传了敦煌艺术，而且还带动了敦煌艺术的研究。如段文杰就是在重庆看了画展后，才被吸引到敦煌来的；另如1944年在成都举办画展时，史苇湘还是四川艺专的一年级学生，正是看了画展，才使他对敦煌艺术产生了热爱，并义无反顾地去了敦煌。以段文杰、史苇湘

murals and holding national exhibitions, Zhang Daqian not only promoted Dunhuang art, but pushed the field of Dunhuang art research forward. For example, Duan Wenjie was attracted to Dunhuang after attending Zhang's exhibition in Chongqing. For Shi Weixiang, who was only a first-year student in the Sichuan Arts College when the exhibition was held in Chengdu in 1944, it was Zhang's exhibition that aroused his interest in Dunhuang art, leading him to go

图 62　张大千于台北摩耶精舍"梅丘"巨石前

Fig.62　Zhang Daqian in Front of a Huge Stone Known as "Plum Hill" in Taipei

为代表的一批以石窟艺术研究著称的敦煌学家，将自己的一生都献给了敦煌，如果没有张大千临摹的敦煌壁画展，他们的人生道路可能就是另外一番景象了。

另外，张大千还对敦煌艺术研究所的成立有促进作用。当洞窟编号开始不久，国民政府监察院院长于右任和甘宁青监察使高一涵在甘肃省军政官员的陪同下视察河西走廊来到敦煌。由于张大千和于右任有深交，相互来往、交谈也就随便多了。有次吃饭时，张大千半开玩笑半认真地说：我张大千是一个小小百姓，只是为了追求艺术事业而四处奔波；莫高窟是国宝，斯坦因、伯希和把许多好东西都偷抢去了，你是政府要员，你有责任为保护我们的国宝说几句话啊！同时，张大千还向于右任建议，应该在莫高窟设立专门的研究机构。于右任表示：回到重庆后就向政府有关方面提出成立“敦煌艺术研究院”的设想。

to Dunhuang with no hesitation. Duan and Shi later became leading experts in Dunhuang art. They were known for their research of cave temple art and devoted their entire lives to Dunhuang studies. Had they not attended Zhang's exhibition of Dunhuang art, their lives would have been totally different.

Finally, Zhang Daqian also promoted the establishment of the National Research Institute on Dunhuang Art. Not long before Zhang started numbering the caves, Yu Youren, head of the Ministry of Supervision, and Gao Yihan, supervisory commissioner of Gansu, Ningxia, and Qinghai, came through Dunhuang on their way to inspect the Hexi Corridor, escorted by Gansu military and political officials. Because of the deep friendship between Zhang and Yu, they communicated with each other quite freely. Once while they were having dinner together, Zhang said, half in jest, “I'm only a civilian, running around in pursuit of the arts. The Mogao Caves are a national treasure, but Aurel Stein and Paul Pelliot have removed most of the treasures. As a government official, you have a responsibility to protect our national treasures.” Meanwhile, Zhang suggested that a special research institute be set up to study the Mogao cave temples, which received the support of Yu.

After Yu returned to Chongqing, he submitted a proposal titled “On the Establishment of the National Research Institute on Dunhuang Art” to the authorities at the end of 1941. In February 1942, the

于右任回重庆后，于1941 年底向政府有关方面提交了《建议成立"敦煌艺术学院"案》，1942 年 2 月，此建议案在《文史杂志》上全文发表。1943 年 1 月 18 日，国民政府行政院通过决议：设立敦煌艺术研究所，隶属教育部管理。当日即成立敦煌艺术研究所筹备委员会，聘请高一涵任筹备委员会主任委员，张维、张大千、王子云、常书鸿、郑通和、张庚由、窦景椿 7 人为筹委会委员。

由于各种原因，张大千没有参与敦煌艺术研究所的组建，但不可否认，他对敦煌艺术研究所的成立也是有贡献的，我们应该给予实事求是的评价。当然，还有张大千破坏敦煌艺术一说，此当另论。

proposal was published in full in the *Journal of Literature and History*. On January 18, 1943, the Executive Ministry of the Nationalist Government agreed to establish the National Research Institute on Dunhuang Art as an agency of the Ministry of Education. On the same day, a preparatory committee was formed with Gao Yihan as chairman, and Zhang Wei, Zhang Daqian, Wang Ziyun, Chang Shuhong, Zheng Tonghe, Zhang Gengyou, and Dou Jingchun as committee members.

Zhang Daqian did not participate in the subsequent founding of the National Research Institute on Dunhuang Art, but his contribution to its establishment cannot be denied.

常书鸿和“敦煌人”

Chang Shuhong and the “Dunhuangers”

这里所说的“敦煌人”，是指“文革”前到莫高窟，对敦煌石窟的保护、临摹、研究作出了贡献的人士。他们之中，有些可能一生都坚守在敦煌，既献了青春又献了子孙，有些只是短暂的停留；有些可能成了享誉国际学界的著名敦煌学专家，有些可能还名不见经传，只是默默耕耘在敦煌大沙漠中的普通人士。无论如何，凡是在过去那种艰难困苦的条件下工作在敦煌的“敦煌人”，都是值得我们景仰的。

常书鸿先生是“敦煌人”的代表，被誉为“敦煌守护神”，他将自己的一生都献给了敦煌。

1935 年底，在法国巴黎留学的常书鸿，偶然在巴黎塞纳河畔的旧书摊上发现了伯希和的《敦煌图录》，并自此与敦煌结下了不解之缘。“拿远古的西洋文艺发展的早期历史与我们敦煌石窟艺术相比较，无论在时代上或在艺术表现技法上，

The term “Dunhuangers” refers to those people who came to Dunhuang before the Cultural Revolution and who made contributions to protecting and recording the items they found in the Mogao Caves. Some of them stayed there all their lives, devoting their lives to the art of Dunhuang; some stayed for only a short time. Some later became renowned Dunhuang experts; some remained unknown, quietly contributing their efforts to the field. In any case, all who worked under the harsh conditions at the time deserve respect and admiration.

Chang Shuhong (1904–1994), the quintessential Dunhuanger, also known as the “guardian of Dunhuang,” dedicated his whole life to Dunhuang studies.

At the end of 1935, Chang, who was studying in Paris, serendipitously came upon Paul Pelliot's *Les grottes de Touen-Houang* (The Caves of Dunhuang) in a market stall that was selling old books by the Seine River, forging a lifelong connection between him and Dunhuang. He once mentioned in his work *Ninety Springs and Autumns: Fifty Years at Dunhuang*, “Compared with the early history of Western art, the art of the Mogao Caves appears to be more technically advanced than contemporaneous works. This

图 63 常书鸿(1904—1994)
Fig.63 Chang Shuhong (1904-1994)

敦煌艺术更显出先进的技术水平。这对于当时的我来说真是不可思议的奇迹。因为我是一个倾倒在西洋文化，而且曾非常自豪地以蒙巴拿斯的画家自居，言必称希腊、罗马的人，现在面对祖国如此悠久灿烂的文化历史，自责自己数典忘祖，真是惭愧之极，不知如何忏悔才是！"(常书鸿《九十春秋——敦煌五十年》。下述引文若无特别注明，皆出于此)因此常书鸿决心离开巴黎到敦煌去。1936年秋天，常书鸿将妻子陈芝秀和

is really incredible to me, for I've been so fascinated by Western culture and been so proud of calling myself a painter of Montparnasse that I couldn't even open my mouth without mentioning Greek or Roman artists. However, our nation has such a splendid culture, and I can't help blaming myself for forgetting my origins. I'm extremely ashamed and don't know how to make up for it!" This experience inspired him to leave Paris for Dunhuang. In autumn of 1936, leaving his wife Chen Zhixiu and daughter Shana behind in Paris, Chang went to Beijing on his own.

女儿沙娜留在巴黎，只身向北平赶来。

1942年，围绕过去河南洛阳龙门浮雕被盗卖的事件，文化界人士正在议论如何继承民族文化遗产和文物保护问题，由于国民党监察院院长于右任的建议，再加上向达、贺昌群等先生的响应呼吁，重庆政府便指令教育部筹备成立"国立敦煌艺术研究所"。

1942年8月，重庆报纸上报道了筹备成立"国立敦煌艺术研究所"的消息，并公布了筹委会名单："陕甘宁青新五省监察使高一涵任主任委员，常书鸿任副主任委员，王子云任秘书，张庚由、郑通和、张大千、窦景椿等任委员。"

当常书鸿决定去敦煌时，于右任先生曾对他说："那里是沙漠，与城市隔绝，生活十分艰苦，如果是没有事业心的人到那里去，那是干不久也干不好的。"其实，即便是在今天，那里的条件也相对是比较艰苦的。而当时敦煌的艰辛，从去敦煌的路途上即可见一斑。

今天我们从兰州去敦煌，不论是乘飞机，还是坐火车、汽车，

In 1942, intellectuals had grown concerned about the removal of relief sculptures from the Longmen Grottoes in Luoyang, Henan Province, sparking discussions about the protection of national cultural relics and heritage sites. Following Yu Youren's advice, which was supported by Xiang Da and He Changqun, the central government in Chongqing designated the Ministry of Education to prepare for the establishment of the National Research Institute on Dunhuang Art.

In August 1942, newspapers in Chongqing reported the news and listed the members of the Preparatory Committee as follows: Gao Yihan as chairman; Chang Shuhong as vice-chairman; Wang Ziyun as secretary; and Zhang Gengyou, Zheng Tonghe, Zhang Daqian, and Dou Jingchun as committee members.

Before Chang decided to go to Dunhuang, Yu Youren warned him, "The place you're going to is in a desert, isolated from city life. Anyone without strong perseverance can't stay there long, and can't do his work well." Even today, the climate and physical conditions in Dunhuang are more forbidding than that of other areas.

Nowadays, travel to Dunhuang from Lanzhou by plane, train, or car is convenient and fast, but it was quite difficult at that time, and the hardships of

都是比较方便而迅速的，但在当时却是很艰难的。1943 年 2 月 20 日，常书鸿一行乘一辆敞篷卡车从兰州出发，经过整整一个月的旅行，于 3 月 20 日下午才到安西。从安西到敦煌，连破旧的公路都没有了，只能靠“沙漠之舟”骆驼。因“当时兰新公路只经过安西，从安西到敦煌 120 公里没有公路”。他们经过瓜州口、甜水井、疙瘩井三夜的宿营，到第四天才到达莫高窟。这在今天简直是天方夜谭。

“当时，一提起塞外戈壁滩，不少人便谈虎色变，对于长期去那里工作，则更是望而却步，无人问津了。”常书鸿先生在兰州时，想招去敦煌的工作人员都是很困难的。最初“由郑通和调来天水中学校长李赞亭任秘书”，后在一个偶然的机会，“碰到一个在西北公路局工作的国立北平艺专学生龚祥礼。他(与我)一见如故，欣然应允随我前往敦煌，并且又由他介绍了一名小学美术教员陈延儒和我们一块去……后来，又经过和省教育

the journey can be extrapolated from Chang's experience. On February 20, 1943, Chang and his team got a ride in an open truck from Lanzhou, and, after an entire month on the road, arrived at Anxi in the afternoon of March 20. However, there was no road from Anxi to Dunhuang, requiring them to ride camels for the remaining 120 kilometers. After three nights of camping in Guazhou, Tianshuijing, and Gedajing, they finally arrived at the Mogao Caves on the fourth day. The hardships they suffered and endured on the journey were beyond imagination.

"In those days, many people would turn pale at the mere mention of the Gobi desert, not to mention the idea of working there for a long term," Chang recalled. When he was in Lanzhou, it was extremely difficult to recruit anyone who was willing to work in Dunhuang. Chang wrote, "Initially, Li Zanting, principal of Tianshui High School, was appointed by Zheng Tonghe to be the secretary of our team. After that, by chance I met a student of mine, Gong Xiangli, who was working in the Northwest Highway Bureau after graduating from the National Art College in Beiping (Beijing). Since we were already well-acquainted with each other, Gong readily agreed to work with me, and he also recommended an art teacher in a primary school, Chen Yanru, to join us... Later, with the assistance of the Provincial Education Department, a clerk named Liu Rongzeng, was recommended by the Provincial Highway Bureau. In addition, I still needed to

厅交涉，由省公路局推荐了一位文书，名叫刘荣曾。最后还缺少一名会计，没有办法，我只有到教育厅举办的临时会计训练班去招聘。开始，这个班四十几个人中没有一人愿意应招。半个钟点以后，才有一个穿着长布衫名叫辛普德的人站起来说，他愿意去敦煌。他说他原在武威工作，因为受到马家迫害才来兰州的。这一下总算解决了班子问题”。

李浴先生 1944 年到敦煌，1946 年初离开。据他回忆：“研究所初建时，研究人员有所长常书鸿及其夫人陈芝秀，还有罗继美、史岩、张民权、董希文及其夫人张琳英，此外还有苏莹辉、邵芳等都是先我而到的。其中罗、史二先生都是在我到达之前即离去。随后张民权也走了。接着来了周绍淼和乌密风夫妇和赵冠州先生，赵冠州也很快离去，次年又来了潘絜兹……当时的行政人员在总务主任之下设有文书一人、庶务二人、会计一人共五人，工友、厨师和饲养员共六人”。

常书鸿等人初到敦煌时，

recruit an accountant from those who were taking a short-term bookkeeping course held by the Education Department. At the beginning, no one among the 40 students of the class was interested in the job. Half an hour later, Xin Pude, who had previously worked in Wuwei, and had immigrated to Lanzhou because of persecution from the Ma clan, accepted the job. Anyway, the problem with a lack of staff was eventually solved.”

Li Yu arrived in Dunhuang in 1944 and left in early 1946. He recalled, “At the very beginning, the researchers at the National Research Institute on Dunhuang Art were director Chang Shuhong and his wife Chen Zhixiu, Luo Jimei, Shi Yan, Zhang Minquan, Dong Xiwen and his wife Zhang Linying, Su Yinghui and Shao Fang. All of them arrived earlier than me. However, some of them left after only a short period. For example, Luo Jimei and Shi Yan had already left before my arrival. Then Zhang Minquan and Zhao Guanzhou left too. Later, Zhou Shaomiao, his wife Wu Mifeng, and Pan Xiezi came... The administrative staff at that time was only five people, including a director of general administration, a clerical worker, two clerks in charge of general administration, and a bookkeeper. Besides these, there were six other employees, including workers, cooks, and animal attendants.”

When Chang Shuhong arrived, Li Yu added, “Cattle and sheep were grazing in front of the caves. At night, gold miners took

"窟前还放牧着牛羊，洞窟被当作淘金沙人夜宿的地方。他们在那里做饭烧水，并随意毁坏树木。洞窟中流沙堆积，脱落的壁画夹杂在断垣残壁中随处皆是。洞窟无人管理，无人修缮，无人研究，无人宣传，继续遭受大自然和人为毁损的厄运"。因此，他们面临的第一任务就是战风沙，筑围墙。在当时那种艰难困苦的环境中，他们克服了常人难以想象的困难，竭尽全力地从事清除积沙，治理环境，保护洞窟，砌筑围墙等当时所能做的一切保护工作。据常书鸿在其自传中回忆："这里物资昂贵，有钱也买不到东西。千佛洞孤处沙漠戈壁之中，东面是三危山，西面是鸣沙山，北面最近的村舍也在 30 里戈壁滩以外。在千佛洞里除我们之外，唯一的人烟是上寺一老一少两个喇嘛，下寺一个道人。因此，工作和生活用品都得到县城去买，来回路程有八九十里，走戈壁近路也要七八十里，而我们唯一的交

shelter in the caves. They boiled water for cooking, and freely cut down trees for firewood. Drifting sand had piled up in the caves, and mural fragments had fallen apart and were mixed in with broken pieces of wall plaster, scattering everywhere. Under a lack of management, maintenance, or recognition, the caves suffered from both natural and human destruction." Therefore, the first task for the team was to build walls to protect the cave temples against wind and sand. Under challenging circumstances, they made every effort and overcame tremendous difficulties while clearing sand, managing the environment, building walls, and protecting the caves. Chang recalled in his autobiography, "There are no supplies here, and we cann't buy anything even if we had a lot of money. Mogao is isolated in the Gobi desert, with the Sanwei Mountain to the east and the Mingsha Mountain to the west. The nearest cottage to the north is more than 30 *li* (9 miles) away. Besides us, there are only two lamas, one old and one young, living in the upper temple, and a Taoist in the lower temple. So we have to buy rations and supplies in the county seat, with a round-trip journey of about 80–90 *li* (25 to 28 miles). The shortcut through the Gobi desert is around 70–80 *li* (22 to 25 miles), while our only means of transport is a borrowed ox cart with wooden wheels. It still takes at least a day and a night for a round-trip journey with the cart."Apart from the lack of materials and supplies, the loneliness and isolation from society was even more terrible:

图 64　1944 年，国立敦煌艺术研究所全体职工合影
Fig.64　Staff of the National Research Institute on Dunhuang Art, 1944

通工具是一辆借来的木轮老牛车，往返至少一天一夜。”除了这些物质方面的困难外，“还有一个更可怕的困难，是远离社会的孤独和寂寞。在这个周围 40 里荒无人烟的戈壁沙洲上，交通不便，信息不灵，职工们没有社会活动，没有文体娱乐，没有亲人团聚的天伦之乐”。“记得画家张大千在 1943 年初离开莫高窟时，半开玩笑地对我说：‘我们先走了，而你却要在这里无穷无尽地研究保管下去，这是一个长期的——无期的徒刑呀！’”

正如史苇湘先生所说：“这里与

"On this desolate Gobi desert, extending for nearly 40 *li* (12 miles), the transportation is poor, and we have no access to outside information, and workers have no social activities, no entertainment, and no contact with their families." He added, "The experience reminded me of the joke Zhang Daqian made as he was leaving the Mogao Caves in early 1943, 'We're on our way out, but you have to stay here to work. The situation you face is just like being sentenced to life in prison!'"

Shi Weixiang also mentioned the hardships, "The place we are in is completely isolated from the outside

外面的世界完全是封闭的，听不见新闻，看不见内地的新书杂志，仅有的一份兰州出版的《和平日报》要半个月到二十天才能到达莫高窟，看病购物要骑毛驴进城，从城上回来的人才讲一点在县城里道听途说的'新闻'。"

正是在这种艰难困苦的条件下，有些人无法忍受便不得不离开莫高窟。如常书鸿的夫人陈芝秀于1945年初说去兰州治病，但她到了兰州后，立即登报发表声明：与常书鸿脱离夫妻关系——离婚。面对妻子的离去、家庭的破裂，在选择事业还是选择家庭这一关键时刻，常书鸿曾有过犹豫，但最终下定了决心："家庭和事业都牵绕着我的心，但最终我还是决定以事业为重，让她走吧！"

1945年7月，随着抗日战争的胜利，国立敦煌艺术研究所接到国民党教育部发来的一道命令，宣布撤销敦煌艺术研究所，命令研究所把石窟交给敦煌县政府。随后，"中央研究院接管我们所的通知也收到了，并汇来了一笔钱。但是，由于日本战败投降，一些职工希望尽快回到过去的敌占区与亲属团聚，有的已无心再

world. News, books, and magazines are inaccessible. It takes about 20 days for the only available newspaper—*Peace Daily*, published in Lanzhou—to reach the Mogao Caves. We have to ride a donkey to the county seat to see a doctor or to go shopping. Those coming back from the county share the gossip and local news they heard there."

Some members of the team could not bear the hardship, so they chose to leave. For example, Chang's wife Chen Zhixiu went to Lanzhou to see a doctor in early 1945. However, upon her arrival there, she made a statement in the local newspaper that she was divorcing Chang. Facing his wife's departure and the break-up of his family, Chang found himself in a dilemma, but eventually he made up his mind. "Both family and career are important in my life, but I have to concentrate on the cause. Let her go!"

In July 1945, after the Chinese victory in the War of Resistance Against Japanese Aggression, an edict from the Kuomintang Ministry of Education was issued, announcing the dissolution of the National Research Institute on Dunhuang Art and asking Chang to relinquish all the cave temples to the authority of the Dunhuang County government. Chang recalled, "Soon, the notification about the Academia Sinica taking over our affairs was also received, attached to a sum of

待在这个边陲荒凉之地，想尽早离开这里，因而，接着而来的就是一个散伙‘复员’的狂潮”。这时，董希文、张琳英夫妇走了，李浴走了，周绍淼、乌密风夫妇走了，潘絜兹走了。到了1945年冬天，“先后来所工作的人大都走了”。

李浴先生在回忆当时的经历感受时说：“1945年8月15日日本投降，抗日战争胜利了。这消息传到千佛洞却是一个月以后的事，闻讯无不欢欣鼓舞，兴奋之情难以言表。可是稍一定神，故乡亲人之思就顿时倍增，八年流亡他乡的滋味应该结束了，所以人人都要东归，先是阎文儒（该团工作结束后，原拟受聘留所任研究员）走了，苏莹辉走了，大雪纷飞中又送走了邵芳，继之董希文夫妇带着孩子也走了，我当然也急欲回到中原与亲人团聚……潘絜兹家眷在兰州，他当然也要走，于是我俩偕行，于1946年初告别了千佛洞。当时乌密风（夫妇）正在敦煌县

money. But because of the Japanese surrender, some of the staff hoped to return to the formerly occupied areas to reunite with their families as soon as possible; some, having no intention of staying in such a desolate place, wanted to leave quickly. Then came a frenzy of ‘demobilization’ or disbandment. Following this trend, the couple Dong Xiwen and Zhang Linying left; so did Li Yu, the couple Zhou Shaomiao and Wu Mifeng, as well as Pan Xiezi. By the winter of 1945, most of the staff who once worked in the institute had left.”

Li Yu recalled his experience at the time, “On August 15, 1945, we witnessed the surrender of the Japanese invaders and our victory in the War of Resistance Against Japanese Aggression. However, the good news didn’t reach Mogao until one month later. Upon hearing the news, the excitement of the staff was beyond description. But once they calmed down, they were overwhelmed by homesickness. The eight-year exile had finally come to an end, and all were longing to return home to reunite with their families. At first Yan Wenru, a candidate for a position as a researcher at the institute, left, and so did Su Yinghui. Then, Shao Fang departed on a snowy day. Later, Dong Xiwen, together with his wife and children, also went away. I myself was eager to get back to the Central Plains to see my family members... Of course, Pan Xiezi wanted to go too, for his family was in Lanzhou. So we two departed in early 1946. The couple Wu Mifeng and Zhou Shaomiao were in

城，他俩听说我们走了之后，自然也是不安于位而东归了。就是这样，研究所的专职研究人员全部都走光了，于是常先生不能不离开敦煌回重庆。”

除了生活上的艰难困苦，精神上的寂寞难熬之外，当时敦煌艺术研究所的科研条件也非常差，不仅没有基本的资料《大藏经》、“二十四史”等，甚至就连一架照相机都没有。

尽管如此，在研究所成立之初的一段时间，即从 1943 到 1945 年，敦煌艺术研究所的同仁们仍然做出了一些成绩。在这些为数不多的研究人员中，或因时间过短，或因兼职而影响研究工作，但大家都踏踏实实做出了一些研究成果，如董希文留下了非常精彩的《萨埵饲虎图》等摹本，邵芳留下了一幅宏大而精美的盛唐《西方净土变》，周绍淼、乌密风留下了数幅藻井、边饰、龛楣等图案，潘絜兹也留下了一些唐、宋壁画摹本，苏莹辉留下了敦煌碑刻文字考。

1946 年，常书鸿在重庆又招聘了中央大学艺术系毕业生郭世清及其妻子刘缦云，国立

Dunhuang County at the time, and when they heard of our departure they naturally couldn't bear staying there any longer, so they left soon after. In a very short period, all the researchers in the institute left, one after another. At last, Chang had to leave Dunhuang for Chongqing."

Apart from the hardships and the loneliness, the research conditions in the institute were very poor. Not only did they lack basic reference texts such as the *Tripitaka*, and *Twenty-Four Histories*, they did not even have a camera.

Nevertheless, during the period between 1943 and 1945, the researchers in the institute made some progress. Dong Xiwen created a wonderful reproduction of *Prince Sattva Sacrificing Himself to Tigers*; Shao Fang produced a facsimile of the magnificent *Illustration Painting of the Western Pure Land* from the High Tang period; Zhou Shaomiao and Wu Mifeng made paintings of decorative motifs and patterns found in the caves, including the *zaojing* (caisson) ceiling patterns, surrounding trim or borders, and niche lintels; Pan Xiezi produced copies of murals from the Tang and Song dynasties; and Su Yinghui conducted textual research on Dunhuang inscriptions.

In 1946, Chang recruited new members for his team, including Guo Shiqing and his wife Liu Manyun, both graduated from the Fine Arts Department of the National Central University, Ling Chunde from the Sculpture

图 65　矗立在敦煌研究院的常书鸿塑像
Fig.65　Statue of Chang Shuhong at the Dunhuang Academy

艺专雕塑系毕业生凌春德；在成都招聘了四川省立艺专图案系毕业生范文藻和在艺专任教的霍熙亮，“另外搭车前往敦煌的，还有四川省立艺专教授沈福文夫妇”；在兰州，段文杰“希望随我到敦煌工作……我接受了他来敦煌工作的要求”。

1947 年夏天，敦煌艺术研究所又增添了一批年轻人，有孙儒僩、黄文馥、欧阳琳、李承仙、薛德嘉、萧克俭等人。1948

Department of the National Art Institute in Chongqing, Fan Wenzao from the Pattern Department of the Sichuan Provincial Art College, and Huo Xiliang, who was teaching at the same college. In addition, Shen Fuwen and his wife—professors at the Sichuan Provincial Art College—also hitchhiked to Dunhuang, as well as Duan Wenjie, who came at Chang's invitation.

In the summer of 1947, several young people became members of the institute, namely Sun Ruxian, Huang Wenfu, Ouyang Lin, Li Chengxian, Xue Dejia, and Xiao Kejian. In the winter of 1948, Shi Weixiang

年冬天，史苇湘也来了。这批生力军的到来，不仅使研究所充满了朝气，而且使停顿了的不少工作得以开展起来，临摹壁画的队伍也十分齐整了。

如史苇湘先生是 1948 年 9 月底到敦煌的，当时只有 24 岁。他在《初到莫高窟》一文中说："当时生活非常严峻，这里的一群知识分子却能埋头专心工作，一日两餐白水煮面条和清汤白菜、萝卜，维持着生命的最低要求，但是在精神上都非常富有，上洞下洞，孜孜不倦，天天如此，毫无怠意。很容易就接受了这种精神的感染，谈石窟里的事情就成为生活中的重要内容。……

"到莫高窟才一个多月，我就受到先行者们的感染，生活虽然艰苦，以段文杰为首的一群年轻人，情绪总是那么乐观、饱满，在常书鸿先生的领导下，能够在这里坚持下去。我逐步理解他们甘心投身在这片戈壁滩上，行为就是无限悲壮的誓词，因为莫高窟并不能任凭风吹雪打，任凭虎去狼来，虽然这群人在当时尚无回天之力来抢救

came as well. This arrival of new blood brought not only vitality to the institute; it also helped them to resume the work that had stopped. At the same time, a team responsible for mural reproduction was also established.

Shi Weixiang, one of the team members, came to Dunhuang in late September, 1948, when he was only 24 years old. In the article "My First Visit to the Mogao Caves," he wrote, "Although life there was very tough at the time, the intellectuals could put their minds wholeheartedly into their work. They only had two meals a day, and both were boiled noodles with cabbage and radishes—the minimum requirement for survival. But they were rich in spirit, copying the murals cave by cave, day by day. Sharing stories about the caves had become an important part of their lives... I was greatly inspired by the forerunners, even though I had come to the Mogao Caves for only a month.

Despite their hard life, this group of young people—Duan Wenjie and his colleagues—were always so optimistic and energetic. They had been dedicated to their work here for many years, under the leadership of Chang Shuhong. I gradually came to understand their dedication and the solemn vow they had made in the Gobi desert. They firmly believed the Mogao Caves should not be allowed to be damaged or neglected, although they may not have

它，却不能让它自生自灭。……

“当时生活的困难，已到了最低点，几个月发不出工资，仅有的一点经费养活不了一辆破卡车，留在这里的人，也没有经济能力‘逃回’内地。难怪在我之前已经来过多少青年画家和学人，都由于这个难熬的生活环境和种种原因先后离去。临到 1948 年冬天，莫高窟就只剩下常书鸿先生和我们七个年轻的业务人员。”

段文杰先生也回忆说：“新中国成立前七年中，先后在研究所工作的专业人员和事务人员达三十人之多。但由

been able to completely protect or rescue them.”

He added, “We were suffering the most difficult living conditions, working without salary for several months. The remaining funds couldn't cover the expenses of the old truck. Those wanting to go back couldn't even afford the journey. It was no wonder that many young painters and scholars had left before my arrival, one after another. By the winter of 1948, only Chang and another seven young people had stayed in Mogao.”

图 66　常书鸿故居(摄影：张先堂)

Fig.66　Former Residence of Chang Shuhong (Photo by Zhang Xiantang)

图 67 段文杰(前)、樊锦诗(右)和作者(摄于 2006 年 12 月 22 日)
Fig.67 Duan Wenjie (Center Front), Fan Jinshi (Right), and the Author (Left), December 22, 2006

于环境艰苦、社会腐败，大多在黎明前的黑暗中先后离去，坚持到敦煌解放的只有十四人，其中专业人员只有七人，但他们都是敦煌文物研究事业的开创者。"除常书鸿先生外，这七个年轻人就是段文杰、史苇湘、孙儒僩、欧阳琳、李承仙、霍熙亮、黄文馥。我们不应忘记他们。

Duan Wenjie recalled, "During the seven years before liberation, the number of professionals and other employees in the institute was as many as 30. However, most of the staff gradually left, and as a result, there were only 14 staying there, of whom only seven were professionals, namely myself, Shi Weixiang, Sun Ruxian, Ouyang Lin, Li Chengxian, Huo Xiliang, and Huang Wenfu. They were truly pioneers in the

敦煌解放时，当时的敦煌艺术研究所全体员工不到20人，他们全部被留用。1950年8月22日，西北军政委员会文化部文物处赵望云处长、张明坦副处长受中央文化部的委托，率工作组来莫高窟正式接管敦煌艺术研究所，并宣布：从1950年8月1日起“敦煌艺术研究所”更名为“敦煌文物研究所”，直属文化部文物事业管理局。据孙儒僩先生回忆，当时“我虽曾表示过想离开敦煌回四川老家的意向，但经不住张处长的三言两语，很快就放弃了自己的打算。”

中华人民共和国成立后，全国许多地方各方面的条件都比以前好了，但莫高窟仍然是比较艰苦的。据施萍亭（即施娉婷）先生回忆，“即使日历翻到1962年，莫高窟还没有电”；“喝的是苦水”；莫高窟离城25公里，没有汽车，只有一挂马车，“为数不多的职工子女，上学必须进城，星期六用马车接回来，晚上赶紧消灭衣服上的虱子，星期天用马车摇着送回去。”

research of Dunhuang cultural relics. We will never forget them.”

The staff at the institute numbered less than 20 when Dunhuang was liberated, all of whom stayed later. On August 22, 1950, Zhao Wangyun, director of the Cultural Relics Department of the Ministry of Culture in the Northwest Military and Political Committee, and Zhang Mingtan, deputy director, were entrusted by the Central Ministry of Culture to Mogao with a delegation to officially take over the National Research Institute on Dunhuang Art. They announced that the institute was to be renamed the Research Institute on Cultural Relics of Dunhuang under the administration of the Cultural Relics Bureau of the Ministry of Culture, starting from August 1, 1950. Sun Ruxian commented, “At that time, I initially intended to leave Dunhuang and go back to my hometown—Sichuan—but I soon gave up that idea after being persuaded by Director Zhang.”

After the founding of the People's Republic of China, living conditions became better in many parts of the country, but few changes had taken place at Mogao. Shi Pingting shared her memories, “In 1962, there was no electricity there, and the drinking water was bitter. The Mogao Caves were 25 kilometers away from the city, and the only vehicle was a cart. Since the children of the staff had to attend school in the city, they had to be picked up on Saturdays and sent back on Sunday evenings by cart after their parents had hurriedly killed the lice that clung to their

虽然“敦煌的生活、工作是苦的。然而，敦煌人除了因孩子上学不便而感到有点内疚以外，他们似乎不感到什么苦。人们常常能听到临摹工作者、保护工作者从窟内传出的川剧、秦腔、民歌、小调，他们面对佛、菩萨，有时竟那样忘情。资料室不但白天开门，晚上也开门，煤油灯擦得锃亮，看看心里也光明。被称为‘活字典’的史苇湘先生每晚必到，以供同志们‘备查’。著名的第465窟(俗称欢喜佛洞)孤零零坐落在石窟群的北端，离我们的住区——中寺、上寺很远，李其琼女士临摹该窟时，带上干粮，中午不回家，为的是节省时间，并争到光线充足的黄金时间。”

敦煌是艰苦的，“敦煌人”是有真本领的。如果他们为了个人的幸福，或为了孩子的将来，想离开敦煌是很容易的。如被摘了“右派”帽子的史苇湘、孙儒僩、李其琼，那时候“都是刚步入中年、精力旺盛的人，如果他们想离开敦煌，易如反掌。但是，他们谁也没有如此想”;“文革”中，段文杰、贺世哲等先生都被打倒，甚至被开除党籍和公职送回

clothes.”

These difficult living conditions didn't bother the Dunhuangers, except that they felt somewhat guilty for the inconvenience experienced by their children in attending school. In the cave temples, Sichuan Opera, Shaanxi Opera, folk songs and popular tunes could often be heard, sung by the mural copiers and custodians, who—under the gaze of the Buddhas and bodhisattvas—were intently consumed with their work. The door to the reference room was open throughout the day, with a polished kerosene lamp lighting the way for all. Shi Weixiang, known affectionately as a walking dictionary, went there every night to answer questions from colleagues. Cave 465 (the Mandkesvara Cave or Yab-Yum Cave, colloquially known as the Happy Buddha Cave), was located alone at the northern end of the caves, far from the residential area—the middle temple and the upper temple—so Li Qiqiong usually brought her lunch there, to save time and get enough sunlight to copy the murals.”

Life in Dunhuang was primitive, but the Dunhuangers were truly courageous and strong-willed. When Shi Weixiang, Sun Ruxian, Li Qiqiong had their “rightist label” removed, they were only middle-aged and still energetic. If they had wanted to leave for the sake of their own happiness or for the future of their children, it would not have been difficult. However, such a

老家，“文革”后“给他们落实政策，还是没有一个人要求离开敦煌，都回到了莫高窟”。

“敦煌人”是有真才实学的，他们能耐得住寂寞，能面壁10年、20年，甚至30年，一步一个脚印，踏踏实实地从事着自己执着追求的事业。他们就是那样的执着，以敦煌为家，与菩萨做伴，守护着莫高窟。他们的科研成果可能并不是很多，但都是无水分的“干货”，是能够留给后代的。

今天，固然生活、工作等各方面的条件都比以前好了很多很多，但我们似乎就是缺少点什么，就是无法和我们的先辈比，缺乏他们的敬业精神，缺乏他们的献身精神。

敦煌研究院现任院长樊锦诗女士在《为了敦煌的久远长存》中说：“以常书鸿、段文杰为代表的一代又一代的有志者，离开了繁华的城市和温暖的家园，从祖国各地来到了人烟稀少的大漠深处，为了保护和研究祖国的稀世瑰宝，甘愿过着清贫的生活，奉献自己的青春，甚至自己的一生。几代人

thought never occurred to them. During the Cultural Revolution, Duan Wenjie and He Shizhe were expelled from the Party and sent back to their hometowns. After the Cultural Revolution, the accusations against them were withdrawn and they regained their positions and reputations as well. Still they asked to return to Dunhuang and to the Mogao Caves once again.

The Dunhuangers were both knowledge-able and persistent. They had been copying murals on their own for 10, 20, even 30 years, step by step, resolutely engaged in the pursuit of their work. So steadfast were they that they took Dunhuang as their home and the Buddha as their company, and naturally protected the Mogao Cave shrines as though they were guarding their own home. Their achievements were a legacy for future generations.

Frankly speaking, our living conditions today in all aspects are much better than those in the past, but it seems that we lack something, something that cannot compete with our predecessors—the commitment and dedication to the cause.

In her article “For the Eternal Existence of Dunhuang,” Fan Jinshi, director of the Dunhuang Academy, wrote, “Promising youth represented by Chang Shuhong and Duan Wenjie gave up their bustling city life and the comforts of home to gather in the sparsely populated desert. They were willing to endure a primitive existence, dedicating their youth and their lives to protecting the rare treasures

图 68　敦煌文物研究所部分职工合影(摄于 1950 年秋)
Fig.68　Members of the Research Institute on Cultural Relics of Dunhuang, Autumn of 1950

薪火相传，恪尽职守，不懈奋斗，开拓探索,为敦煌文物的保护作出了自己的贡献。”

这何尝不是樊锦诗他们这一代“敦煌人”的真实写照和宣言呢!

因此,我们永远不能忘记那些“敦煌人”,我们应该永远记着常书鸿、段文杰、史苇湘、霍熙亮、潘絜兹、李承仙、欧阳琳、孙儒僩、李其琼、关友惠、万庚育、张学荣、李云鹤、刘玉权、贺世哲、施娉婷、潘玉闪、李永宁、孙修身、樊锦诗、李振

of the motherland. For several generations these researchers in Dunhuang have been fulfilling their duties, dedicating their unwavering efforts to the protection of the cultural relics of Dunhuang.”

Fan Jinshi's comment is indeed an appropriate description and definition of the Dunhuangers, isn't it?

The Dunhuangers should never be forgotten. As such, here is a roster of their names: Chang Shuhong, Duan Wenjie, Shi Weixiang, Huo Xiliang, Pan Xiezi, Li Chengxian, Ouyang Lin, Sun Ruxian, Li Qiqiong, Guan Youhui, Wan Gengyu,

图 69　常书鸿先生故居内景一角
Fig.69　Chang Shuhong's Former Residence

甫、窦占彪、龚祥礼，等等，等等。当然，还有许多"敦煌人"，我连他们的名字都还不知道。

他们之中，有些已经去世，有些也已步入老年。近来，我常常想，随着这批"敦煌人"的离世退休，不仅仅使我们失去了学术上的老师，更重要的是我们失去了精神上的导师，使我们在做人做事方面缺少了楷模。

他们，是永远值得我们学习的！

Zhang Xuerong, Li Yunhe, Liu Yuquan, He Shizhe, Shi Pingting, Pan Yushan, Li Yongning, Sun Xiushen, Fan Jinshi, Li Zhenfu, Dou Zhanbiao, and Gong Xiangli.

Actually, there are more Dunhuangers whose names remain unknown, among whom, some have already passed away; some are now in their old age. With the Dunhuangers passing away or gradually retiring, not only has the world lost some of its great teachers, but it has also lost its spiritual mentors as well. They illuminate the road of life, and without them, living is like sailing without a lighthouse.

Their academic achievements, especially their spirits are examples for us to learn.

图 70　段文杰先生荣获敦煌文物和艺术保护研究终生成就奖颁奖大会
于 2007 年 8 月 23 日在兰州举行

Fig.70　Duan Wenjie Receiving the Lifetime Achievement Award for Research on the Conservation of Cultural Relics and Art in Dunhuang, August 23, 2007, Lanzhou

图 71　敦煌研究院院史陈列馆院内(摄影:张先堂)

Fig.71　Courtyard of the History Exhibition Hall of the Dunhuang Academy (Photo by Zhang Xiantang)

图 72　常书鸿先生之墓(摄影:张先堂)

Fig.72　Tomb of Chang Shuhong (Photo by Zhang Xiantang)

遗响千年：敦煌的影响

Dunhuang: Its Everlasting Impact

敦煌文艺创作

Dunhuang Literary and Artistic Achievements

有一首现代诗歌《大漠敦煌》，作者署名为秋酿醇酒，是这样描述敦煌的沧桑的：

我多想带上装满梦的行囊
牵一只骆驼去那风沙弥漫的远方
我多想沿着遥远又遥远的古道
寻找我梦中的大漠敦煌

穿过祁连山的六月飞雪
走进炎风吹沙的大漠
我寻一把先人遗留在那里的石斧
看它是否还能劈出四千多年的火光

追赶丝绸之路落下的夕阳
跋涉在曾经鼓角争鸣的河西走廊
我想找到三苗人留下的陶器
让它盛满历史的冷热和苍茫

我想听到羌笛穿透千古的余音
在荒原的夜空里哀怨悠扬
借着大漠的冷月寒光
我多想找回乌孙人失散的牛羊

在漫漫狂野中赶路
我多想举起月氏人的宝刀将夜空划亮
我望见浩瀚的沙海如血的残阳
远处传来铁蹄铮铮烈马奔腾的轰响
一支剽悍的胡骑消失在流沙的尽头
远离了草原和毡房

The modern poem "Dunhuang in the Desert," authored by Qiuniang Chunjiu (pen name of the author Ma Ke), describes Dunhuang as follows:

How I want to take a bag full of dreams
Lead a camel into the distance through blowing sandstorms
How I want to go down the remote and distant road
Search for Dunhuang desert in my dreams

Through the June snow in the Qilian Mountains
Into the desert with scorching winds and blowing sand
I found an axe left there by people of the past
See if it can still blaze as it did four thousand years ago

Chasing the falling sunset on the Silk Road
Trekking in the Hexi Corridor that has seen shots of gunpowder
I want to find pottery left by the Sanmiao people
Let it fill history with its boundless vicissitudes

I want to hear the Qiang flute echo with the flight of time
In the wasteland night sky sorrows rising and falling
By cold moon light in the surrounding desert
How I hope the Wusun people's lost sheep and cattle are found

Rushing towards the long way through the wilds
How I want to spark the night with the Yuezhi people's sword
I see the vast sand sea in the blood-like setting sun
From the distance come galloping horses with their rumbling sound
A wild Hu rider disappearing at the end of the sands
Away from the grasslands and yurts on land

我望见张骞出使西域归来的马队
马踏飞燕的嘶鸣声扬四方
我望见汉武的狼烟扬起旌旗遮日的豪壮
飘逝在风萧萧路漫漫的边关

那鸣沙山千年不绝的鸣响
每一声吟唱
都是英雄泯血长笑的悲壮
那月牙泉甘洌清澈的水塘
每一个眼神
都曾凝视过扬鞭的牧人拓荒的农夫

玉门关的残垣断壁
望断多少远行的商队往来的使者
阳关三叠的千古绝唱
又有多少故人更尽一杯酒从此不见回故乡

我站在汉长城古烽燧遗址上
似乎还能听到
一腔长风万里的呼啸
我站在魏晋隋唐的古墓旁
似乎还能看到
边塞诗人雪山长云孤城遥望的豪情和惆怅

几度春秋风与火
东来西往的驼队穿过大漠莽莽
曾经几载云和月
边城要塞通向了海纳百川的大唐

I saw Zhang Qian's mission returning from the Western Regions
Galloping horses treading flying swallows, the sound of neighing all around
I saw the grandeur of Emperor Wu with fluttering streamers blotting out the sun
Fading in the frontier with the whistling winds and desolate road

On Mingsha Mountain a thousand years of incessant ringing
Every singing
Is the hero's everlasting bloody laughing
The Crescent Moon Spring sweet clear pool
Every looking
Having every herdsman and farmer gazing

The Yumen Pass ruins
Witnessed numbers of travel caravan messengers
Through the ages in Yangguan Pass a three-stanza masterpiece poem
How many people drank a cup of wine to leave and never come back home

Standing on the ruins of ancient Han Great Wall watchtowers
I seem to hear
A long wind howling through thousands of miles
Standing beside the ancient tombs of the Wei, Jin, Sui, and Tang dynasties
I seem to see
A frontier poet overlooking snowy mountains with pride and sorrow

Ever-changing ages of wind and fire
East and west the caravans cross the boundless desert
Once every few months or years
From border towns to the inclusive Tang Dynasty

我的大漠我的敦煌啊
你已不是金戈铁马厮杀遍野的战场
你丝绸铺路
你名声远扬
……

追踪远古消失的绿洲
注视大漠不朽的胡杨
我寻着崖壁上的佛光
看见风卷僧衣的乐僔和尚
在石壁上开凿了第一个洞窟
在穷荒中点燃了第一炷香火
一代代虔诚的僧侣随他而来
创造出佛洞悬空的圣堂

天空移动的云彩
遮不住三危山的金黄
莫高窟这座千佛神奇的宝藏
在沙漠中沉睡了一千年

岁月的寒暑
剥蚀了多少绚丽的画卷珍贵的佛像
屈辱的年代
劫持了多少无价之宝流落他乡

尽管大漠景象如此苍凉
尽管丝绸之路如此漫长
神秘的敦煌啊
你玄妙神奇的经书壁画令人心驰神往

My desert, my Dunhuang
No fighting places in the battlefield can be found
With the Silk Road
Your reputation everywhere follows along
...

Tracing the ancient disappearing oasis
At the desert immortal poplars gaze
I searched the cliffs of the Buddha's light
Saw the monk Lezun in weathered clothing tight
Excavating the first cave on the cliff
In harsh drought lit the first incense
Generations of pious monks following
Creating the sanctuary with the Buddha cave floating

Clouds moving in the sky
Cannot cover the golden glory of the Sanwei Mountain
The Mogao Caves, a Thousand Buddha magical treasure
Sleeping in the desert for one thousand years

Through time's vissicitudes
How many magnificent and precious Buddha pictures were eroded
In the age of humiliation
How many priceless treasures lost their home

Though the desert scene so desolate
Though the Silk Road so long
Mysterious Dunhuang
Your magical sutras and murals are so fascinating

你举世闻名的丝路花雨让人沉醉难忘
美丽的敦煌啊
流光溢彩的故事有你大漠落日的悲怆
灿烂辉煌的历史有你光辉夺目的一章

我多想借反弹琵琶的神韵止住千年黄沙
我多想用飞天飘逸的梦想擦去百年彷徨
我多想牵来一股溪流为你栽上一排胡杨
我多想乘春风度玉门让梦露宿在你的身旁

敦煌所蕴含的深厚历史文化，激发了国内外一大批作家、艺术家的创作灵感，围绕着敦煌的历史和艺术，创作出了许多优秀并影响深远的文学艺术作品。

The world-famous narrative dance "The Rain of Flowers Along the Silk Road" is so mesmerizing
Beautiful Dunhuang
Colorful stories show your desert paths of the setting sun
Glorious history has your brilliant chapter in song

How I want to borrow the magic of playing the *pipa* in reverse to stop the drifting eroding sand
How I want to use the elegant apsaras to erase a hundred years of hesitation
How I want to bring a stream to plant a line of poplar trees
How I want to take a breeze through Yumen Pass to let dreams be with you

The profound historical culture rooted in Dunhuang inspired a large number of writers and artists to create numerous and influential literary artistic works.

井上靖的《敦煌》及其影响

Inoue Yasushi's Influential Work: *Dunhuang*

井上靖(1907—1991),既是日本著名的作家,又是酷爱敦煌艺术的画家,还是中日文化交流的使者,在日本颇具名望。他生前曾任日本文艺家协会理事长、日本笔会会长、日中文化交流协会会长。

井上靖自中学起就酷

Inoue Yasushi (1907–1991) was prestigious in Japan for his varied career, including being a famous Japanese writer, a passionate Dunhuang art painter, and a promoter of Sino–Japanese cultural exchange. During his life, he served as director of the Japanese Association of Art, chairman of the Japanese Pen Association, and chairman of the Japan–China Cultural Exchange Association.

Inoue Yasushi excelled in literature from his middle school days onward. His novels received

图 73 井上靖(1907—1991)
Fig.73 Inoue Yasushi (1907–1991)

爱文学，进入京都大学哲学系学习时，创作的小说就曾多次获奖。大学毕业后在大阪每日新闻社任记者、编辑多年，1951 年辞去报社职务，专心从事文学创作，开始了其职业作家的生涯。

井上靖自 1955 年起开始创作以中国古代历史为背景的小说，令人惊奇的是，他当时还不曾踏上中国国土一步，但由于他熟读了许多中国古代的文献典籍，从而对中国历史文化有相当深刻的认识。井上靖不但对中国的历史、文化倾慕不已，而且还对中国的西北地区及丝绸之路怀有一种特殊的感情。他以我国古代西域风土人情、历史掌故为题材，用文学的笔触，赋以丰富的想象，创作出了《楼兰》《敦煌》《异国的人》《漆胡樽》《昆仑采玉》等优秀的作品。其中《楼兰》《敦煌》两书获得日本“每日艺术大奖”。此外，他还以中国的历史及古代名人为背景撰就了如《杨贵妃》《苍狼》《孔子》等佳作。

在《敦煌》的写作过程中，井上靖还得到了国际著名敦煌

several awards when he was studying in the Philosophy Department of Kyoto University. After graduation, he worked in the Osaka Daily News Agency as a reporter and editor. He resigned in 1951 to devote himself to professional literary writing.

In 1955, he began writing historical novels on ancient China. Despite never stepping on Chinese soil before, he had a good command of Chinese history and culture, for he had read ancient Chinese classics extensively. He not only admired Chinese history and culture but also had a special interest in northwestern China, especially the Silk Road. Taking customs and historical allusions in ancient Western Regions as subjects, he produced a series of outstanding literary works, such as *Kingdom of Kroraina / Loulan*, *Dunhuang*, *People from Exotic Places*, *The Qihu Goblet* (a goblet used for parties in ancient China), and *Jade Quarrying in the Kunlun Mountains*, among which the first two won "Daily Art Awards." Based on Chinese history and renowned historical figures, he created other masterpieces, for instance *Yang Guifei*, *The Blue Wolf: The Epic Tale of the Life of Genghis Khan and the Empire of the Steppes*, and *Confucius*.

During the creation of his work *Dunhuang*, Inoue Yasushi was given generous assistance from Fujieda Akira, a famous Dunhuang researcher in the Humanities Institute of Kyoto University.

图 74　井上靖著《敦煌》
Fig.74　*Dunhuang* by Inoue Yasushi

学家、京都大学人文科学研究所藤枝晃先生的鼎力相助。作者将《敦煌》故事定格在公元 11 世纪上半叶，北宋与辽国交恶，西夏李元昊趁机崛起并占据敦煌地区近一个半世纪之久的历史大背景之下，采用章回体小说的范式写作，全书共分十一回：

The writer set the background of *Dunhuang* in the first half of the 11th century when the Northern Song (960–1127) became an enemy of the Liao (907–1125). Taking advantage of this situation, Li Yuanhao in the Western Xia rose up and took over Dunhuang for a century and a half. In the serial-chapter novel format, *Dunhuang* had 11 chapters.

第一回	**Chapter One**
湘中秀士醒梦悟道	Hunan scholar awakens to the truth
河西蛮女骇世惊俗	Hexi beauty amazes the world
第二回	**Chapter Two**
身陷凉州赵行德当兵	Zhao Xingde becomes a soldier when trapped in Liangzhou
心系汉土朱王礼许愿	Zhu Wangli makes wishes to pledge loyalty to the Han Dynasty
第三回	**Chapter Three**
顿生恻隐行德怜香惜玉	Zhao Xingde shows compassion to a woman
忍受天命王女移情别恋	Princess dismisses doomed fate and loves for another man
第四回	**Chapter Four**
玉殒香消证心迹	True love lasts with beauty fading
青灯黄卷归佛门	Bronze lamps and aged manuscripts return to the Buddhism
第五回	**Chapter Five**
驻瓜州朱王礼纳小妾	Zhu Wangli takes a concubine in Guazhou
访兴庆赵行德聘秀才	Zhao Xingde sits for the Civil Service Examination
第六回	**Chapter Six**
旧情未了将军怒斥娇儿	A general scolds his child for showing affection
积怨难消太守责怪家兄	A prefecture chief blames his older brother for enduring rancor
第七回	**Chapter Seven**
报仇雪恨朱王礼兵变	Zhu Wangli mutinies in revenge
丧魂落魄曹延惠弃城	Cao Yanhui loses the city in terror
第八回	**Chapter Eight**
三僧人发愿保经卷	Three monks vow to preserve the sutras
曹贤顺立志守沙州	Cao Xianshun determines to defend Shazhou
第九回	**Chapter Nine**
朱王礼出征托后事	Zhu Wangli entrusts his affairs before fighting
赵行德抄经了夙愿	Zhao Xingde fulfills his wish in Buddhist transcription
第十回	**Chapter Ten**
走投无路沙州城放火	Setting fire to Shazhou in desperation
移花接木千佛洞藏经	Preserving Buddhist sutras in the Thousand Buddha Caves
第十一回	**Chapter Eleven**
百年征战兴衰皆成往事	Hundreds of years of conquests and defeats become history
千载蒙尘瑰宝再显辉煌	Thousands of years of weathered treasures emerge glory

小说《敦煌》通过特定的人物刻画、情节编排，寄予了作者对历史的认知，有着深厚的人文内涵。其故事内容概况是：主人公赵行德上京投考，误了考期，正在失望茫然之际，却被一位被掳掠并即将被处死的西夏妇女倔强的行为所震惊，并从其身上感到了西夏国崛起的希望。这一震动，也使他不再迷恋功名，毅然前往西夏学习西夏文。在途中，他历经坎坷，被听命于西夏的汉族首领所率军队俘虏，但幸运的是得到了大字不识几个的队长朱王礼的赏识和重用。在攻打回鹘占据的甘州城时，在烽火台上偶遇回鹘公主，并将她藏于民房内，后来，渐生恋情，私订终身。赵行德为了实现自己的志向去西夏首都学习，恋恋不舍地与回鹘公主离别。但赵行德到了西夏后，却醉心于学术研究，误了当初他们所定的归期。待他归来时，回鹘公主早已被西夏王李元昊抢去做了妃子，苦苦等待赵行德的回鹘公主不忘当初

Through specific characters and plots, *Dunhuang* showcases the writer's view of history. This view is saturated with abundant humanistic connotations. Zhao Xingde, the protagonist, misses the imperial examination in the capital. Feeling intense loss and disappointment, he is then stunned by the indomitable behavior of a kidnapped and quickly-executed Western Xia woman. Feeling the hope of the Western Xia, he is no longer infatuated with fame but decides instead to head for the Western Xia to learn the Tangut language. On his way, he is captured by troops led by a Han chief who has taken orders from the Western Xia. Fortunately, he is highly esteemed and respected by the illiterate team leader, Zhu Wangli. When attacking Ganzhou that has been taken over by the Uyghurs, he comes across a Uyghur princess on a watchtower and hides her in a house. Later, they fall in love with each other and are secretly engaged. In order to achieve his goal of learning the language of the Western Xia, he departs from his Uyghur princess with great reluctance. However, in the Western Xia, he is so absorbed in his studies that he fails to return in time, and when he does, he finds that the Uyghur princess has already been taken as an imperial concubine by Li Yuanhao, King of the Western Xia. However, the Uyghur princess does not forget their love. Seizing an opportunity to be alone while others flock to a military parade, she commits suicide by jumping off the city wall to reveal her true love for Zhao. In extreme agony, Zhao Xingde

的表情，乘阅兵时跳下城墙自尽。赵行德在痛苦万分之下对李元昊顿生仇恨，与同时暗恋回鹘公主的朱王礼率军叛变。在与西夏军残酷的斗争中，他们退守到敦煌，朱王礼战死。在西夏大军焚城之际，于阗王族后裔、西域商人尉迟光，为了给自己从敦煌曹太守那里骗取的钱财，以及乘战争所发的横财找一个安全的藏匿之所，千方百计知道了千佛洞的底细，在他藏宝的同时，赵行德为了纪念他所钟爱的回鹘公主、抢救城中寺院的佛经，也乘机将万卷经典藏封于洞窟中。尉迟光想乘混战于夜晚盗宝，反被闪电击中暴亡。故事在敦煌化为一片火海中结束。

小说《敦煌》，后来又被改编为同名电影。1988 年的电影《敦煌》是为了纪念中日邦交正常化 10 周年而由中日双方联合摄制的。影片的所有场景全部在中国西北部实景拍摄完成，拍摄时期，还特意修建了敦煌古城外景地，据专家们考证，历史上的敦煌城原貌大抵如此。现今敦煌古城外景地已成为敦煌著名的旅游景点。

suddenly burns with hatred for Li Yuanhao, joining forces with Zhu Wangli to commit mutiny. Zhu Wangli has also borne a secret love for the Uyghur princess. In fierce fighting with the Western Xia army, they retreat to Dunhuang and Zhu Wangli dies in battle. When Dunhuang is on fire, Yuchi Guang, a descendant of the Khotan royal family, and Western Region merchant makes every effort to find out information about the Thousand Buddha Caves, so as to look for a secure place to stash the money swindled from governor of Dunhung Prefecture and his war booty. While Yuchi is doing this, Zhao Xingde seizes the opportunity to seal 10,000 Buddhist sutras in the cave for the sake of commemorating his beloved as well as saving the Buddhist sutras. Yuchi Guang, intending to steal the treasures at night in tangled warfare, is struck dead by lightning. With Dunhuang burning, the story ends.

The novel *Dunhuang* was adapted into a film with the same name later. The film *Dunhuang* in 1988 was also released to commemorate the 10th anniversary of the stabilization of Sino-Japanese relations. All the live-action scenes in the film were shot in northwestern China. As part of the film-making process, some buildings and roads outside Dunhuang were created as location shots. According to textual research by experts, the buildings and roads which were constructed for the movie closely resemble the original appearance of ancient

影片由日本著名导演佐藤纯弥执导。佐藤纯弥曾拍摄过许多广为中国观众熟悉的电影作品，如《追捕》《远山的呼唤》《新干线大爆炸》《一盘没有下完的棋》等优秀影视作品。他最为著名的作品是《人证》，片中的那首动人的《草帽歌》，在许多中国观众的心目中留下了深刻的印象。

与小说相比，电影《敦煌》稍有改编。它描述了宋朝年间，落第书生赵行德偶然认识西夏女子，对此新兴国家大感兴趣，决定探访。途中被西夏军俘虏，编入由汉人组成的外国人部队，并跟队长朱王礼结为生死之交。后来赵行德与王族女子斯鲁比娅共浴爱河，但因事分手两年，回来时爱人已以死殉节。他在万念俱灰之下赴敦煌埋首整理经书。朱王礼策动兵变，部队全被歼灭，敦煌亦成一片火海。

电影《敦煌》中所演绎的藏经洞历史，是一种合理的想象和虚构。故事中，敦煌的统治者曹太守未尝不是一位爱书、爱古董成癖的人，然而他的爱

Dunhuang. At present, these movie sets form a famous tourist attraction.

The film was directed by Junya Sato, a famous Japanese director, who had directed many well-received films popular with Chinese audiences, such as *Man Hunt, A Distant Cry from Spring, The Bullet Train* (also known as *Super Express 109*), and *The Go Masters*. His masterpiece was *Proof of The Man*, in which the theme song "An Old Straw Hat" greatly impressed the majority of the Chinese audience.

Compared with the novel, the film *Dunhuang* had some slight differences. It describes how the poor scholar, Zhao Xingde in the Song Dynasty, comes across a woman from the Western Xia and becomes so interested in this emerging country that he decides to make a visit. On his way there, he is enslaved by Western Xia soldiers and put into a foreign army made up of Han people, where he maintains a close friendship with the captain, Zhu Wangli. Later, Zhao Xingde and the princess of the Uyghur fall in love with each other but are forced by circumstances to break up. When he returns back two years later, he finds his lover has committed suicide. In despair, he goes to Dunhuang and devotes himself to learning sutras. Zhu Wangli plots a mutiny, in which the whole army is destroyed, and Dunhuang burns in a great fire.

The history of the Library Cave in the film *Dunhuang* is mostly fictional. In the film, the governor of Dunhuang, Cao, is for the most part a person fond of books and antiques. However,

是毁灭性的，在西夏军已破沙州，即将攻来之时，他居然要让那些无价的宝物，历代人花了多少心血撰写出来的书卷典籍，连同敦煌一起陪他自焚。而作为小小书记官的赵行德，却在敦煌城被破焚毁之际，悄悄带了一队挑夫，用马匹、骆驼，把那些经卷运到莫高窟某一处佛窟中封藏起来，把那些凝聚了无数人虔诚心愿的经卷埋藏在最安全的地方。在动荡、战乱、飘浮不定的历史环境下，如赵行德般的小人物，宁愿舍弃性命、尽己所能保存人类宝贵的文化遗产——数以万计的佛教经典和文书资料，使之流传后世，着实令人感动。电影《敦煌》中塑造的这种人物性格、品质的鲜明差别，突出了人性中善恶的两面，很是令人深思。

20 世纪 70 年代之后，井上靖曾数次来中国，专门踏上西域丝绸之路，仔细追寻古人留下的每一处遗迹。正是由于井上靖孜孜不倦地创作并介绍中国的文化和艺术，强烈地表现出他对中国的一片热爱之情，从而赢得了中国人民的尊敬与赞誉，作为第一个被北京大学授予名誉博士的日本人，井上靖当之无愧。

his love is so destructive that he intends to selfishly makes these priceless treasures, which cost the sweat and toil of many generations, burn with him when the Western Xia attacks Dunhuang. However, while Dunhuang is burning, Zhao Xingde, a humble clerk, leads a group of porters with horses and camels, secretly taking the sutras and sealing them in one of the Mogao cave temples. Thus, the sutras with sacred content written by diverse people are preserved in the safest place. During this turbulent historical period, selfless people like Zhao Xingde would rather give up their lives and preserve the precious cultural relics of humanity. Therefore, tens of thousands of classical Buddhist sutras and documents are able to be passed down to future generations. This story has moved many people. The vivid disparities of characters in the film *Dunhuang* contrast the good and the evil in human nature, which is also thought-provoking.

After the 1970s, Inoue Yasushi came to China several times, visiting the Silk Road in the Western Regions and walking in the footsteps of people from times past. Because of his tireless work and support of Chinese culture and art, he won both respect and praise from the people of China, which makes him the first Japanese citizen to receive an honorary PhD from Peking University.

中国舞剧的经典——敦煌舞剧《丝路花雨》

Classical Chinese Narrative Dance: "The Rain of Flowers Along the Silk Road"

20世纪70年代末、80年代初，随着中国改革开放号角的吹响，迎来了中国艺苑百花争艳的春天。博大精深的敦煌壁画艺术，为艺术家的文艺创作提供了可资借鉴的形象资料，也激发了他们的创作灵感。1978年创作排练的大型民族舞剧《丝路花雨》就是其中的代表。

1979年5月23日，为庆祝中华人民共和国成立30周年，《丝路花雨》正式在人民大会堂首演。剧本由艺术家赵之洵执笔。女主角英娘由贺燕云、傅春英饰演；男主角神笔张由仲明华饰演，伊努斯由李为民饰演；主要男配角强人窦虎由张稷饰演，市曹由贾世铭饰演。敦煌舞剧《丝路花雨》讲述的是唐代一对莫高窟画匠父女和波斯商人的感人故事。《丝路花雨》连同序幕与尾部，共8个场景，现将其主要内容简介如下：

序幕：在悠扬的乐声中，拉开序幕。“飞天女神”在天宇飘

China witnessed a huge growth in the arts during the late 1970s and early 1980s. The murals of Dunhuang have inspired artists to create many choreographed dramas, among which "The Rain of Flowers Along the Silk Road" in 1978 has been considered the most outstanding.

To celebrate the 30th anniversary of the founding of the People's Republic of China, "The Rain of Flowers Along the Silk Road" was first performed in the Great Hall of the People in Beijing. The libretto was written by Zhao Zhixun. The original cast included the protagonist, Master Painter Zhang played by Zhong Minghua; the heroine Yingniang, Zhang's daughter, played by He Yanyun and Fu Chunying; Enus, a Persian merchant, played by Li Weimin; Douhu, a bandit, played by Zhang Ji; and the local magistrate, played by Jia Shiming. With eight scenes, it tells a moving story about fictional events set in the Tang Dynasty (618–907) involving Master Painter Zhang, his daughter Yingniang, and a Persian merchant.

The opening prologue begins with orchestral music, and pairs of flying apsaras strew flowers in the sky. The bells on

荡，将朵朵云花撒向人间……唐代丝绸之路上，远处，驼铃声中，古道上走过西域商队，风沙骤起，画工神笔张救起了困倒在沙漠里的波斯商人伊努斯，他结识了一位挚友，但是爱女英娘却被强人窦虎掳去。

第一场：数年之后，敦煌市场。丝绸相交，歌舞相望。神笔张终于找到了女儿，但出落得美丽动人的英娘已沦为百戏班子的歌舞伎，在街头卖艺；伊努斯为救命恩人仗义疏财，为英娘赎身，父女得以团聚。

第二场：莫高窟中，神笔张按照女儿的舞姿，画出了敦煌壁画的代表作——反弹琵琶伎乐天。市曹觊觎英娘的美貌，企图占有英娘。与其让女儿身陷火坑，莫如让女儿远走他乡，神笔张将爱女托付给伊努斯，市曹诡计未逞，罚神笔张带枷画窟。

第三场：英娘与波斯人民朝夕相处，互切技艺，在如梭的光阴中结下了深厚的情谊。伊努斯奉命使唐，英娘也随之

camels clang in the distance. The Silk Road from the Tang Dynasty appears, with traveling merchants. All of a sudden, a gale of wind arises. Enus, a Persian merchant, is caught in the resulting sandstorm. Master Painter Zhang and Yingniang see Enus and save his life, who, feeling indebted to them, becomes their friend. Yingniang is then kidnapped by a bandit named Douhu.

Act I is set several years later. At a prosperous market in Dunhuang, Master Painter Zhang finds his daughter Yingniang in the crowd, who unfortunately has been forced to dance for the crowds in exchange for money. Enus then brings enough money to buy back Yingniang's freedom so that Zhang and his daughter may be reunited to have a happy life.

In Act II, inspired by his daughter's dance movements and her pose of holding the *pipa*, Master Painter Zhang succeeds in finishing the famous mural *Celestial Musician Playing the Pipa in Reverse*. The local magistrate attempts to buy Yingniang by force. Master Painter Zhang, after thinking it over, tells his daughter to go to Persia with Enus for her freedom. Unable to accomplish his evil plan, the local magistrate explodes with rage and punishes Zhang to paint in the Mogao Caves with shackles on his feet.

Act III shows how Yingniang has been happily living with the Persian people, and has developed a deep friendship with them. She is to leave Persia for her homeland with Enus, who will go to China as an ambassador.

回到了离别日久的故土。

第四场：莫高窟中神笔张思女心切，梦幻中神游了他所彩绘的天宫幻境。河西节度使进洞朝香，观赏壁画，欣然为神笔张解除了枷锁。

第五场：阳关外，烽燧下。市曹为泄私愤唆使强人窦虎拦劫波斯商队。为了友谊，神笔张燃烽火报警，救伊努斯于危难之中，自己却血染大漠。

第六场：敦煌二十七国交易会。商贾云集，歌舞喧腾，五彩缤纷，富丽堂皇。节度使与各方来宾欢唱一堂。英娘化装献艺，潜入会场，揭露了市曹的罪状。大唐节度使怒斩恶人，剪除了丝绸路上的隐患。

尾声：十里长亭，宾主话别。中外人民的传统友谊源远流长，绵延千秋，丝绸之路上洋溢着友谊之歌。

舞剧《丝路花雨》具有较强的历史性和浓郁的浪漫主义气息，反映了唐王朝经济文化的繁荣，以及热爱和平的中外人民之间的纯洁友

Act IV depicts that Master Painter Zhang misses his daughter so much that he dreams he meets his daughter in the fairyland. When Zhang awakens from his dream, the military commissioner of Hexi comes into the cave. He appreciates Zhang's painting and orders his men to remove the shackles from Zhang.

Act V is set outside the Yangguan Pass. The local magistrate decides to take revenge on Enus and lets Douhu rob the Persian caravan. In order to save Enus, Master Painter Zhang tries to climb up to the top of a watchtower to warn Enus, but is shot and killed by Douhu.

Act VI takes place at the Twenty-seven Nations Fair. The military commissioner welcomes merchants from different nations with various performances. Yingniang, dressed up as a dancing girl, accuses the local magistrate of looting the Persian caravan and killing Master Painter Zhang. The military commissioner orders that the magistrate and Douhu be executed at once.

The epilogue begins with the appearance of a pavillion on the stage. The military commissioner bids his guests a warm farewell, revealing that the friendship between the Chinese and other peoples will endure forever.

"The Rain of Flowers Along the Silk Road" is a historical and romantic narrative dance which reflects the cultural and economic prosperity of the Tang Dynasty as well as the pure friendship between China and other nations. The main character Yingniang's dance is an authentic representation of dance styles

图 75 《丝路花雨》演出海报

Fig.75 Poster for "The Rain of Flowers Along the Silk Road"

谊。舞剧借用歌舞伎英娘真实地再现了敦煌壁画中优美的舞姿风格，其中许多舞蹈场面绚丽多彩，如敦煌集市上的百戏，莫高窟中的反弹琵琶舞，波斯花园中的刺绣舞、马铃舞、黑巾舞，梦幻中的柘枝舞、凭栏仙女舞、美音鸟舞，二十七国交易会上的盘中舞、印度舞、土耳其舞、霓裳羽衣舞、新疆舞等。舞剧所用各种服饰二百多套、三千多件，美轮美奂，引人入胜。

舞剧《丝路花雨》在改革开放之初的中国文艺界刮起一股强劲的敦煌艺术旋风。《丝路花雨》在人

found in Dunhuang murals. There are other kinds of beautiful dances as well, including various acrobats at the Dunhuang fair; "dancing while playing the *pipa* in reverse" in the Mogao Caves; the embroidering dance, the horse bell dance, the black scarf dance in the Persian garden; the *zhezhi* fantasy dance, the fairy dance, and the bird dance; the plate dance, the Indian dance, the Turkish dance, the rainbow and feather dance, and the Xinjiang dance at the Twenty-seven Nations Fair. The narrative dance is lavish and fascinating, with the display of over 3,000 costumes in the whole performance.

"The Rain of Flowers Along the Silk

民大会堂成功初演后，又在北京演出28场，获得文化部颁发的“创作一等奖”和“演出一等奖”。1979年11月1日在人民大会堂做专场文艺演出，受到各级领导和艺术家们的高度赞许。1981年6月，《丝路花雨》作为“文化使者”，应外国友人邀请，出国进行为期一个月的文化交流，演出23场，受到各地观众的热烈欢迎。1982年，《丝路花雨》荣登世界第一大剧院——意大利米兰斯卡拉大剧院，成为亚洲第一个进入世界最高艺术殿堂的演出团体，并由此拉开了中国艺术表演团体出访各国、开展文化交流的序幕，同年在巴黎第十二届国际舞蹈节演出时，也深受好评。1982年3月，《丝路花雨》由西安电影制片厂拍摄成彩色宽银幕艺术片。1999年“《财富》全球论坛·上海年会”举行，《丝路花雨》作为唯一的歌舞祝贺节目参加演出。

《丝路花雨》剧组先后到朝鲜、法国、意大利、日本、泰国、西班牙、土耳其、德国、南斯拉夫等四十多个国家和港澳台地区访问演出，在海内外引起了极大反响，深得好评，被誉为“中国民族舞剧的典范”“东方的天鹅湖”“中国民族舞剧的新成果”。1994年在中华民族20世纪舞蹈经典评比中荣获“经典作品金像奖”，被誉为“中国舞

Road” was a tremendous success in the field of Chinese arts in the late 1970s. It has been performed 28 times in Beijing since its premiere in the Great Hall of the People and was awarded “First Prize for Creativity” and “First Prize for Performance” by the Ministry of Culture. A special performance was held in the Great Hall of the People on November 1, 1979 , which won high praise from experts and leaders. In June 1981, as an“ambassador of culture,” “The Rain of Flowers Along the Silk Road” was invited to perform in foreign countries 23 times, attracting large local audiences. In 1982, as the first Asian performance group, it presented in the world-top theater of art—the Teatro alla Scala in Italy. Since then, Chinese art groups began their visits to various countries for cultural exchanges. It was well received in the 12th International Dance Festival in Paris the same year. The Xi’an Film Studio released a version of the story as a color wide-screen film in March 1982. In the Fortune Global Forum—Shanghai Annual Meeting in 1999, “The Rain of Flowers Along the Silk Road” was welcomed as the only dance program.

“The Rain of Flowers Along the Silk Road” has been praised as a

剧的里程碑”。

《丝路花雨》二十多年来长盛不衰，在国内和世界各地演出千余场，成为中国“舞剧舞台的常青树”。2005年《丝路花雨》以“演出年轮、场次最多的舞剧”成功入选上海大世界吉尼斯纪录，成为“中国舞剧之最”。

二十多年来，《丝路花雨》不但创造了中国舞剧久演不衰的纪录，而且以浓郁的民族色彩和东方情调，以及集古代艺术之大成，为中国舞蹈走向世界提供了有益的启示。其后，甘肃艺术家们创作、演出的《飞天》《天姿馨曲》《唐韵胡旋》《千手观音》《编钟乐舞》《大梦敦煌》《敦煌古乐》《悠悠雪羽河》《天马萧萧》《敦煌情韵》等大型舞剧，都是在《丝路花雨》经验基础上的开拓和创新。

在2004年举行的《丝路花雨》演出25周年纪念活动中，甘肃省委宣传部、甘肃省文化厅在兰州举行了纪念演出并召开座谈会，宣布启动“《丝路花雨》复排提高再创辉煌工程”，以使这一经典舞剧的艺术水

"Model of Chinese National Narrative Dance," the "Swan Lake of the East," and the "New Fruit of Chinese National Narrative Dance" since it played in the countries including Korea, France, Italy, Japan, Thailand, Spain, Turkey, Germany and Yugoslavia, as well as in the areas such as China's Hong Kong, Macao and Taiwan. It was awarded the "Gold Statue Award for Classics" and was considered as a "Landmark for Chinese Narrative Dance."

With thousands of performances both at home and abroad for more than 20 years, "The Rain of Flowers Along the Silk Road" has become the "Evergreen of Narrative Dance" in China. It appears in the Shanghai Guinness Records and was acclaimed as "Best Chinese National Narrative Dance" in 2005 since it was the most frequently performed narrative dance for so many years.

As a masterpiece of ancient art, "The Rain of Flowers Along the Silk Road," with its unique oriental performing features, has led Chinese narrative dances to the world. Additionally, it has inspired artists to create even more works such as "Flying Apsaras," "Sweet Melody of Heavenly Beauty," "Rhymes of Tang and Whirling of Hu," "Thousand-Armed Avalokitesvara (*Guanyin*)," "Chime-bell Music and Choreography," "Dunhuang, My Dreamland," "Ancient Music of Dunhuang," "A Mother's Love," "Neighing Heavenly Horses," and "The Charm of Dunhuang."

At the celebration of the 25th anniversary

图 76 《丝路花雨》剧照

Fig.76 Performance of "The Rain of Flowers Along the Silk Road"

准，得到进一步提高，从而更好地适应不断变化的新形势，并利用这一品牌进行产业开发，促进甘肃文化产业的发展。工程的主要内容包括：制订《丝路花雨》的两个版本，一个完全保留经典剧目的原貌，供研究和特殊群体欣赏之用，另一个将充分运用现代艺术理念和表现手法进行复排，以增强其艺术感染力，更好地体现时代精神，等等。

21 世纪，相信注入活力的敦煌舞剧《丝路花雨》这一文化精品仍将演绎令世界瞩目的舞台"神话"。

of its birth in 2004, the Gansu Provincial Party Committee Publicity Department and the Gansu Cultural Department held a meeting in Lanzhou to launch the "Rehearsal and Improvement Project of 'The Rain of Flowers Along the Silk Road'" which aimed to improve the classical dance and to further develop Gansu's cultural industry. The project preserved the original dance for study and appreciation on the one hand; on the other hand it was revised with modern ideas and techniques meaning to intensify its artistic impact and present contemparary spirit.

The new century has witnessed and will achieve the amazing success of "The Rain of Flowers Along the Silk Road" on various stages all over the world.

敦煌乐舞结硕果

Other Achievements in Dunhuang Music and Dance

博大精深的敦煌文化是敦煌乐舞的母体。敦煌遗书和壁画中的故事、舞蹈、音乐等资料给文艺工作者的艺术创作提供了用之不竭的素材。通过富有感染力的舞台艺术表演，敦煌文化逐渐为越来越多的观众所喜爱。同时，新的舞台艺术剧，又成为传播和弘扬敦煌文化的最好载体。

敦煌壁画中的舞蹈风格，主要有两种:一为中原舞。悠扬婉转，挥袖而舞，“长袖善舞”是其特点。壁画中的人物双手持长长的锦带(长巾或长绸)起舞，锦带在其周身左右回旋，上下飘举。有的神情开朗奔放，有的温婉妩媚，有的动作疾驰矫健，有的轻盈柔曼。每组有一个或两个跳舞的舞伎，伴奏的乐伎少的两人，多的达三四十人。一为西域民族舞。性格爽朗，感情激扬，歌舞节奏强烈是其特点。双人舞《飞天》是艺术家创作的第一部取材于敦煌壁画的舞蹈，1954年由著名舞蹈家戴爱莲编剧。

The eclectic and profound history and culture of Dunhuang is the origin of its performing arts. The stories, dance, and music as found in the Dunhuang manuscripts and murals provide inexhaustible resources for the creations of writers and artists. Dunhuang culture is drawing the attention of more and more people through appealing performances. Meanwhile, new stage arts have become the best exporter for the promotion and transmission of Dunhuang culture.

There are two choreography styles which appear in Dunhuang murals: the Central Plains dance, and the exotic dances from the Western Regions. The former is featured with melodious rhythms and long waving sleeves. The characters in the murals dance with long, bright, colorful silk ribbons or narrow scarves in both hands that sway up and down. The mannerisms of the dancers vary greatly—ranging from cheerful and unrestrained, vigorous and fast, to gentle and graceful, and soft and slow. In each group, there are one or two dancers, while accompanying ensembles of musicians may include two to thirty or forty people. The latter is characterized by bold intensity, passionate emotions, and strong rhythms. As

《飞天》成功地运用了戏曲中的“长绸舞”，把它加工为独立的纯舞蹈艺术。舞蹈追求的不是敦煌壁画的描摹再现，而是以绸带飞扬瞬间的舞姿造型和流畅、滑翔、腾跃的步伐，表现翱翔天宇的一种意境——寄予人类的希冀与向往。

自以敦煌为题材的舞剧《丝路花雨》成功演出之后，甘肃文艺工作者围绕敦煌艺术继续大做文章，创作出了一系列如《千手观音》《敦煌古乐》《敦煌组舞》《西出阳关》《大梦敦煌》《敦煌神韵》《敦煌韵》等音乐、舞蹈作品，使敦煌艺苑再结硕果。现撷取其中的一些简介如下：

《千手观音》

在2005年央视春节联欢晚会上，舞蹈《千手观音》受到观众的极大欢迎。《千手观音》舞蹈的最早雏形出现在《丝路花雨》之中。在《丝路花雨》中有一段舞蹈叫作“六臂神”，由三个人站成一列，重叠起来，不停变换手臂姿势。这一段舞蹈在舞台上一经表

the first choreographic work inspired by the Dunhuang murals, “Flying Apsaras” was created by the famous dancer Dai Ailian in 1954. It successfully absorbs the essence of the “long silk dance” as in traditional Chinese opera, refining it into a pure dance form. The objective of “Flying Apsaras” is not to re-depict the Dunhuang murals, but to show people's hopes and expectations represented by the choreography with flying silk and smooth, gliding steps.

With the success of the Dunhuang-themed dance “The Rain of Flowers Along the Silk Road,” artists in Gansu Province continued creating works based on Dunhuang art, such as “Thousand-Armed Avalokitesvara (*Guanyin*),” “Ancient Music of Dunhuang,” “Suite Dance of Dunhuang,” “West of the Yangguan Pass,” “Dunhuang, My Dreamland,” “The Romance of Dunhuang,” and “Rhymes of Dunhuang,” which make Dunhuang art more abundant and diverse. The following provide further information:

“Thousand-Armed Avalokitesvara (*Guanyin*)”

Broadcast on CCTV's New Year's Gala in 2005, the performance of “Thousand-Armed Avalokitesvara” won wide praise from audiences. The prototype of this dance derived from “The Rain of Flowers Along the Silk Road,” in which one dance was named the “Six-Armed Deity.” Three dancers were in a line, one behind the other, constantly changing their arm postures. It

图 77 舞蹈《千手观音》剧照

Fig.77 Performance of "Thousand-Armed Avalokitesvara (*Guanyin*)"

现，便给观众留下深刻印象。

《千手观音》原创于甘肃省艺术学校，是高金荣教授根据敦煌莫高窟第 3 窟的千手千眼观音壁画所创作的，当时命名为《敦煌手姿》，舞蹈的主题画面就是一个叠面，似孔雀开屏，突出了敦煌舞垂、扬、俯、仰等千变万化的手姿。1991 年，甘肃省艺术学校的学生演出了以“千手观音”为基本造型的舞蹈《敦煌手姿》，1998 年在北京演出时，根据舞蹈史学家王克芬的建议更名为《千手观音》。

《敦煌神韵》

《敦煌神韵》是集《丝路花雨》与《敦煌乐舞》之大成的作品，全剧时长 90 分钟，敦煌舞蹈、音乐贯穿始终。舞剧部分由《丝路花雨》中的精彩片段《霓裳羽衣舞》以及《水月观音》《妙音反弹》《西凉乐舞》《唐韵胡旋》《丝路情韵》等 8 个舞蹈组成，千姿百态的飞天仙子在缥缈动人的伎乐中翩翩起舞，把人们带入心驰神往的佛国世界。

created a sensation onstage and impressed audiences.

“Thousand-Armed Avalokitesvara” was originally created in the Gansu Provincial Art School by Professor Gao Jinrong based on the mural of Thousand-Armed and Thousand-Eyed Avalokitesvara in Cave 3 at Mogao, although it was originally named “The Mudras of Dunhuang.” The main image and theme of this dance consists of an overlapping effect, like a peacock spreading its tail, highlighting the ever-changing hand postures or mudras, including hanging, weaving, falling, and rising. In 1991, students in the Gansu Provincial Art School performed “The Mudras of Dunhuang” based on the same choreography as “Thousand-Armed Avalokitesvara.” In 1998, when performed in Beijing, following the advice of Wang Kefen, a dance historian, it was renamed “Thousand-Armed Avalokitesvara.”

“The Romance of Dunhuang”

“The Romance of Dunhuang,” a synthesis of “The Rain of Flowers Along the Silk Road” and “Dunhuang Musical Dances,” is 90 minutes in length with Dunhuang music and dance throughout. The entire dance is an integration of eight fragments, including “Rainbow and Feather Dance” (the highlights from “The Rain of Flowers Along the Silk Road”), “Water-Moon Avalokitesvara,” “Echoes of Sublime Music,” “Western Liang Musical Dances,” “Rhymes of Tang and Whirling of Hu,” and “The Sentiment of the Silk Road.” Apsaras in various postures

图 78 舞蹈《敦煌神韵》剧照

Fig.78 Performance of "The Romance of Dunhuang"

dance to the melodious music, transporting people to the longed-for Buddha world.

《敦煌韵》

《敦煌韵》是由甘肃省歌剧院创作完成的。这台大型乐舞共分为乐舞《天宫伎乐》、舞《美音鸟》、歌《阳关三叠》、舞《妙音反弹》、乐《太平乐》、舞《千手观音》、歌《秦王破阵乐》、乐舞《鸣沙月》、歌《望江南》、舞《香音神》、歌《玉关情》和《莫高盛世》等 12 个篇章。演奏用的仿古乐器均取材于敦煌

"Rhymes of Dunhuang"

"Rhymes of Dunhuang" was created by the Gansu Opera House. This large-scale musical dance consists of 12 acts: "Musical Dances of the Heavenly Palace," "The Bird with Beautiful Sound," "Parting at the Yangguan Pass," "Echoes of Sublime Music," "Music for Peace and Tranquility," "Thousand-Armed Avalokitesvara," "Music of King Qin Breaking up the Enemy's Front," "Moon over the Mingsha Mountain," "Yearning for the South," "Gandharva the God of Fragrance," "The Sentiment of Jiayu Pass," and

图 79　舞蹈《敦煌韵》剧照
Fig.79　Performance of "Rhymes of Dunhuang"

壁画，是根据莫高窟壁画中的古代乐器制作的。通过歌、舞、乐一体的全新模式，陆续展示了“九色鹿”“步步生莲”等佛经故事。该乐舞最摄人心魄的莫过于舞蹈和背景的恢宏壮阔，以及160种华丽、美轮美奂、光怪陆离的服饰。由于使用了高科技手段，使舞台的气氛被烘托到前所未有的艺术高度和绝妙境地。其中“妙音反弹”一场，12位伎乐天反弹琴瑟的集体舞姿比《丝路花雨》的独舞更显得多姿多艺，异彩纷呈。整个场景的主色调为金色，堪称金碧辉煌、相得益彰。

《敦煌韵》成为继《丝路花雨》《敦煌古乐》《大梦敦煌》之后，又一个根植于敦煌文化的舞台艺术精品，成为以歌舞表现敦煌文化的“活化石”。

《敦煌情韵》

乐舞剧《敦煌情韵》是为庆祝澳门回归祖国两周年暨澳门旅游塔会展娱乐中心落成而专门创作的，节目大多取材于敦煌壁画。2001年12月19日在澳门演出。在敦煌壁画背景下，

"Mogao's Golden Age." The period musical instruments replicated for the performance are based on those seen in the Mogao murals. Through new forms of music, song, and dance, it brings to life such Buddhist legends as the "Nine-Colored Deer" and the "Step-by-Step Lotus." The most appealing aspect is the splendor of the choreography and the stage sets, as well as 160 different gorgeous and fascinating costumes. Advanced technology makes the performance reach an unprecedented artistic height. "Echoes of Sublime Music," jointly performed by 12 musician-dancers, is even more spectacular than the solo dance in "The Rain of Flowers Along the Silk Road." The dominant golden hue of the scene complements the dance perfectly.

"Rhymes of Dunhuang" is another outstanding artistic achievement rooted in Dunhuang culture, along with "The Rain of Flowers Along the Silk Road," "Ancient Music of Dunhuang," and "Dunhuang, My Dreamland." It represents a "living example" of historical Dunhuang culture in music and dance.

"The Charm of Dunhuang"

The musical dance "The Charm of Dunhuang," performed in Macao on December 19, 2001, was especially created to commemorate the second anniversary of Macao's return to the motherland and the completion of the Macao Tourist Tower

由玉笛、玉排箫、曲项琵琶、莲花琴等仿唐乐器演奏的敦煌古乐悠悠响起，十多位身穿黄色长裙、头顶荷花灯的"水月观音"翩翩而至，她们模仿敦煌壁画中千姿百态的飞天观音造型，轻舒柔臂，慢展长袖，一举手、一投足，充满绝妙的艺术魅力和异域的神秘之美，仿佛那一个个姿态优美的飞天从壁画中降临人间。飞天乐舞、敦煌古乐、西凉乐舞、民族新音乐《天上人间》……节目精彩纷呈，背景不断变幻，时而是飞天仙女，时而是苍凉大漠，使置身于现代化剧院里的澳门观众，仿佛瞬间来到了遥远的敦煌莫高窟，与诸神对话，听千佛祝福，时间与空间、历史与现实在这里浓缩，引人遐思飞扬。最后，仙女们手持花篮，将一片片象征吉祥的花雨撒向观众，把最美好的祝福带给澳门人民。《敦煌情韵》以婀娜

Convention and Exhibition Center. Most of the work takes its inspiration from the Dunhuang murals; the jade flute, jade panpipes, *pipa*, and lotus *qin* are period instruments based on those of the Tang Dynasty, which produce melodious ancient Dunhuang music. More than 10 "Water-Moon Avalokitesvara" dancers in long yellow skirts and with lotus lanterns on their heads, perform in the manner of the apsaras in Dunhuang murals, waving their arms gently and slowly spreading their long sleeves. Every movement is filled with amazing artistic charm and mysterious, exotic beauty, as if several graceful apsaras have come to life from the Dunhuang murals. "Immeasurably Vast Difference" is a synthesis of music and dance from different dynasties and regions. As a splendid choreographic work, it presents vivid visual imagery in different scenes. For example, the performance includes a scene of apsaras as well as a scene of the desolate and forbidding desert. By frequently changing scenes, the performance seems to have a magic that transported audiences from the theater in Macao to the distant Mogao Caves. It is as if audience members were talking with different Buddhist deities and receiving their blessings. Time and space, past and present were all frozen, capturing people's boundless imagination. At the end of the performance, celestial maidens with flower baskets in hand scatter auspicious flower petals like falling rain to the audience, bestowing best wishes to the people of Macao. "The Charm of Dunhuang" was loved and applauded by Macao audiences for its graceful and charming dances, distinctive melodies, and lush performances. Major media outlets in

迷人的舞姿，独具特色的韵律，精彩的演出，令澳门观众如痴如醉，全场不时响起热烈的掌声，澳门各大媒体以“敦煌情韵动濠江”为题进行了详细报道。演出获得了极大成功，为澳门回归祖国两周年增添了不少喜庆色彩，并在濠江掀起了一股“敦煌热”。

《敦煌古乐》

敦煌曲谱发现后，即引起了学术界和音乐学界的关注，在众多的研究者中，甘肃敦煌艺术剧院原院长、著名敦煌学者席臻贯先生慧眼独具，紧紧抓住了诗、乐、舞三位一体这个中国古代音乐的根本特点，经过多年的探索研究，于 1991 年底将敦煌古谱成功释解，全卷包括《品弄》《倾杯乐》《急曲子》《长沙女引》《撒金沙》《伊州》《水鼓子》等 25 首曲谱，原原本本地复活了世人难得一闻的“唐乐”。新解乐谱旋律优美流畅，古韵跃然。文曲缠绵而高妙，武曲雄健而激昂，堪与唐代诗

Macao described in great detail the ways in which “The Charm of Dunhuang” shocked Macao (also called Haojiang). The performance’s success added much festive flavor to the second anniversary of Macao’s return to China, a new upsurge of “Dunhuang heat” in Macao.

“Ancient Music of Dunhuang”

The discovery of Dunhuang music drew the attention of both academia and music circles. Among numerous scholars, Xi Zhenguan, the former president of the Gansu Dunhuang Art Theater and a famous Dunhuang scholar, grasped the essence of ancient Chinese music: it was a three-dimensional synthesis of poetry, music, and dance. After many years’ research, at the end of 1991, he successfully finished his annotation of Dunhuang ancient musical works. The whole volume consists of 25 works, including “Appreciation,” “*Qingbei* Music,” “Allegro Music Score,” “Changsha Girl Prelude,” “Sprinkling the Golden Sand,” “Yizhou,” and “Water Drum Melody,” all of which bring the rare music from the Tang Dynasty to life. The newly transposed ancient musical scores are elegant and full of an archaic atmosphere. The civil music is lingering and sublime, while the military music is bold and inspiring, matching the poetry and murals from the Tang Dynasty. Therefore, the successful decoding of “Ancient Music of Dunhuang” won high acclaim from both domestic and international academic authorities and news media. In September 1992, the

图 80 乐舞《敦煌古乐》剧照

Fig.80 Performance of "Ancient Music of Dunhuang"

歌、壁画相匹配，国内外学术权威和新闻媒体高度评价了《敦煌古乐》谱破解的成功。1992 年 9 月，配有唐代诗词的录制音带由敦煌文艺出版社和甘肃音像出版社在国内外发行，有三盘录音磁带，并附有详细说明和席臻贯先生所著“敦煌乐谱新译”《敦煌古乐》精装书一本。

随后，在席臻贯先生的主持下，

Dunhuang Literature and Art Publishing House and Gansu Audiovisual Publishing House jointly released three musical recordings with poetry from the Tang Dynasty, together with background notes and a hardcover book *New Annotations of Dunhuang Music: Ancient Music of Dunhuang* by Xi Zhenguan.

Subsequently, under the leadership of Xi Zhenguan, Xu Qi, Zhang Jufang,

甘肃敦煌艺术剧院舞蹈家许琪、张聚芳、张强将《敦煌古乐》以敦煌乐舞壁画为素材编创为大型乐舞，在第四届中国艺术节上引起强烈反响，获中国文化部第五届“文华新剧目奖”和“挖掘古典音乐奖”。

and Zhang Qiang, dancers from the Gansu Dunhuang Art Theater adapted "Ancient Music of Dunhuang" into a large-scale musical dance, receiving positive reviews at the 4th China Arts Festival, and winning the 5th Wenhua New Play Award as well as the Award of Classical Music Exploration issued by Ministry of Culture of PRC.

舞剧《大梦敦煌》

Narrative Dance: "Dunhuang, My Dreamland"

2000年7月，敦煌藏经洞发现百年纪念活动在莫高窟九层楼前的广场隆重举行。由兰州歌舞剧院文艺工作者历经两年艰辛创作完成的大型舞剧——《大梦敦煌》也在此进行大型实景演出，舞剧的悲情故事以及将莫高窟、月牙泉、鸣沙山融为一体的精美画面，赢得了与会专家、学者以及广大观众的喜爱。

《大梦敦煌》是一部富于传奇色彩的四幕舞剧，它以敦煌艺术宝库的千百年创造历史为背景，以青年画师莫高与大将军之女月牙的感情经历为线索，以浓烈的笔墨，刻画了青年画工莫高不断追求艺术至高境界的坚忍形象，歌颂了忠贞不渝、纯洁炽热的爱情，演绎出了一场中国版的“罗密欧与朱丽叶”式的悲凄爱情故事。

舞剧《大梦敦煌》的分幕内容大体如下：

序幕：一百年前的一个偶然机会，看守莫高窟的道士王圆箓惊奇地发现了一个藏满经卷的洞窟，当他从浩如烟海的敦煌遗书中打开一

"Dunhuang, My Dreamland," the culmination of two years of hard work from artists in the Lanzhou Song and Dance Theater, was performed in the square in front of the Nine-Storey Tower at the Mogao Caves to celebrate the 100th anniversary of the discovery of the Library Cave. It won great attention from all walks of life with its impressive story mixed with the Mogao Caves, the Crescent Moon Spring, and the Mingsha Mountain.

"Dunhuang, My Dreamland" is a narrative dance in four acts. Based on the long history of Dunhuang arts, it tells a love story between a young painter, Mogao, and a general's daughter, Yueya. It depicts Mogao's perseverance in pursuing the arts and extols true love similar to that between Romeo and Juliet.

The synopsis of "Dunhuang, My Dreamland" is as follows:

The prologue relates how a hundred years ago, Wang Yuanlu, a monk taking care of the Mogao Caves, is surprised to discover a secret cave full of sutras. When he opens a scroll from so many manuscripts, a profound story begins,

幅画卷时，一个动人的故事如梦如幻般地展开了……

第一幕:很久很久以前的西北大漠，自中原西行而来的青年画师莫高为追求艺术的最高境界，身背装满画工工具的小布包，不辞辛苦前往敦煌。在途中，莫高饥渴难耐，生命垂危，他的眼里始终亮着朝圣者虔诚而执着的光芒。极度的衰竭，使莫高眼前出现了奇美的幻觉:大片的美景从沙海中飘然而起;五色的神鹿在绿洲中驰过。突然，一支在沙漠中凯旋的军团路过这里，士兵们发现了这个执迷而又羸弱的青年画师，便粗俗地围住他嬉戏逗弄。女扮男装的少年将军月牙拨开众人，好奇地查看这个孤身一人徒步沙漠的年轻画师。之后，她喝住士兵，甩给莫高一只羊皮水囊，却又任性地抽走了画师背上被其视同生命的画稿。三危山前，众多的工匠与当地的市井百姓、商贾官吏、民间艺人以及出资建窟的供养人等，熙攘往复，一派喧闹景象。凭着那只水囊走出沙漠的莫高，终于找到了他神往已久的敦煌。疲惫与喜悦交织在一起，他似乎要向每一个人表达心中的激动。

第二幕：新窟开凿，市井欢娱。洞窟内，莫高面对新壁浮想联翩，

like something out of a movie.

Act I depicts the artist Mogao from the Central Plains going to Dunhuang for artistic pursuits. In the northwestern desert, a young painter named Mogao goes to Dunhuang to achieve his artistic dream. He nearly dies from hunger and thirst on his journey. Suffering from extreme exhaustion, he hallucinates magnificent scenery with colorful deer running across the desert. All of a sudden, an army group passes by, with some soldiers harassing Mogao. Yueya, dressed as a man, watches him with curiosity and reproaches others who make fun of Mogao. She leaves him a waterskin made from sheep's hide, but removes the drawings from his bag. At the foot of the Sanwei Mountain, many people including craftsmen, local residents, merchants, officials, folk artists, and Buddhist donors come and go, making it a prosperous place. Mogao reaches Dunhuang—a place he has dreamed of—with the waterskin given by Yueya. Weary though he is, he cannot help sharing his excitement with others.

Act II relates the construction of a cave shrine. All the workers are cheerful. In the cave stands Mogao, staring at the wall and contemplating how to draw a sacred picture that

他要把自己虔诚的信念与全部的才华倾注于笔尖，勾勒出心中最神圣的艺术境界。又想起从中原一路带来的画稿被人抢去，心中不禁怅然若失。料想不到的是，一日，莫高与少年将军月牙再度相逢，不过此时月牙脱去铠甲，恢复了女儿装。月牙带着画轴，由乳娘陪伴着来到洞窟里寻找莫高。在对艺术的共同痴迷中，月牙对莫高了解加深，调皮任性的月牙，渐渐地为外表朴实憨厚而内心情感丰富的莫高所吸引；而莫高也被性格活泼、聪慧亮丽的月牙所打动，二人由陌生到熟悉，进而渐生好感，萌生了爱情。在莫高对自己来敦煌虔诚心愿的诉说中，在莫高所绘壁画那神奇境界的辉映下，二人的心慢慢地贴在了一起。闻讯而来的大将军带兵闯进洞窟寻找女儿，却见莫高与月牙正在一处，不由大怒。将军欲杀莫高，被月牙阻拦；大将军耻于女儿与穷画师来往，为阻止他们交往，强带月牙离去，留下莫高孤独一人在洞窟中。

第三幕：将军行营大帐中，为断绝女儿与贫穷画师莫高的恋情，大将军逼迫女儿门当户对地择婿出嫁。王公贵胄，纷至沓来，他们在月牙面前或逞其威猛，或彰其富贵，

expresses his pious faith in art. He feels lost when thinking of his drawings taken away by Yueya. One day, Mogao unexpectedly meets Yueya again, who is not wearing a suit of armor this time. Although she once disguised herself as a male, now she wears women's clothing and reveals her femininity. They gradually get acquainted with each other and fall in love over their common interest in art. Upon knowing this news, the general rushes to the cave with his soldiers, looking for his daughter. Flying into a rage, he intends to kill Mogao, but is prevented by Yueya. To put a stop to their relationship, the general forces Yueya to go back home, leaving Mogao alone in the cave.

Act III depicts the general recruiting a husband for his daughter. In the army tent, the general decides to marry Yueya to a nobleman. She refuses all the nobles who vie for her hand, as she misses Mogao so much. Upon learning that the general is recruiting a husband for Yueya, Mogao disguises himself to enter the general's tent with the help of folk artists. Yueya recognizes Mogao who is among the dancers but is afraid to acknowledge him. The two lovers can only watch each other in tears. Later, the general finds out the truth and bursts into

以求月牙芳心，但均遭拒绝。心中思念月牙的莫高，得知将军大营中正在招亲，情急之下，乔装打扮，在民间艺人的帮助下混进大将军的营帐；在舞蹈中，莫高的身姿为月牙认出，但此地此境，二人心中纵有千言万语，却只能相看泪眼。大将军识破了莫高的真实身份，怒不可遏，欲杀莫高。月牙再次在父亲的剑下救出心爱的莫高。月黑风高，月牙出逃。军营里火焰熊熊，杀气冲天，大将军率军追向敦煌。

第四幕：阴暗的洞窟里，莫高潜心作画，一幅精美的壁画即将完成。突然，急促的马蹄声把心爱的月牙带到了莫高眼前。二人悲喜交集，相拥在一起。他们互诉衷肠，发誓生死一处，永不分离。重兵围困的洞窟中，面对血与火的威逼，月牙再次拯救了莫高，并为爱付出了生命的代价。大将军面对女儿的鲜血，震撼于女儿的刚烈，突然变得苍老，终于在惭愧中放下手中的屠刀。莫高在巨大的悲怆中，将心上人月牙的躯体沉入清澈的月牙泉中。之后，莫高完成了敦煌艺术的绝唱。从此莫高窟灿烂辉煌，月牙泉清纯秀丽，艺术、爱情，朝夕相守，直到永久……

《大梦敦煌》整个舞剧极富浪漫气息，通过令人柔肠百转、荡气回肠的爱情传奇故事，形象地再现了博大精深的

anger. He orders his men to kill Mogao. Yueya stops her father and then runs away from her family. Then, the general, boiling with anger, pursues her in a chase to Dunhuang.

In Act IV, Mogao is focused on painting in the dim cave. He is about to finish a mural when to his surprise Yueya comes to him on horseback. They weep with joy and swear to be together forever. The general orders his soldiers to capture Mogao, and although Yueya saves Mogao she is killed in the process. Her father seems to age overnight at the death of his daughter and from guilt over his own cruelty. Mogao, grieving over the loss of his lover, places Yueya's body in the Crescent Moon Spring. From then on, he is devoted to his painting and succeeds in finishing countless Mogao murals. Since then, the Mogao Caves become more and more significant and the Crescent Moon Spring more and more beautiful. Art and love are united together for eternity.

"Dunhuang, My Dreamland" portrays the profound artistic creations in the Mogao Caves through a romantic and sad love story.

图 81　舞剧《大梦敦煌》剧照 1
Fig.81　Performance of "Dunhuang, My Dreamland"

敦煌莫高窟艺术的创作过程。

由于相同的敦煌艺术文化背景，有许多观众将《大梦敦煌》和《丝路花雨》相提并论，并简单地以"姊妹篇"来定义两者的关系，其实二部舞剧之间有许多明显的区别：

一是两者创作的时代背景不同。舞剧《丝路花雨》创作于 1979 年，而《大梦敦煌》则完成于 2000 年，两部舞剧创作时间相差二十余年，其间，时代发生了巨大的变化。因此在完全不同的时代背景下，两个作品呈现

Due to a similar artistic and cultural creation background, "Dunhuang, My Dreamland" is considered a complementary companion to "The Rain of Flowers Along the Silk Road." However, there are significant differences between them.

First, they were created during different time periods. "The Rain of Flowers Along the Silk Road" was produced in 1979, whereas "Dunhuang, My Dreamland" in 2000. There have been great changes in the performing arts during 21 years between these two works, and each presents different means of artistic expression and has exerted its own influences on Chinese folk dances.

给观众的是完全不同的艺术景观。两者带给中国民族舞蹈发展的影响，也都是各不相同的。

二是舞剧反映的主题不同。由于两者时代背景不同，舞剧所反映的主题自然也就有着巨大的差异。《丝路花雨》首演时，刚刚从几十年的“阶级斗争”现实中走出来的人们，还不能放弃“这个世界是由好人和坏人组成的矛盾世界”的观念，所以，即便是在强调中外友谊交流的故事中，也难免要带上阶级斗争的色彩。文艺作品的结局几乎千篇一律，以好人打败坏

Second, they reveal different themes. People held the view that "the world was made up of good and evil" when "The Rain of Flowers Along the Silk Road" premiered, since they had just witnessed a long-term class struggle. Therefore, it follows a certain line—justice triumphing over evil, although it mainly emphasizes friendship between Chinese and Westerners; while "Dunhuang, My Dreamland" focuses on human nature through a love story between the poor painter Mogao and the noble heroine Yueya. It reflects the deep thinking of

图 82　舞剧《大梦敦煌》剧照 2

Fig.82　Performance of "Dunhuang, My Dreamland"

人、正义战胜邪恶的大圆满而收场。而《大梦敦煌》的主题则关注的是普遍的人性，通过讲述穷画工莫高与贵族女月牙之间的"死恋"故事，最终体现的是对于生命、理想、爱情的深深思考。因此与《丝路花雨》相比，《大梦敦煌》的主题完成了从"阶级斗争"到人性和爱情的变化，打上了时代变迁的烙印。

三是艺术再现敦煌文化的创作手段和表达方式不同。《丝路花雨》的舞蹈是由敦煌壁画模仿而来，是把壁画中的静态人物画面拿到现实中来，再人为地把它串联起来；而《大梦敦煌》的舞蹈是为剧情创编出来的，是用舞蹈在讲述一个凄美动人的爱情故事，《大梦敦煌》的舞蹈是用来写人的。

life, ideal and love. Therefore, the themes of the two dances reveal the changes from class struggle to human nature and love, marking the characteristics of different times.

Third, they employ different techniques of expression. The choreography in "The Rain of Flowers Along the Silk Road" is based on the styles found in the Mogao murals. It transforms static characters from the Dunhuang murals to figures in real life. However, the dance in "Dunhuang, My Dreamland" is choreographed for telling a poignant love story to the audience and is designed to serve as a vehicle for the characters.

遗响千年：敦煌的影响

Dunhuang: Its Everlasting Impact

世界关注敦煌

Dunhuang: Attracting Worldwide Attention

敦煌是中国的，又是全人类的，世界只有一个敦煌。敦煌在中国，但敦煌学在世界，是国际学术潮流中的一门显学。这主要体现在以下几个方面：

第一，敦煌本身的国际性。敦煌石窟是佛教艺术的结晶，它的存在本身就是中外文化交流的结果，因为佛教从印度发祥后不断东传，在传播的过程中，许许多多的石窟寺得以开凿，莫高窟就是其中之一。佛教是一个世界性的宗教，作为佛教石窟之一的莫高窟，内容丰富而又被完整地保存下来，它自然也就成了世界关注的中心。

除了佛教这一世界主题外，敦煌的艺术也是世界的，如敦煌壁画上发现的玻璃器皿，表现出了萨珊波斯的艺术风格，由此可以探讨西亚地区玻璃器皿的制造工艺。

敦煌文书虽然以汉文文书为主，但也有以梵文、回鹘文、于阗文、龟兹文、突厥文、粟特文、西夏文、叙利亚文、八思巴文等文字书写的资料。这些资料自然属于世界性的，也就引起了各国学者的关注，如近年来国内外学者对粟特的重视与研究就是一例。在敦煌的考古中，也发现了一些其他国家的文物。

Dunhuang, as a place name, lies in China; as a branch of learning, it is a source of wealth both for Chinese and all humankind. With more and more international attention being paid to it, Dunhuang studies has become an influential field of academia for several reasons.

To begin with, Dunhuang itself is eclectic and international in nature. The Dunhuang Caves are the essence of Buddhist art as well as the combination of Chinese and international cultural exchange. Since the birth of Buddhism in India, it continued its spread eastward. Many cave temples and rock-cut architecture had been explored, and the Mogao Caves were among them. Buddhism is a multicultural religion, with the Mogao Caves serving as a kind of symbol. As its rich and profound content has been preserved almost completely intact, Dunhuang has become a focal point of the world.

Besides Buddhism, Dunhuang's art is multicultural as well. For example, the glass vessels discovered in the Dunhuang murals display the art style of Sassanian Persia. These show the manufacturing process of glass vessels of the Western Asia.

The majority of Dunhuang manuscripts are in Chinese, but they are also written in other languages, such as Sanskrit, Uyghur, Khotanese, Kuchean, Turkic, Sogdian, Tangut, Syriac, and Phags-pa. The manuscripts have garnered attention at home and abroad. An example is that in recent years, domestic and international scholars have expanded research on Sogdian. Also, in the archaeological exploration of Dunhuang, a number of cultural relics from other countries have been discovered.

第二，文献收藏的国际性。敦煌文献从发现之始，就遭到了各国探险家的欺骗掠夺，绝大部分被劫往世界各地，目前被收藏在中国、英国、法国、俄罗斯、日本、德国、美国、韩国、印度、瑞典、丹麦等十几个国家的几十个博物馆、图书馆中。其中以位于北京的中国国家图书馆（约16000卷）、伦敦的英国国家图书馆（约13300卷）、巴黎的法国国家图书馆（约6000卷）和圣彼得堡的俄罗斯科学院东方学研究所（约18000卷）收藏最多，因此，北京、巴黎、伦敦和圣彼得堡，就被称为敦煌文献的四大收藏中心。

正是由于敦煌文献分散收藏在世界各地，各国博物馆、图书馆的工作人员就要对其进行登记、整理、研究，从而在世界许多国家，都有了敦煌学的研究。

第三，研究的国际性。由于敦煌本身的国际性，就使得各国的学者都要从主观上关注它、研究它，而文献收藏的国际性，又在客观上形成了对其整理、研究的国际性和国际交流。因此，世界上许多国家，尤其是收藏敦煌

Second, Dunhuang manuscripts are international in scope. Since the discovery of the Library Cave, Dunhuang manuscripts have been removed by explorers from all over the world. At present, the majority have been preserved in museums and libraries in over 10 countries, including China, Britain, France, Russia, Japan, Germany, the United States, South Korea, India, Sweden, and Denmark. Of these about 16,000 volumes are in the National Library of China, about 13,300 in the British Library, about 6,000 in la Bibliothèque nationale de France, and about 18,000 in the Institute of Oriental Manuscripts of the Russian Academy of Sciences. Therefore, Beijing, Paris, London, and St. Petersburg are known as the four depositories of Dunhuang manuscripts.

Just as Dunhuang manuscripts are scattered around the world, the staff in those national museums and libraries have to do related work including cataloguing, classification, and studying, and thus Dunhuang studies have been within the research of many countries.

Third, the research on Dunhuang is international. Dunhuang itself has attracted the attention of scholars from various countries. Meanwhile, the collection of Dunhuang documents has accelerated its international collation, research, and exchange. Therefore, many countries in the world, especially those preserving relevant documents, have had their own research institutes with experts excelling in Dunhuang studies. They have sponsored international conferences, and published academic works as well. Of course, scholars have their own emphasis on doing research: Chinese scholars focus on the traditional subject of books, making great achievements in history, literature, and unique

文献的国家，都有专门的敦煌学研究机构和研究人员，都曾举办过敦煌学方面的国际会议，都有许多敦煌学方面的论著。就其研究的主旨来看，中国学者在传统的四部书，尤其是历史、文学以及得天独厚的石窟研究方面成就卓著；日本学者则在宗教方面独树一帜；欧美学者，尤其是法国学者在民族语言、历史研究方面建树较多。

第四，国际合作的典范。由于敦煌文献所涉及的范围广泛，文字又多，而且许多还是死文字(即现在已经消失、不再使用的文字)，因此，许多方面都需要各国学者通力协作、联合攻关，如已经出版的《英藏敦煌文献》《俄藏敦煌文献》《法藏敦煌西域文献》等，就是国际合作的典范。可以说，还没有哪一门学科，像敦煌学一样迫切需要国际合作，也没有哪一门学科像敦煌学一样有着如此广泛、密切的国际合作。

国际敦煌项目(IDP)就是国际敦煌学界合作的结晶。1993 年，中国国家图书馆、英国国家图书馆等收藏机构倡议成立国际敦煌项目。1994 年，英国国家图书馆设立了专门的机构——国际敦煌项目(IDP)，现在它已经成为英国国家图书馆的一个重要部门。国际敦煌项目的成立，为世界敦煌文献收藏机构搭建了一个合作交流的平台，各收藏机构共

Buddhist rock-cut architecture; Japanese scholars have special and profound views on religion; whereas European and American scholars, especially French scholars, focus more on scripts and languages as well as historical research.

Fourth, the cooperation and joint efforts in Dunhuang studies are international. Dunhuang literature involves a wide range of documents, scripts, and languages, with many dead languages. Therefore, cooperation and joint research are needed by scholars far and wide. Previous publications including *Dunhuang Manuscripts in British Collections, Dunhuang Documents Held in Russia,* and *Dunhuang and Western Region Manuscripts Held in France* set good examples for international cooperation. It can be said that few subjects demand more international cooperation than Dunhuang studies, and few subjects embody more international cooperation than Dunhuang studies.

The International Dunhuang Project (IDP) is the manifestation of international cooperation in Dunhuang academic circles. In 1993, bibliographic institutions including the National Library of China and the British Library proposed setting up an international Dunhuang project. In 1994, the British Library established a specialized group—IDP, which has grown to become an important center of research. The IDP has built a platform for cooperation and exchange among worldwide agencies to discuss issues such as conserving and cataloguing the documents. So far, several international

商解决保护、编目的问题，并已召开了几次国际学术会议，如1997年在伦敦召开的“二十世纪初叶的敦煌写本伪卷”学术研讨会就是由该项目举办的。同时，各收藏机构还倡议共同建立一个完整的网上数据库，将目录资料与高质量的数字化图像相链接，并附有其他相关资料，使各国学者能充分利用世界各国的收藏品。经过数年的努力，网上数据库已于2002年正式开通，研究者可以利用网络查找有关的敦煌文献和研究成果。

2003年初在日本京都宣告成立的“敦煌学国际联络委员会”，是适应新时期敦煌学研究的发展而组建的。刚成立的时候共有干事8人，即中国4人、英国1人、法国1人、日本2人；2004年又增加了俄罗斯1人；2005年又增加了美国1人、德国1人、哈萨克斯坦1人。目前共有8个国家的12位学者任联络委员会的干事。由此可见，它是一个真正国际性的联络机构。

“敦煌学国际联络委员会”成立后，已开展了一些卓有成效的工作，如编辑《敦煌学国际联络委员会通讯》，主持了2005年俄罗斯所藏敦煌吐鲁番文物的考察；2006年9月，在南京成功举办了“转型期的敦煌学：继承与发展”国际学术研讨会。

academic conferences have been organized. The conference on "Forgeries of Dunhuang Manuscripts in the Early Twentieth Century" held in London in 1997 was hosted by the IDP. At the same time, agencies have also jointly initiated establishing a complete online database, in which descriptive data and qualified digital images are linked, together with other relevant information, so that scholars can make full use of the resources. After several years of work, the online database was officially opened in 2002. Now researchers can have access to relevant literature and research achievements in Dunhuang via the platform.

In early 2003, with the development of Dunhuang studies in the new era, the Dunhuang International Liaison Committee was established in Kyoto, Japan. There were only eight members at first: four Chinese, one British, one French, and two Japanese; in 2004, one Russian member joined; in 2005, one American, one German, and one Kazakhstan joined as well. There are currently twelve scholars from eight countries in the committee, making it a truly international agency.

The Committee has accomplished some noteworthy achievements, such as editing *Communications of the International Liaison Committee of Dunhuang Studies*, hosting an expedition of Dunhuang and Turfan cultural relics stored in Russia in 2005, and holding the international academic conference "Dunhuang Studies during the Transitional Period: Inheritance and Development" in September 2006 in Nanjing, China.

平山郁夫的敦煌情结

Hirayama Ikuo in Dunhuang

平山郁夫，日本著名画家。1930年6月生于日本广岛。1952年毕业于东京美术学校日本画科。1984年任日中文化交流协会副会长。1992年任日中友好协会会长。创作、出版有《敦煌鸣沙》《敦煌三危》《平山郁夫画集：从西到东》《丝绸之路素描集》《敦

Hirayama Ikuo, a renowned Japanese Nihonga painter, was born in Hiroshima in June 1930. He graduated from the Department of Japanese Painting at the Tokyo Art College in 1952. He was appointed as vice president of the Japan-China Cultural Exchange Association in 1984 and president of the Japan-China Friendship Association in 1992. During his career, he created and published several works, including *Mingsha Mountain of*

图83　平山郁夫(1930—2009)
Fig.83　Hirayama Ikuo (1930-2009)

煌——历史之旅》等作品。

1945 年，时为初中生的平山郁夫，经历了广岛原子弹爆炸这场人类的劫难，并从此留下了毕生的痛苦回忆。“原爆”使他无法摆脱人生的虚无感和地狱般的记忆，并由此患上了“原爆后遗症”。他是一位九死一生的幸存者，从此以后，他一直从事反映渴望和平的绘画创作。从中国改革开放的 20 世纪 80 年代初期开始，他曾前后十多次来到日本文化源泉的佛教传播地——敦煌莫高窟，进行考察研究、写生和讲学。

与佛教的结缘，使平山郁夫的画风大变。平山郁夫以佛教、释迦牟尼传记、佛画、佛教遗迹等为题材作画，创作出了诸如《佛教传来》《大楼炭经转轮王品图》《入涅槃幻想》《受胎灵梦》《建立金刚心图》等画作。他自喻如那些翻山越岭，穿过沙漠，用自己的生命来传播佛教的人们，要使自己从中得到拯救。在这期间，一位

Dunhuang, Sanwei Mountain of Dunhuang, Hirayama Ikuo Painting Work: From West to East, The Collection of Sketching the Silk Road and *Dunhuang: A Journey Through History.*

In 1945, when Hirayama was a junior high school student, Japan witnessed the Hiroshima atomic bomb explosion—a catastrophe for all its citizens. The explosion left him with a lifetime of painful memories, unable to rid himself of the emptiness and bitterness of life or recover from the trauma of the atomic bomb. As a survivor who narrowly escaped, he engaged in the creation of paintings reflecting a desire for peace. Beginning in the early 1980s when China implemented its policy of reform and opening up, Hirayama visited the Mogao Caves in Dunhuang dozens of times—a holy land of the Buddhist religion, a spiritual foundation of Japanese culture—to explore, sketch, and give lectures.

Having faith in Buddhism greatly changed his style of painting. With thematic source material of Buddhism, the biography of Sakyamuni Buddha, Buddhist artworks and monuments, Hirayama created a number of paintings, including *The Transmission of Buddhism, Chakravartin King in the Sutra of Creation and Destruction, The Illusion of Entering Nirvana, The Fairy Dream of Pregnancy,* and *Portrait of a Bodhisattva.* When creating a work, he always compared himself to those who had trudged over mountains and deserts to transmit Buddhism. He himself was eager to achieve spiritual salvation through his paintings as well.

中国古代的高僧——玄奘，引起了他的注意：在古代交通不怎么发达的情况下，是什么精神力量驱使这位高僧不畏艰险酷暑，寂寞孤独，西去求法？他思考的结果是佛教，是一种具有巨大感召力的精神文化。

除了以佛教题材创作之外，平山的画大多以玄奘的旅途和丝绸之路为题材。1980年，日本奈良药师寺主管筹资兴建玄奘三藏院。时年50岁的平山决心自费绘制表现玄奘“西天取经”的《大唐西域壁画》，以奉纳在玄奘三藏院内，从而完成自己的夙愿——将玄奘三藏走过的神圣之路展示在世人面前。平山郁夫创作的巨幅《大唐西域壁画》，高2.16米，长40米，有7个部分、13个画面。它们分别是：朝阳，晨雾中的长安大雁塔，途经嘉峪关，新疆高昌故城，西方净土须弥山，阿富汗巴

During one period, the Chinese Buddhist monk Xuanzang (Hsuan Tsang) captured his imagination. He wondered, “What force drove this monk, conquering so many difficulties, suffering intense cold and heat, to pursue a pilgrimage for Buddhist sutras in such forbidding conditions and in total solitude?” Eventually, he had the answer: it was Buddhism—a spiritual culture with universal appeal.

Besides Buddhism, his paintings also focus on Xuanzang's westward journey and the Silk Road. In 1980, the Yakushi-ji Temple in Nara invited Hirayama to paint a large-scale mural illustrating the travels of Xuanzang. Hirayama, at the age of 50, committed to painting *The Mural of the Western Regions of the Tang Dynasty* at his own expense with the purpose of venerating Xuanzang, and in return realizing his dream—illustrating the sacred road of Xuanzang to the world. The great painting is 2.16 meters high, 40 meters long with 7 subjects and 13 panels, including the “Big Wild Goose Pagoda,” “The Jiayu Pass,” “Ancient Ruins of Gaochang,” “Mount Meru,” “Bamiyan Caves,” “The Deccan Plateau” and “Ajanta Caves in the Moonlight.” The seven subjects show a complete scene of a day from morning to night. Meanwhile, he also creates a 25-meter-long painting *The Blue Sky of the Silk Road* displayed in the Imperial Palace in Tokyo. *The Mural of the Western Regions of the Tang Dynasty*, for which Hirayama spent nearly 40 years planning and 20 years creating, represents the peak of his artistic career. In order to gather source materials, he came to China several times, treading the Silk Road 70 times, traveling 800,000 kilometers and creating more

米扬石窟，印度德干高原的黄昏，月夜下的印度阿旃陀。这 7 幅画的画面构成了一日从早到晚的图景。同时，平山还在为展示壁画而修建的殿堂顶部画了一幅 25 米长的《丝绸之路蓝色天空》。《大唐西域壁画》是平山郁夫先生一生艺术生涯的结晶，他为这幅壁画构思了近 40 年，创作了 20 年。为获取创作素材，他多次来到中国，踏察丝绸之路 70 多次，行程 80 多万公里，总共作画 6000 多幅。每当遇到什么阻力和困难时，他始终把玄奘当作自己的榜样。他说玄奘取经历经 17 年，吃的苦、遇的险比自己要多得多。在丝绸之路上，每到一地他都要细细体会："玄奘是否在此休息过"，"玄奘会有什么感受"？如果说 1959 年平山郁夫以《佛教传来》在日本美术界崭露头角，那么其后相继创作的《入涅槃幻想》《大唐西域壁画》等画作，则使他成为日本最顶尖的画家。

平山郁夫的中国之旅始于 1975 年 6 月。此后，他数次来到中国。1976 年，楼兰遗址掘出女尸，平山郁夫以此为题材，画出《鄯善国妃子》(又名《楼兰公主》)。1977 年，平山郁夫成为中华人民共和国成立后首批获准访问西藏地区的日本人。1978 年，平

than 6,000 paintings. Whenever he encountered problems, he always took Xuanzang as his model. He mentioned that Xuanzang, in his 17-year pilgrimage for Buddhist sutras, suffered much more than what he had endured. Whenever he arrived at a place along the Silk Road where Xuanzang once passed through, he always asked himself, "Did he ever stop here? What did he feel then?" If *The Transmission of Buddhism* first established his reputation in the art circles of Japan in 1959, then his following paintings *The Illusion of Entering Nirvana* and *The Mural of the Western Regions of the Tang Dynasty* made him one of Japan's top artists.

He first came to China in June of 1975, later returning several times. In 1976, inspired by a female body unearthed in the ruins at Loulan, Hirayama created his work *Imperial Concubine of the Shanshan Kingdom* (also known as *The Loulan Princess*). In 1977, he was part of the first group of Japanese to visit Tibet after the founding of the People's Republic of China. In 1978, he flew to Xinjiang, visiting a number of sites and historical relics that he had been interested in seeing, including the Tianshan Mountains,

山郁夫飞往新疆，看到了向往已久的天山、高昌国故址、交河故城、汉代都护府的所在地库车、苏巴什、和田等地。1986 年 9 月 15 日，平山郁夫抵达他向往的楼兰。而敦煌更是让平山郁夫心驰神往，魂牵梦萦：敦煌是日本的艺术之根。

出于对敦煌的热爱，平山郁夫积极推动日本各界参与对敦煌文物的保护。1982 年和 1983 年，作为“东京艺术大学敦煌壁画调查团”团长的平山郁夫多次来到敦煌。1988 年，兼任中国敦煌研究院客座研究员。此后，他又获联合国教育科学文化机构任命，成为亲善大使。这些荣誉，更加使他意识到在人类文化遗产的保护方面自己所肩负的责任。1988 年 1 月，平山郁夫在日本发起建立“文化财保护振兴财团”倡议，召开发起大会，为保护敦煌遗产展开了募捐筹款活动。同年 5 月，日本经济新闻社联同“文化财保护振兴财团”设立事务所，在东京日本桥三越百货店举办了“平山郁夫素描新作展”，开展了“共同努力保护敦煌遗迹”的活动，为作示范，他率先捐献了卖

the site of Gaochang, the Jiaohe ruins, the seat of the Protectorate of the Han Dynasty—Kucha, the Subashi ruins and the Khotan City. On September 15, 1986, he arrived in Loulan, a place he was also keen to visit. Of all these places, Dunhuang is the one that foremost occupies his mind, for it contains the roots of Japanese art.

Out of his interest in Dunhuang, Hirayama actively encouraged Japanese people from all walks of life to participate in the protection of the cultural relics there. Between 1982 and 1983, as the head of a research group for Dunhuang murals at Tokyo National University of Fine Arts and Music, he had an opportunity to visit there many times, serving as a visiting scholar in 1988 at the Dunhuang Academy. He was also appointed as a goodwill ambassador by UNESCO. These honors have made him truly realize his own responsibility in the protection of world cultural heritage. In January 1988, Hirayama launched the “Cultural Property Protection and Revitalization Consortium” in Japan, and a special fund-raising event was held to protect the legacy of Dunhuang. In May of 1988, Nikkei news media, together with the Consortium established an office and sponsored events such as “The New Sketches Exhibition of Hirayama Ikuo” in the Mitsukoshi Department Store in

画所得的两亿日元。1988年8月，平山郁夫陪同竹下登首相访问中国并担任敦煌之行的向导。在他一系列卓有成效的努力下，为敦煌筹集了近10亿日元资金，这为敦煌研究院后来建立“敦煌石窟维修保护陈列馆”起了举足轻重的作用。平山郁夫把对保护人类敦煌的深厚感情也扩展到中国以外的国家，在英国博物馆，就有专辟的“平山郁夫敦煌文物修复室”。除了英国博物馆外，其他大凡有敦煌文物的外国国立博物馆都有他的敦煌文物修复室以及修复敦煌文物项目。作为一名虔诚的东方艺术朝圣者，平山郁夫认为:“作为一个艺术家，谁都愿意为敦煌做些事情，有的人成功了，有的只是没有成功。因为我得到很多人的帮助和支持，所以就成功了。敦煌壁画放在英国博物馆就是西欧文化和亚洲文化很好的对比，我作为亚洲的一员，当然就愿意做这个工作。”

平山郁夫在积极推动保护敦煌遗产的同时，还倾注全力资助敦煌学研究和人才的培

Nihonbashi district in Tokyo, which launched joint-effort activities to protect the ruins of Dunhuang. To provide an example for others, he himself donated 200,000,000 Japanese yen by selling his own paintings. In August 1988, Hirayama escorted Prime Minister Noboru Takeshita in a visit to China, serving as the guide to Dunhuang. Through a series of fruitful efforts, nearly one billion Japanese yen was raised, which played a vital role in building the Dunhuang Conservation and Protection Exhibition Hall by the Dunhuang Academy. Hirayama has also promoted the protection of Dunhuang in other countries besides China. For example, there is the Hirayama Studio for the Conservation of Dunhuang Relics in the British Museum. In addition, any Western national museum with Dunhuang relics possesses a restoration room or projects named after him. As a devout Asian art pilgrim, he said, “Any artist is willing to do something for Dunhuang. Some succeeded, while some didn't. I made it only because of the support and assistance from others. That Dunhuang murals are preserved in the British Museum is a good cultural contrast between Western Europe and Asia. As an Asian, undoubtedly, I am willing to do this work.”

Apart from actively promoting the protection of Dunhuang's heritage, Hirayama has also been committed to the research on Dunhuang studies and the cultivation of

养。1986年，他在中央工艺美术学院设立“平山郁夫奖学金”，接受中央美术学院、中央工艺美术学院的聘请，担任客座教授。1989年，平山郁夫担任东京艺术大学校长，在学校设立了“敦煌研究基金”，促成中日两国互派研究生交流学习。1990年，捐赠100万美元设立联合国教科文组织“丝绸之路基金”，资助敦煌学研究。

正是因为有了如平山郁

talents. In 1986, he set up the Hirayama Ikuo Scholarship at the Central Academy of Fine Arts and Crafts and served as a visiting professor there. Meanwhile, he was also a visiting professor in the China Central Academy of Fine Arts. In 1989, he served as president of the Tokyo National University of Fine Arts and Music, where he set up the Dunhuang Research Fund to contribute to scholarly exchange between Chinese and Japanese postgraduates. In 1990, he donated $1,000,000 to establish the Silk Road Fund under UNESCO with the aim of supporting research on Dunhuang studies.

The Japanese people's interest in

图84 平山郁夫参观段文杰先生敦煌艺术研究60年成就展

Fig.84 Hirayama Ikuo at Duan Wenjie's Exhibition on 60 Years of Dunhuang Art Achievements

夫这样热爱、了解中国文化，宣传保护敦煌的有识之士的积极努力，使远在异域的日本民众也对敦煌产生了深情的向往。来到敦煌莫高窟的游客，细心一点就会发现这里挂有一个日本姑娘的画像。这是为什么呢？原来这位叫越智佳织的大学生生前向往敦煌，但是后来不幸死于车祸，她的母亲把准备给她到中国留学的200万日元捐给了敦煌研究院。据了解，每年到敦煌旅游的外国游客中，日本人就占到了一大半。日本前首相海部俊树说，不到敦煌，就算不得一个有文化的日本人。长期关心敦煌保护的日本友人平山郁夫说："作为一个画家，我孜孜以求的是日本美的源流。可是，这种源流在什么地方呢？那就是遥远的敦煌。"平山郁夫曾要求他任校长的东京艺术大学的学生，每年至少去敦煌一次，亲自看看日本文化的原典，否则不能毕业。

平山郁夫对敦煌的热爱和投入，也得到了中国政府和人民的认可和嘉奖。在2000

Dunhuang, to a great extent, is inseparable from Hirayama's passion for Chinese culture and the positive efforts made by those advocating and protecting Dunhuang. Tourists to the Mogao Caves, if they look carefully enough, will wonder why there is a portrait of a Japanese girl there. It comes from a touching story: a female college student named Echi Kaori intended to visit Dunhuang, but unfortunately she was involved in a car accident and died. Her mother donated 2,000,000 Japanese yen—originally planned to be her funds for study in China—to the Dunhuang Academy. It is estimated that the Japanese account for half of all international tourists coming to Dunhuang every year. The former Japanese prime minister Ama Shunki once stated, "He who never comes to Dunhuang is not a well-educated Japanese." Hirayama said, "As a painter, I have been striving ceaselessly for the origin of Japanese aesthetics. But, where is it? Dunhuang is actually its source." When he was president of the Tokyo National University of Fine Arts and Music, he required students to go to Dunhuang at least once a year to see the origins of Japanese culture, and if not, they could not graduate.

Hirayama's dedication to Dunhuang also received recognition and praise from the Chinese government and people. On July 29, 2000, a special event, "Commemorating the 100th Anniversary of the Discovery of

图 85 平山郁夫在段文杰先生敦煌文物与艺术保护研究 60 年座谈会上
Fig.85 Hirayama Ikuo at Duan Wenjie's 60 Years of Dunhuang Heritage and Conservation Conference

年 7 月 29 日于敦煌九层楼前广场举行的“纪念敦煌藏经洞文物发现暨敦煌学百年”活动中，平山郁夫以其杰出的贡献与常书鸿、段文杰、邵逸夫、季羡林、饶宗颐、潘重规同时获得了由国家文物局、甘肃省人民政府颁授的“敦煌文物保护研究特殊贡献奖”。2002 年 9 月 27 日，又荣获了中国政府颁发的“文化交流贡献奖”。

曾经有记者问他：“有人说，世界上最爱敦煌的人，除了张

the Library Cave and the Founding of Dunhuang Studies" was held in the square in front of the Nine-Storey Tower at the Mogao Caves. Hirayama, together with Chang Shuhong, Duan Wenjie, Shao Yifu, Ji Xianlin, Jao Tsung-I (Hong Kong), and Pan Chonggui (Taipei), won Dunhuang Relics Conservation and Research Special Award sponsored by the National Cultural Heritage Administration and the Gansu Provincial People's Government. On September 27, 2002, he was awarded the Cultural Exchange Contribution Award by the Chinese government.

Once he was asked by a reporter,

图 86　平山郁夫(左二)、樊锦诗(左一)等在段文杰先生临摹的《都督夫人出行图》前留影

Fig.86　Hirayama Ikuo (Second from Left) and Fan Jinshi (Far Left) in Front of *Procession of the Governor's Wife*

大千、于右任、常书鸿，还有就是您。您对敦煌艺术的修复、保护所贡献的心力和资金已被刻写在敦煌的碑林中，您对敦煌情感的源头是什么？”

平山郁夫深情地回答说：“我在孩提时代，从历史书中知道了敦煌，知道了敦煌的意义所在。我亲身访问敦煌是在 1979 年。我

"It's said that you're the one who loves Dunhuang the most in this world, along with Zhang Daqian, Yu Youren, and Chang Shuhong. What you've done in the restoration and protection of Dunhuang art has been inscribed in the Stele Forest in Dunhuang, but what's the source of your interest?"

Hirayama answered with deep feeling, "When I was a child, I learned about

觉得通过敦煌的壁画不仅可以看到日本文化的传承，还可以了解东亚文化的共性。在敦煌石窟，从4世纪开始一直到14世纪，1000年的壁画，奇迹般留在敦煌，这是一个世界的奇迹。我作为日本的艺术家，作为一个日本民族的成员，对过去的中国给予日本的恩惠铭记在心，如果我们有条件的话就应该报答一下。现在中国强大了，但20年、30年以前，中国确实是没有精力也没有条件去保护敦煌的。当时在敦煌从事研究的第一线的人就很着急，如果这样下去的话，敦煌就眼看被湮灭了，他们很痛苦，所以我当时的心情同样很着急，我有条件的话就很愿意贡献自己的一点微力。我就是这么一个心情，多年来我就是以这个心情一直从事保护敦煌的事业。”

Dunhuang from history books, and then got to know the significance of it. I first personally visited Dunhuang in 1979. I believe Dunhuang murals can not only reflect the heritage of Japanese culture, but also let us recognize the common characteristics of East Asian culture. From the fourth century to the fourteenth, more than 1,000 years have witnessed the existence of the murals in the Dunhuang Caves, which is, to some extent, a wonder of the world. As a Japanese artist and as an ordinary person, I should treasure this favor from the Chinese in my memory and repay it as much as possible. China is now developing fast, but 20 or 30 years ago, it was really hard to get the funding or the manpower to protect Dunhuang. The field survey researchers in Dunhuang were very anxious, and so was I. If nothing had been done for Dunhuang, it would turn to ruins some day, so my intention was to do a little contribution with my own power. With such a grateful heart, I have been engaged in the cause of protecting Dunhuang for many years.”

敦煌文物保护研究特殊贡献奖

Dunhuang Relics Conservation and Research Special Award

2000年7月至8月，为纪念敦煌藏经洞发现暨敦煌学百年，敦煌研究院在莫高窟举办了“2000年敦煌学国际学术讨论会”。会议期间的7月31日晚上，在莫高窟九层楼广场，国家文物局和甘肃省人民政府举行了隆重的颁奖仪式，对半个世纪以来在敦煌文物保护研究中作出特殊贡献的7位个人和3家机构给予表彰，并授予“敦煌文物保护研究特殊贡献奖”。国家文物局和甘肃省人民政府的表彰决定说：

敦煌莫高窟是中华民族优秀的历史文化遗产，作为我国首批公布和列为世界文化遗产名录的全国重点文物保护单位之一，得到了各级政府和社会各界的一贯关心和保护。特别是我国学者在极其艰苦的条件下，克服困难，在从事敦煌文化遗产的研究和保护中，做了大量卓

From July to August 2000, the Dunhuang Academy hosted its annual conference titled the “2000 International Conference on Dunhuang Studies” at the Mogao Caves for the sake of celebrating the centenary of the discovery of the Dunhuang Library Cave and the founding of Dunhuang studies. On the evening of July 31, in the square of the Nine-Storey Tower at the Mogao Caves, the National Cultural Heritage Administration and the Gansu Provincial People's Government jointly held a special ceremony to commend seven people and three institutions for their great dedication to research on Dunhuang relics in the past half century and to award them the Dunhuang Relics Conservation and Research Special Award. The commendation decisions by the National Cultural Heritage Administration and the Gansu Provincial People's Government are as below:

The Mogao Caves are an outstanding historical and cultural heritage of China. Being a Major Historical and Cultural Site Protected at the National Level, and one of the first sites in China designated as a UNESCO World Cultural Heritage Site, they draw attention from all walks of life and are under preservation by the government at all levels. Chinese scholars in particular have overcome many hardships in extremely arduous situations and achieved much

有成效的工作，为中国人文社会科学的繁荣发展和敦煌学的创立作出了杰出贡献。一些国际友人和文物保护研究机构，投入人力、物力和先进技术，给予了热情支持。经过文物工作者的辛勤努力，使莫高窟成为世界上现存规模最大、保存最完整、保护最好的石窟寺。为了鼓励和弘扬保护优秀文化遗产的奉献精神，在纪念敦煌藏经洞文物发现暨敦煌学百年活动中，国家文物局、甘肃省人民政府决定对曾经在敦煌文物保护和研究中作出贡献的常书鸿、段文杰、季羡林、饶宗颐、邵逸夫、潘重规、平山郁夫(日本)和中国敦煌研究院、日本东京国立文化财研究所、美国盖蒂基金会予以表彰，并授予“敦煌文物保护研究特殊贡献奖”。

在受表彰的个人和机构中，常书鸿、段文杰先生，在大漠戈壁中默默地奉献，几十年如一日，在极其艰苦的条件下，从事敦煌石窟艺术的临摹、研究工作，开创并推动了敦煌文物的保护事业，

in the study of Dunhuang cultural relics, which lays a solid foundation for the prosperity of Chinese humanities and social sciences as well as for the establishment of Dunhuang studies. International friends and research institutes for cultural relics conservation have won great appreciation for their dedication of manpower, materials, and advanced technology. Through the great efforts of cultural relics researchers, the Mogao Caves have become the largest, most complete and best preserved rock-cut architecture in the world. In the ceremony, the National Cultural Heritage Administration and the Gansu Provincial People's Government commended and recognized those who had made contributions to the conservation and research of Dunhuang relics with the Dunhuang Relics Conservation and Research Special Award, including Chang Shuhong, Duan Wenjie, Ji Xianlin, Jao Tsung-I, Shao Yifu, Pan Chonggui, and Hirayama Ikuo, together with institutions such as the Dunhuang Academy, Tokyo National Research Institute of Cultural Properties, and the Getty Foundation.

Among them, Chang Shuhong and Duan Wenjie have wholeheartedly dedicated themselves for decades in the Gobi desert to copying and researching Dunhuang cave temple art, which initiated and promoted the preservation of Dunhuang relics. They have been honored as “the patron saint of Dunhuang.” Not only was Ji Xianlin committed to Dunhuang studies with his profound

他们将自己的一生都献给了敦煌，被誉为“敦煌的守护神”。季羡林先生不仅以深厚的学养致力于敦煌学研究，而且还以崇高的学术声望积极培养、扶持中青年敦煌学者。潘重规和饶宗颐先生是台港地区敦煌学的开创者，他们不仅个人成就卓著，而且还创办刊物、培养人才，推动了台港地区敦煌学的发展。香港爱国人士邵逸夫先生是享有国际声望的实业家，1984 年，他向敦煌研究院捐献港币 1000 万元。敦煌研究院利用这笔捐款，为莫高窟、榆林窟、西千佛洞的 560 余个洞窟安装了铝合金门，为莫高窟的 100 余个洞窟安装了用于保护壁画的玻璃屏风。日本著名画家、社会活动家、联合国教科文组织亚洲大使平山郁夫先生，非常热爱敦煌艺术，曾创作了多幅以丝绸之路、敦煌为题材的美术作品；在东京艺术大学担任教授、校长期间，积极倡导绘画专业学生以观察、学习敦煌艺术为必修课；他将举办个人画展所筹集的 2 亿日元捐赠

knowledge, he also cultivated and supported middle-aged and young scholars with his prestigious academic reputation. Pan Chonggui and Jao Tsung-I were pioneers of Dunhuang studies in Taiwan and Hong Kong. Not only did they make significant personal achievements, but they also issued publications and trained young talents, which stimulated the development of Dunhuang studies in Taiwan and Hong Kong. Shao Yifu, a patriot in Hong Kong, as well as an internationally renowned industrialist, donated 10 million Hong Kong dollars to the Dunhuang Academy in 1984. With this fund, the Dunhuang Academy purchased and installed aluminum doors on almost 560 caves in the Mogao Caves, the Yulin Caves, and the Western Thousand Buddha Caves, as well as mural- protection glass screens for nearly 100 caves at Mogao. Hirayama Ikuo, the Japanese painter, social activist, and UNESCO goodwill ambassador, was so keen on Dunhuang art that he created a number of works with the theme of the Silk Road and Dunhuang. As a professor and president of Tokyo National University of Fine Arts and Music, he advocated observing and studying Dunhuang art as a compulsory course for painting majors. Furthermore, he raised 200,000,000 Japanese yen from his own art exhibitions, donating it to the Dunhuang Academy, which later served as a research fund. On behalf of the Cultural Property Protection and Revitalization Consortium, he

图 87　李承仙代表常书鸿接受敦煌文物保护研究特殊贡献奖(摄影:孙志军)
Fig.87　Li Chengxian Receiving the Dunhuang Relics Conservation and Research Special Award on Behalf of Chang Shuhong (Photo by Sun Zhijun)

图 88　郑阿财代表潘重规接受敦煌文物保护研究特殊贡献奖(摄影:孙志军)
Fig.88　Zheng Acai Receiving the Dunhuang Relics Conservation and Research Special Award on Behalf of Pan Chonggui (Photo by Sun Zhijun)

图 89 段文杰接受敦煌文物保护研究特殊贡献奖(摄影:孙志军)

Fig.89 Duan Wenjie Receiving the Dunhuang Relics Conservation and Research Special Award (Photo by Sun Zhijun)

敦煌研究院，成为敦煌研究院的保护研究基金；他代表日本文化财保护振兴财团捐赠高精度的保护仪器，极大地推动了敦煌研究院的保护研究事业。

敦煌研究院是目前全世界最大的敦煌文物保护研究专业实体，经过以常书鸿、段文杰、樊锦诗为代表的三四代人艰苦奋斗，在敦煌文物的保护、研究、弘扬方面做出了举世瞩目

endowed high-precision conservation instruments to the Dunhuang Academy, lending momentum to its work.

The Dunhuang Academy is currently the largest professional institution in the world for the preservation of Dunhuang relics. Through the hard work of three to four generations, represented by Chang Shuhong, Duan Wenjie, and Fan Jinshi, the Dunhuang Academy has made remarkable achievements in the preservation, research, and promotion of Dunhuang heritage. Since 1988, the Tokyo National Research Institute of Cultural Properties and the Getty Conservation Institute have been cooperating with the Dunhuang Academy in terms of the scientific conservation of

图 90 饶宗颐接受敦煌文物保护研究特殊贡献奖(摄影:孙志军)
Fig.90 Jao Tsung-I Receiving the Dunhuang Relics Conservation and Research Special Award (Photo by Sun Zhijun)

图 91　樊锦诗代表敦煌研究院接受敦煌文物保护研究特殊贡献奖(摄影:孙志军)

Fig.91　Fan Jinshi Receiving the Dunhuang Relics Conservation and Research Special Award on Behalf of the Dunhuang Academy (Photo by Sun Zhijun)

的成绩。日本东京国立文化财研究所和美国盖蒂保护研究所，自1988年以来，就和敦煌研究院合作进行敦煌石窟的科学保护研究，在科学仪器、先进技术、人才培养和科学管理等方面，给敦煌研究院的保护工作给予了极大的帮助，为敦煌石窟的保护作出了重要贡献。

“敦煌文物保护研究特殊贡献奖”的奖牌用铝合金材料制成，整体设计古朴典雅、庄重大方，其图案取材于唐画像砖。这块唐画像砖是1944年西北科学考察团夏鼐、向达、阎文儒等先生在敦煌佛爷庙

the Dunhuang Caves with scientific instruments, advanced technology, talent cultivation, and scientific management, contributing to the development of the Dunhuang Academy as well as the preservation of the Dunhuang Caves.

The medal for the Dunhuang Relics Conservation and Research Special Award is made of aluminum alloy; the design is simple and elegant with its pattern deriving from a Tang Dynasty molded brick. In 1944, this brick, with the design of a Hu person and a camel, was excavated by Xia Nai, Xiang Da, and Yan Wenru, members of the scientific research expedition to northwestern

图 92 柴剑虹教授给季羡林先生转交敦煌文物保护研究特殊贡献奖证书
Fig.92 Chai Jianhong Giving the Dunhuang Relics Conservation and Research Special Award to Ji Xianlin

唐墓考古发掘时发现的，画面有一胡人牵着骆驼。被称为“沙漠之舟”的骆驼，是古代东西方经济文化交流的主要交通工具，选用胡人拉驼的画像砖，既表示敦煌是古代丝绸之路的重镇、东西方文化交流的枢纽，寓意敦煌和丝绸之路有着密切关系；同时还以骆驼吃苦耐劳、忠实可靠、乐于奉献的精神品质，寓意受奖者执着追求、无私奉献的高尚品德。

China, while doing the archaeological tomb work of the Tang Dynasty at the site of Foyemiao, Dunhuang. Camels, known as "ships of the desert," were the major transportation mode for the economic and cultural exchange between the East and the West in ancient times. The chosen brick reflects the significant location of Dunhuang for cultural exchanges between the East and the West along the ancient Silk Road, and also represents the close connection between Dunhuang and the Silk Road. Moreover, it illustrates the spirit of diligence, loyalty, reliability, and dedication of the award-winners through the camels' features.

世界文化遗产——敦煌莫高窟

World Cultural Heritage: the Mogao Caves in Dunhuang

敦煌位于甘肃省河西走廊的西端，它地处青藏高原北部边缘地带，是一个高山、沙漠、戈壁环绕的小绿洲。

敦煌有着灿烂悠久的历史。汉武帝派遣张骞出使西域的前后，派霍去病率兵攻打河西的匈奴。匈奴败亡，汉王朝“列四郡，据二关”，即建立了包括敦煌郡在内的河西四郡，并在敦煌郡城的西面，设置了玉门关和阳关，作为扼守西域进入河西、中原的门户。

由于敦煌南枕祁连，西控西域，是汉王朝西边的重镇，也是中西交通、贸易南北两道上的分合点，遂成为东西方文明交汇的枢纽。它既是东来僧侣、使节、商人步入中原的最初落脚点，也是西去僧侣、使臣和商人告别故国的地方。当时，凡罢都护、废屯田之时，汉政府派人迎接吏士，“出敦煌，迎入塞”就算完成了使命。对当时的旅行者来说，“西出

Dunhuang, located at the western end of the Hexi Corridor in Gansu as well as at the northern edge of the Qinghai-Tibet Plateau, is an oasis surrounded by mountains and the Gobi desert.

Dunhuang has a long and brilliant history. Around the time Emperor Wu (157-87 BC) sent Zhang Qian to the Western Regions, he designated Huo Qubing to lead soldiers in an attack against the Xiongnu in Hexi. After their defeat, the Han government set up four prefectures in Hexi with Dunhuang as one of them. They also founded the Yumen Pass and the Yangguan Pass in the western part of Dunhuang, which served as gateways for the people from the Western Regions entering Hexi and the Central Plains.

With the benefit of having the Qilian Mountains in the south and advantages of controlling the Western Regions in the west, Dunhuang became a hub for Eastern and Western trade and cultural exchanges. It served as the first destination for monks, ambassadors and businessmen entering the Central Plains, as well as being the final point for those in the Central Plains going westward. At the time, whenever removing frontier command officers or abandoning

阳关"就意味着凄凉的离别,"生还玉门"就象征着幸福的重聚。

丝绸之路不论有几条道路,也不论其走向怎样变化,敦煌都是其唯一不变的吐纳口,即史籍所称"咽喉之地"。通往西方的丝绸之路,都是"发自敦煌",然后经伊吾、高昌、鄯善而达中亚、欧洲。世界上四大文化体系曾在这里留下了灿烂的篇章和深厚的历史沉淀,正如季羡林教授所说:"在人类绚丽多彩、异彩纷呈的历史创造中,有四种文化范围最广,自成体系,光芒四射。它们是希腊文化、伊斯兰文化、印度文化和中国文化。而这四个文化体系汇流的地方只有一个,就是中国的敦煌和新疆地区,再没有第二个。"

敦煌莫高窟是一处集建筑、绘画、雕塑三者于一身的世界艺术殿堂,是世界上现存规模最为宏大、保存最为完好的佛教艺术宝库,被誉为"东方艺术明珠"。1961年,莫高窟被国务院列为全国重点文物保护单位。1987年,联合国教科文组织公布敦煌莫高窟为世界人类文化遗产保护单位。1991年,联合国教科文

reclaimed wasteland, the Han government would send people to welcome and see off the officers in Dunhuang. For travelers then, "going westward from the Yangguan Pass" indicated a sad farewell, while "coming back to the Yumen Pass" meant a happy reunion.

No matter how many roads were created along the Silk Road or how many changes took place in their orientation, Dunhuang was always a linchpin of the Silk Road. The Silk Road toward the West began from Dunhuang, and passed through Yiwu, Gaochang, and Loulan to Central Asia and Europe. Four major cultures in the world left their splendid historical traces there. Just as Ji Xianlin said, "In all of human history, four major distinctive cultures—Greek, Islamic, Indian, and Chinese cultures—shine with radiance. The unique place where they converged is found only in Dunhuang and the Xinjiang area."

The Mogao Caves, combining architecture, paintings, and sculptures, serve as a treasure trove of world Buddhist art, being the largest and best preserved site of its kind. It is known as the "pearl of Oriental art." In 1961, it was designated by the State Council as a Major Historical and Cultural Site Protected at the National Level. In 1987, it was inscribed on the list of UNESCO World Cultural Heritage Sites and was awarded

图 93　莫高窟的标志——九层楼

Fig.93　Symbol of the Mogao Caves: the Nine-Storey Tower

组织授予莫高窟“世界文化遗产”证书。

敦煌除了举世闻名的莫高窟之外，现存的石窟寺遗址、古墓葬群、汉长城、关隘、古城、烽燧、古驿站等文物景点和独特的自然风光同样引人入胜，令人流连忘返。作为莫高窟的姊妹窟榆林窟，俗称“万佛峡”，位于安西县城西南 75 公里的榆林河（亦名踏实河）畔，现存唐、五代、宋、西夏、元等朝代洞窟 42 个。虽没有

the World Cultural Heritage Site Certificate in 1991.

In Dunhuang, besides the world-renowned Mogao Caves, there are other distinctive and fascinating sights and historical landmarks, including the ruins of cave temples, ancient burial grounds, the Han Dynasty Great Wall, border passes, ancient towns and inns, watchtowers, and more. The Yulin Caves, the sister site of Mogao, are located on the banks of the Yulin River (also called the Tashi River), about 75 kilometers southwest of Anxi County. The existing 42 caves there are from the Tang Dynasty (618–907), the Five Dynasties (907–960), the Song Dynasty (960–1279), the Western Xia Dynasty (1038–1227), and the

莫高窟那样闻名世界，但因其自身特色也别具神韵。特别是五代以后，莫高窟艺术呈明显的衰落趋势，而榆林窟无论从内容、绘画风格，还是艺术水准方面，都显示出其时代特征和独到的艺术魅力。1961 年，榆林窟被国务院列为第一批全国重点文物保护单位，后划归敦煌文物研究所管辖。

敦煌莫高窟不仅因其丰富的壁画、雕塑而享誉全球，而且还因“藏经洞”的发现而蜚声海内外。

1900 年发现的藏经洞(莫高窟第 17 洞)遗书，与其前后出土的殷墟甲骨文、汉晋木简、明清档案被并称为 20 世纪中国学术文化的“四大发现”。敦煌文书共有五万多件。大部分是汉文写本，少量为刻印本，汉文写本中佛教经典占 90%以上。除汉文文书外，还有古藏文、梵文、回鹘文、于阗文、龟兹文等多种少数民族文字文书。敦煌文书的发现是研究中国与中亚历史、地理、宗教、经济、政治、民族、文学、艺术、科技等的重要资料，因此

Yuan Dynasty (1271–1368). Although its fame fails to match that of the Mogao Caves, the Yulin Caves also are worth visiting. After the Five Dynasties, the Mogao Caves displayed an obvious decline in its artistic quality, while the Yulin Caves continued to reveal extraordinary artistic features as far as content, painting style, and artistic level are concerned. In 1961, it was designated by the State Council as a Major Historical and Cultural Site Protected at the National Level, later under the jurisdiction of the Research Institute on Cultural Relics of Dunhuang.

The worldwide fame of the Mogao Caves, however, lies not only in its proliferation of murals and sculptures, but also in the discovery of Cave 17—the Library Cave.

The manuscripts discovered in the Library Cave in 1900, together with oracle bone inscriptions from the Yin Dynasty (1600–1046 BC) ruins, bamboo and wooden slips of the Han and Jin dynasties, and documents from the Ming and Qing dynasties are known as the four great discoveries of Chinese academic culture from the 20th century. There are more than 50,000 Dunhuang manuscripts, most of which are written in Chinese, with over 90% being Buddhist sutras. Other than Chinese manuscripts, there are some in other languages, such as ancient Tibetan, Sanskrit, Uyghur, Khotanese, and Tocharian. Additionally, engravings, woodblock-printed copies, and rubbings are part of the

图 94 世界文化遗产——莫高窟

Fig.94 World Cultural Heritage: the Mogao Caves

敦煌遗书被称为“中国中古时代的百科全书”“古代学术的海洋”。藏经洞的发现让全世界为之震惊，引起国内外学者们的极大兴趣和广泛研究，并因此而形成了“因地名学”的国际性显学——敦煌学，成为“一代学术之新潮流”。除文书外，藏经洞还有

collection. The Dunhuang manuscripts are essential materials for the thorough research of almost all aspects of China and Central Asia, such as history, geography, religion, economy, politics, nationality, literature, art and science. Therefore, they are known as the “encyclopedia of Medieval China (221–960)” as well as the “ancient academic ocean.” The discovery of the Library Cave not only stunned the world, but attracted great interest and extensive study of domestic and international scholars. As a result,

上千件的绢画、版画、刺绣和大量书法作品被发现。

20 世纪末，敦煌莫高窟又有了新的发现，即在莫高窟北区的考古发掘中，清理了 243 个洞窟，敦煌莫高窟再次引起世界的瞩目。

敦煌遗书被发现后，绝大部分都流散到了世界各地，主要的收藏地有北京、巴黎、伦敦和圣彼得堡。

莫高窟绵延千年的文化及藏经洞中的无价之宝，是我们为之骄傲的文化遗产，但同时也是我们民族的一段伤心历史。

Dunhuang studies—an international subject based on its toponym came into being, developing into a new trend of an academic generation. Besides manuscripts, over a thousand silk paintings, prints, embroideries, and a large number of calligraphy works have been excavated from the cave as well.

At the end of the 20th century new discoveries were made at Mogao, with archeologists finding 243 caves on the north section, once again drawing the world's attention.

After their discovery, most of the Dunhuang manuscripts were dispersed all over the world, mainly in Beijing, Paris, London, and St. Petersburg.

The everlasting culture of Mogao and the priceless relics in the caves not only bear China's cultural heritage, but also relate a sad chapter in the history of China.

图 95　敦煌石窟保护研究陈列中心外景(摄影:张先堂)

Fig.95　Panorama of Conservation and Exhibition Center of Dunhuang Caves (Photo by Zhang Xiantang)

图 96 敦煌石窟保护研究陈列中心内景一角(摄影:张先堂)

Fig.96 Inner View of Conservation and Exhibition Center of Dunhuang Caves (Photo by Zhang Xiantang)

图 97 道士塔

Fig.97 Taoist Stupa

莫高窟北区考古新发现

New Discoveries on the North Section of the Mogao Caves

敦煌莫高窟是一座集壁画、雕塑、建筑于一体的石窟，保存至今的石窟崖面还有 1700 多米。这 1700 余米的石窟崖面，按照莫高窟石窟的分布情况被划分为南北两区。以原敦煌文物研究所编号的第 1 窟为界，第 1 窟及其以南为南区，第 1 窟以北为北区。我们以前所提及参观的莫高窟实际上只是南区。南区崖面长 1000 余米，保存着已公布(包括《敦煌莫高窟内容总录》刊布)的莫高窟 492 个洞窟中的 487 个。北区的崖面长 700 多米，也有洞窟数百个，其中只有 5 个石窟编了号，即 461、462、463、464、465 号窟。北区的这 5 个窟与南区的 487 个窟就构成了一般出版物和参观解说中所说的莫高窟 492 个窟。而北区的其他洞窟因大多都没有壁画或塑像，似乎没有多大价值，所以很少被

The Mogao Caves in Dunhuang are collections of murals, sculptures, and architecture. The cliff face of the existing caves is more than 1,700 meters in length. Taking Cave 1 numbered by the Research Institute on Cultural Relics of Dunhuang as the center, it is divided into the north and the south sections according to the distribution of the caves. All caves to the north of Cave 1 belong to the north section; and the remaining caves, including Cave 1 itself, lie on the south section. The cliff face of the south section is more than 1,000 meters long, with 487 caves. According to *General Catalogue of the Mogao Caves*, a total of 492 caves presently remain. The cliff on the north section is 700 meters long. There are hundreds of caves, among which only five—Caves 461–465, are numbered. The combined total number of caves from both the north and south sections is 492, which tallies with that mentioned in publications or guides for visitors. There are those who believe that the other caves on the north section are of limited value as they contain very few murals or sculptures. The Research Institute on Cultural Relics of Dunhuang Art failed to number or recorded any information about the other northern caves, and as a result they were almost entirely forgotten by people except for the five prominent ones

人提及。敦煌文物研究所既未进行编号，也没有对其记录，因此在有关莫高窟的出版物中，除了前述第 461—465 号窟外，北区的绝大多数洞窟也就很少有人提及，几乎被遗忘了。

鸣沙山上的莫高窟，与三危山遥遥相望。大泉河在流经鸣沙、三危两山时，由于受地形的影响，在莫高窟前形成了宽窄不一的河床，南区的河床宽 50 米~60 米，北区的河床宽 60 米~100 米。另外，由于地面和河流、河床等各种因素，使南区和北区的窟前也不相同，南区有高出现河床 1 米~4 米、宽 30 米~200 米的一、二级阶地，这样就有效地保护了南区的下层洞窟，使其免遭洪水冲刷破坏。但同样位于大泉河左岸的北区就没有这样幸运了，因为没有阶地，长期以来，大泉河的河水就一直冲刷着洞窟所在的崖壁，直到 20 世纪 80 年代初修建北区防洪大堤为止。

北区崖面除个别地段由于地质原因没有开凿洞窟外，其他地段都有石窟。北区洞窟的分布情况也和南区差不多，即彼此上下相接，左右毗邻，状如蜂巢。最

mentioned above.

The Mogao Caves at the foot of the Mingsha Mountain lie across but far from the Sanwei Mountain. The Daquan River runs through the Mingsha Mountain and the Sanwei Mountain, forming either wide or narrow riverbeds in front of the Mogao Caves due to the influence of the terrain. The riverbed on the south section is about 50–60 meters wide, while that on the north is about 60–100 meters wide. In addition, due to various factors, the physical formation and architecture of the caves on the north and south sections are completely different: there are overhanging terraces, 1 to 4 meters high and 30 to 200 meters wide on the south, which can effectively protect the southern lower caves from flood erosion damage; the north section, however, previously had no such protection and suffered from natural erosion until the 1980s, when a flood protection dike was constructed.

Caves were constructed on most of the cliff face on the north section except for a few places due to geological limitations. The distribution of caves on the north is similar to that of the south, as the caves are connected or next to each other, similar to a honeycomb. The densest part contains five to six layers of caves. But for thousands of years, the north section suffered both natural and man-made damage, including earthquakes, flooding

密集处，崖面的洞窟上下可达五层或六层。但是千百年来，由于自然和人为的破坏，莫高窟北区崖面的状况及石窟内部，已遭受了巨大的破坏。自然因素主要是大泉河水的泛滥、骤降的暴雨以及突发的地震，而洪水和暴雨对崖壁的冲刷，是造成北区洞窟崩塌的根本原因。人为的因素则主要是外国探险家和国人的乱挖乱掘。

早在中华人民共和国成立前的 20 世纪 40 年代，即敦煌艺术研究所时期，史岩先生曾将分布在鸣沙山长达 1700 余米崖面的石窟，由南到北划为 11 段，其中 1 至 8 段在南区，9 至 11 段在北区。在 20 世纪 70 年代的敦煌文物研究所时期，为了保护北区高层石窟免遭游人的破坏，对从底层洞窟顶部通往高层洞窟的 8 个供上下用的过道洞进行了封堵，从而使高层洞窟内的壁画和文物得以较好的保存。到了 20 世纪 80 年代的敦煌研究院时期，在北区石窟前 20 米~30 米处，修建了长数百米、高 1.5 米~1.8 米、顶宽 4 米的防洪大堤和高 1.9 米的金属防护栏，同时还沿防洪大堤内侧进行绿化，这样就对北区崖面进行了

from the Daquan River, and storms. Erosion from floods and storms is the main cause of the collapse of the caves on the north. Human factors include extreme excavation from international and domestic explorers.

During the 1940s, especially before the founding of the People's Republic of China, the National Research Institute on Dunhuang Art was in charge of the Mogao Caves. Shi Yan had divided the cliff face, more than 1,700 meters in length, into 11 sections. Sections 1–8 were on the south and 9–11 on the north. In the 1970s, the Mogao Caves were under the management of the Research Institute on Cultural Relics of Dunhuang. In order to protect the caves on the north section from human destruction, eight passages from the bottom to the top caves were blocked, which helped with the protection of murals and cultural relics in the top caves. In the 1980s, the Research Institute on Cultural Relics of Dunhuang became the Dunhuang Academy. Metal fences approximately 1.9 meters high were constructed 20–30 meters away from the caves, as well as levees or raised banks hundreds of meters long, 1.5–1.8 meters high, and 4 meters wide. Meanwhile, environmental greening work was done along the inner side of the levees. Thus the north cliff face has been effectively preserved.

图 98　莫高窟石窟远景

Fig.98　Distant View of the Mogao Caves

有效的保护。

虽然在 20 世纪 80 年代以前，敦煌研究院及其前身的各个时期都曾对莫高窟的北区石窟有所关注，但从未进行过科学的考古发掘。因此，北区石窟的崖面上到底有多少洞窟，其石窟形制有何特征，这些石窟的用途是什么，在整个莫高窟石窟群中，北区洞窟的地位如何，又属于什么时代，这许多问题都是学术界所关注并迫切需要给予解答的。

正是为了揭开莫高窟北区石窟之谜，经报请上级主管部门批准，敦煌研究院石窟考古研究所的专业人员，

Before the 1980s, although the Dunhuang Academy and its predecessors once kept an eye on the north section of the Mogao Caves, no scientific archaeological excavations were conducted. Answers to questions such as the number, shape, condition, status, and age of the caves on the north section are heavily anticipated by scholars and are urgently needed.

To solve these problems, professionals in the Dunhuang Academy, led by Peng Jinzhang, excavated the north section six times from late June 1988, to late

图 99 莫高窟北区石窟局部
Fig.99 Partial View of the North Section of the Mogao Caves

在彭金章研究员的主持下，从 1988 年 6 月下旬开始，到 1995 年 11 月底止，用了 7 年多的时间，对莫高窟北区进行了 6 次发掘。

经过发掘，在北区崖面共发现洞窟 243 个，再加上以前已经编号的 5 个窟，即第 461—465 窟，北区崖面共有洞窟 248 个。在发掘完毕后，还仿照南区的编号方式，对北区石窟新发现的 243 个洞窟进行了编号。其编号是依据洞窟在崖面的高低，统一由南到北，再由北向南，由下而上呈“S”形往复编号。

November 1995.

Other than Caves 461–465, they discovered 243 new ones which they numbered in similar fashion as the southern caves. The numbering system was conducted from bottom to top, first from south to north, then from north to south, forming an “S” pattern.

After these excavations, Peng Jinzhang and Wang Jianjun edited the report *Caves on the North Section of Mogao*, consisting of three volumes. Volume I, which comprises 94 caves from B1 to B94, was published in

莫高窟北区石窟考古发掘结束后，由彭金章、王建军先生主持编写了发掘报告——《敦煌莫高窟北区石窟》。考古报告共分三卷，其中第一卷包括B1至B94窟，共计94个洞窟，由文物出版社于2000年出版；第二卷包括B95至B156窟以及第462窟、第465窟，共计64个洞窟；第三卷包括B157窟至B243窟以及第461窟、第463窟、第464窟，共计90个洞窟。第二、三卷由文物出版社于2004年出版。

《敦煌莫高窟北区石窟》的编写原

2000 by the Cultural Relics Publishing House. Volume II, which includes 64 caves from B95 to B156 as well as Caves 462 and 465, and Volume III, which includes 90 caves from B157 to B243 and Caves 461, 463, 464, were both published in 2004 by the same publishing house.

The principle of *Caves on the North Section of Mogao* is to elaborate on the shapes and inner structures of the caves, unearthed relics, and excavated ruins. Hence it can provide comprehensive materials for academic research. Each cave in

图 100 东北到西南方向的北区石窟

Fig.100 Caves on the North Section, from Northeast to Southwest

图 101　工作中的彭金章
Fig.101　Peng Jinzhang at Work

则是：不论是石窟形制、内部结构，还是发掘的遗迹、出土的遗物，都务求详尽，以便为学术界提供完整的研究资料。每个窟基本上都由位置、发掘、形制、出土遗物、时代和性质几部分组成，有的窟更详细，如第一卷所载 B47 窟中，除以上各部分外，还刊布了该窟出土的汉文文书 22 件，西夏文残片 2 件，回鹘文文书 1 件以及织物、瓷器、剪纸等。

据唐代石碑记载，莫高窟共有窟龛千余。北区考古新发现洞窟 243 个，如果再加上原编号的 492 个，总

the report is described in regard to its location, condition, age, shape, and unearthed remains. Some are given additional details as well. For example, besides those mentioned above, B47 in Volume I includes 22 Chinese manuscripts, two manuscript remnants in the Tangut language, one document in the Uyghur language, silk fabric, porcelain, and papercuts.

According to records on steles from the Tang Dynasty, there were more than 1,000 caves and niches at Mogao. The newly discovered 243 caves coupled with the previous 492

数就有 735 个了，这与唐代石碑的记载就比较接近了。

以前普遍认为，北区都是画工窟或塑匠窟，是画工、塑匠在开凿石窟时的生活窟。本次考古发现，北区石窟全为僧人所用，是僧众生活、修禅、死后瘗埋的地方，而与画工、塑匠无关，画工、塑匠也没有在这里生活过。

北区的石窟，根据性质共分为六类：第一类，禅窟。里面既无灶、无烟道，又无用火痕迹，是僧人修禅专用的，共有 82 个窟。第二类，僧房窟。里面有炕、有灶、有烟道、有灯龛，相对宽敞，为僧人日常生活所用，共有 50 个窟。第三类，僧房窟附设禅窟。这类窟同时具备生活、修禅两种功能，一般情况是一个室内有炕、有灶、有用火的痕迹，另外一个室内却无灶也无用火痕迹，但却有禅床，这类石窟共有 5 个。第四类，瘗窟。是埋葬僧人骨灰、遗骨、遗体用的，共有 25 个窟。第五类，廪窟。是用来储藏物品的。这类窟面积较小，有土坯砌成的储藏槽，共发现 2 个。第六类，礼佛窟。里面有壁画或塑像，是僧俗举行佛事活动用

caves make a total number of 735, which is close to the Tang records inscribed on steles.

It was commonly believed that painters and carpenters had lived in the caves on the north section, but these archaeological discoveries indicate that the caves were used instead by monastics for residence, meditation, or burial.

The caves on the north section can be classified into six types. The first type, meditation caves, lacking chimneys or stoves, was used for meditation. There are 82 meditation caves altogether. Residence caves, 50 in total, are the second type, used as living quarters complete with a *kang* (a heated stone or brick bed), stove, chimney, and lampshade. The third type, a combination of residential cave and meditation cave, was used for both meditation and as living spaces. In the main chamber of this type there is a *kang* and a stove, but no other household items. There are five of these caves. The fourth type, burial caves, numbering 25 in total, was used to bury the remains of monks. The fifth type, storage caves, is like storage rooms with a smaller area. Two of these caves have been discovered. The last type, caves for Buddha worshipping, with murals and sculptures, was used for holding Buddhist religious ceremonies; two of these have been discovered. These six types of caves in total make up 166. In addition, there are

图 102 《敦煌莫高窟北区石窟》

Fig.102 Caves on the North Section of Mogao

的，这次发现 2 个这类窟洞。以上六类石窟共计 166 个，另外还有 72 个窟因为塌毁而无法判断，有 3 个窟因未开凿完毕而没有派上用场，还有 2 个石窟的性质目前还没有确定。

北区石窟的上述划分，破解

72 caves that cannot be identified due to deterioration or destruction. Three caves are still under exploration and two are uncertain as to their types.

This classification may answer questions put forward among scholars for many years, that is, the role the northern caves play as part of the Mogao Caves. One

了困扰学术界多年的历史之谜。北区石窟是莫高窟的重要组成部分，与南区石窟构成了统一的整体。

莫高窟北区考古，出土的文物也很丰富。铁器、铜器、木器、陶器、瓷器等，都与日常生活和佛事活动有关。棉、麻、毛、丝织品、绣品等纺织品花样繁多。汉文、藏文、梵文、西夏文、回鹘文、叙利亚文、八思巴文等文献则异彩纷呈，其中有些是国内外仅存的，有些是在当地首次

thing remains certain: they cannot be separated from those of the south section.

There are also rich cultural relics found on the north section, including iron, bronze, wood, pottery, and porcelain utensils, as well as various cotton, hemp, wool, and silk textiles and embroidered pieces, which were closely connected to Buddhist activities and everyday life. Besides, there are impressive documents in Chinese, Tibetan, Sanskrit, Tangut, Uyghur, Syriac, and Phags-pa, among which some are newly discovered in this field, and some are unique. For example, *Suijin*, a dictionary explicating vernacular words and *Ksitigarbha Bodhisattva Pūrvapra nidhāna Sūtra*（*Sutra of the Fundamental Vows*

图 103　东南到西北方向的北区石窟

Fig.103　Caves on the North Section, from Southeast to Northwest

发现的。西夏文《碎金》《地藏菩萨本愿经》等都是孤本，汉文的《排字韵五》是久已失传的古佚本。28 枚西夏铁币的出土，则是甘肃河西地区考古的一次大丰收。48 枚回鹘文木活字重见天日，丰富了我们对少数民族活字印刷的认识。1 枚波斯萨珊朝卑路斯王时期铸造的银币，成了中西文化交流的重要物证，填补了有关研究的一项空白。所有这些发现，对全面了解莫高窟开凿的历史，促进敦煌学的发展都有着非常重要的价值。

of the Bodhisattva Ksitigarbha) in Tangut are the only extant copies in the world. *Paizi yun* (book V), a rhyming dictionary of the arrangement of Chinese characters, is so ancient that it had been considered lost. The discovery of twenty-eight Western Xia iron coins is a great find from the Hexi region of Gansu Province. Forty-eight unearthed wooden movable type characters in the Uyghur language have helped people learn more about printing and movable type of the ethnic minorities. A silver coin bearing the image of King Peroz from the Sasanian period of Persia reflects cultural exchanges between China and the West. All these discoveries are of great value in understanding the history of the Mogao Caves and promoting Dunhuang studies.

参考文献(原文)
Works Cited

[1] 刘诗平，孟宪实.敦煌百年——一个民族的心灵历程[M]. 广州：广东教育出版社，2000.

[2] 敦煌研究院. 敦煌图史 [M]. 上海：上海古籍出版社，2000.

[3] 荣新江. 敦煌学十八讲 [M]. 北京：北京大学出版社，2001.

[4] 王重民. 敦煌遗书论文集[C]. 北京：中华书局，1984.

[5] 向达. 唐代长安与西域文明 [M]. 北京：三联书店，1987.

[6] 王子云. 从长安到雅典——中外美术考古游记 [M]. 长沙：岳麓书社，2005.

[7] 潘重规. 列宁格勒十日记 [M]. 台北：台湾东大图书公司，1993.

[8] 李伟国. 敦煌话语 [M]. 上海：上海科技教育出版社，2002.

[9] 彭金章，王建军. 敦煌莫高窟北区石窟 (1~3 卷)[M]. 北京：文物出版社，2000~2004.

[10] 平山郁夫. 平山郁夫全集 [M]. 石家庄：河北教育出版社，2002.

[11] 中国大百科全书总编辑委员会《音乐·舞蹈》编辑委员会. 中国大百科全书·音乐 舞蹈 [M]. 北京：中国大百科全书出版社，1989.

[12] 荣新江. 惊沙憾大漠——向达的敦煌考察及其学术意义 [J]. 敦煌吐鲁番研究，2004(7).

[13] 孟宪实. 伯希和、罗振玉与敦煌学之初始 [J]. 敦煌吐鲁番研究，2004(7).

[14] 向达敦煌通信[J]. 文教资料简报，1980(11/12).

[15] 张弓. 泪眼亲瞻怜落寞 暂接倩影慰故园——关于〈英藏敦煌文献〉的回忆[G]. //中国社会科学院历史研究所. 求真务实五十载——历史研究所同仁述往. 北京：中国社会科学出版社，2004.

[16] 宋家钰.〈英藏敦煌文献〉编辑、出版始末[G]. //中国社会科学院

历史研究所. 求真务实五十载——历史研究所同仁述往. 北京：中国社会科学出版社，2004.

[17] 莫高窟北区洞窟神秘面纱被揭开[N]. 光明日报. 2006-8-25(1).

[18] 尚林. 中英两国交换馆藏敦煌遗书胶卷追述 [J]. 敦煌研究，1991(2).

[19] 资中筠. 袁同礼——中国现代图书馆的先驱[M]. //资中筠. 读书人的出世与入世. 北京：中国社会科学出版社，2002.

[20] 府宪展. 〈敦煌吐鲁番文献集成〉 十四年——以编辑体例和方法为中心[C]. //国家图书馆善本特藏部敦煌吐鲁番学资料研究中心. 敦煌学国际研讨会论文集. 北京：北京图书馆出版社，2005.

[21] 叶文玲. 平山郁夫的“敦煌情结”[J]. 环球采风，2003(4).

[22] 舞剧《大梦敦煌》[N]. 中国青年报，2000-4-19.

[23]《大梦敦煌》体现时代变迁[N]. 北京青年报，2005-1-17.

参考文献(译文)
Translation References

[1] 姜秋霞. 敦煌文化关键词. 北京：外语教学与研究出版社，2019.

[2] 荣新江. 敦煌学十八讲. 北京：北京大学出版社，2001.

[3] 中国社会科学院语言研究所词典编辑室编. 现代汉语词典(第6版). 北京：商务印书馆，2014.

[4] Agnew, N. & Reed, M. & Ball, T. *Cave Temples of Dunhuang: Buddhist Art on China's Silk Road*. Los Angeles: The Getty Conservation Institute, 2016.

[5] Buswell, R. E. & Lopez, D. S. *The Princeton Dictionary of Buddhism*. Princeton: Princeton University Press, 2014.

[6] Du, Doucheng & Wang, Shuqing. *Dunhuang and Silk Road*. Shenzhen: Sea Sky Publishing House, 2005.

[7] Rong, Xinjiang. translated by Galambos, Imre. *Eighteen Lectures on Dunhuang*. Leiden·Boston: Konin-klijke Brill NV, 2013.